UNDERSTANDING DISORGANIZED ATTACHMENT

Theory and Practice for Working
with Children and Adults

David Shemmings and Yvonne Shemmings

Jessica Kingsley *Publishers*
London and Philadelphia

Extracts from Out et al. 2009 on pp.47–49 and pp.167–169 are reproduced by permission of Taylor & Francis Group, www.informaworld.com.
Figure 2.1 from Madigan et al. 2006 on p.60 is reproduced by permission of Taylor & Francis Group.
Extract from Hesse and Main 2006 on p.79 is reproduced by permission of Cambridge University Press.
Figure 5.1 from George and West 2001 on p.111 is reproduced by permission of Taylor & Francis Group.

First published in 2011
by Jessica Kingsley Publishers
73 Collier Street
London N1 9BE, UK
and
400 Market Street, Suite 400
Philadelphia, PA 19106, USA

www.jkp.com

Library of Congress Cataloging in Publication Data
Shemmings, David.
  Understanding disorganized attachment : theory and practice for working with
children and adults / David Shemmings and Yvonne Shemmings.
    p. cm.
Includes bibliographical references and index.
ISBN 978-1-84905-044-9 (alk. paper)
1. Attachment disorder. 2. Attachment behavior. I. Shemmings, Yvonne. II.
Title.
RC455.4.A84S54 2011
616.85'88--dc22
                               2010038817
British Library Cataloguing in Publication Data
A CIP catalogue record for this book is available from the British Library

ISBN 978 1 84905 044 9
eISBN 978 0 85700 241 9

Printed and bound in Great Britain by Bell and Bain Ltd, Glasgow

UNDERSTANDING DISORGANIZED ATTACHMENT

of related interest

Understanding Attachment and Attachment Disorders
Theory, Evidence and Practice
Vivien Prior and Danya Glaser
ISBN 978 1 84310 245 8
eISBN 978 1 84642 546 2
Child and Adolescent Mental Health Series

A Short Introduction to Attachment and Attachment Disorder
Colby Pearce
ISBN 978 1 84310 957 0
eISBN 978 1 84642 949 1
JKP Short Introductions Series

A Practical Guide to Caring for Children and Teenagers with Attachment Difficulties
Chris Taylor
ISBN 978 1 84905 081 4
eISBN 978 0 85700 367 6

Nurturing Attachments
Supporting Children who are Fostered or Adopted
Kim S. Golding
ISBN 978 1 84310 614 2
eISBN 978 1 84642 750 3

Child Development for Child Care and Protection Workers
2nd edition
Brigid Daniel, Sally Wassell and Robbie Gilligan
Foreword by Professor David Howe
ISBN 978 1 84905 068 5
eISBN 978 0 85700 245 7

Understanding and Working with Parents of Children in Long-Term Foster Care
Gillian Schofield and Emma Ward
ISBN 978 1 84905 026 5
eISBN 978 0 85700 489 5

Understanding Looked After Children
An Introduction to Psychology for Foster Care
Jeune Guishard-Pine, Suzanne McCall and Lloyd Hamilton
Foreword by Andrew Wiener
ISBN 978 1 84310 370 7
eISBN 978 1 84642 684 1

The Developing World of the Child
Edited by Jane Aldgate, David Jones, Wendy Rose and Carole Jeffery
Foreword by Maria Eagle MP
ISBN 978 1 84310 244 1
eISBN 978 1 84642 468 7

To the hundreds of social workers and child protection
professionals who help protect thousands of children

Acknowledgements

We thank David Phillips, David Wilkins and Tania Young, not just for contributing to the book but for their expertise in helping to translate theory and research on disorganized attachment into practice with children and families. We also want to pay tribute to the social workers and their team leaders in the London boroughs of Enfield, Merton, Lewisham and Tower Hamlets who have been piloting the ADAM Project. Finally, we must thank Denise Tucker for her expertise and diligence in completing the index for the book.

Contents

Introduction

You are in a park, just watching the world go by. Two young boys, who don't know each other and have never met before, have been taken to the park for the afternoon by their fathers. They are playing near each other on the swings and slides, in an enclosed space. Their fathers, who also don't know each other, start to chat and then tell their sons to be 'good boys' while they quickly go and get a coffee from a stall round the corner, just out of sight of their sons (but the fathers can still see them). Suddenly a dog appears in the enclosure and starts barking. The two dads hear the commotion and run back. You notice that each toddler reacts very differently. The first child, clearly frightened and starting to cry, turns and runs towards his father, who has already moved towards his son and immediately picks him up and soothes him. After some reassurance from his father, the boy is looking back at the dog with renewed interest and excitement at the prospect of playing with it. The second boy's reaction is markedly different: he turns to his father... but as soon as he sees him, he stops in his tracks and looks down. His behaviour changes noticeably: his legs have frozen to the ground, his arms rise as if in slow motion and his hands turn slowly to his face, but never quite cover it.

The first child showed organized attachment behaviour in his reaction to the dog: naturally, he is scared and so turns to a protective figure who comforts and reassures him, thus enabling his son to carry on being captivated and excited by the dog. The second child exhibited the signs of disorganized attachment behaviour. For a variety of reasons, he cannot use his father as an attachment figure most typically because, either consciously or unconsciously, his parenting style is abusively harsh or emotionally cold and helpless. The result is that the child is caught between Scylla and Charybdis, the 'rock and a hard place' of Greek legend: he is terrified *simultaneously* by the dog *and* his father; he is frightened by what should be his haven of safety; he experiences what

Mary Main called 'fear without solution' (Main and Solomon 1990). Frightened in the park, the second boy's father should have offered the solution to the child's terror; instead, his dread of his own father leads to an unsolvable dilemma – 'I need to go to my dad because I'm scared of the dog, but I can't because my dad frightens me too'. Far from being a protective figure, the boy's father is a source of danger. The child is truly in harm's way…but there are two 'harms', one of them a person who is supposed to be his protector *from* harm.

This kind of behaviour was reported by the *Observer* newspaper (16 August 2009) to have been noticed by the grandmother of Peter Connelly (Baby 'P'). Three adults were convicted of unlawfully killing the 17-month-old child and this was a brutal case of child abuse that hit the headlines of the British press during 2009. It was one of the reasons that led us to write this book. The grandmother said that the toddler would become terrified – 'screaming and crawling' (as we shall see, another well-documented sign of disorganized attachment behaviour) – when one of the men entered the room. The child's mother commented that he often did this, because he was frightened of tall people. Peter's behaviour could be seen as a *possible* indicator of disorganized attachment, especially if the situation the child was in when the man entered the room also contained a level of distress. (None of the police officers, social workers or health professionals, who between them made over 60 visits, were aware of the presence of either male, as they both hid whenever anyone came to the house.)

What we are describing are situations when a child's attachment system is activated, but not terminated. Given the options of 'fight, flight or freeze', the child's brain selects the latter as the 'least worst' option. But the immediate solution of shutting down is now known to carry with it serious consequences. The motionless exterior is a façade masking a complex biochemical and neurological process: on the outside all seems calm, but on the inside there is turbulence. In the short to medium term, significant changes in the body's biochemistry take place when stress remains high and unregulated. This produces hormone imbalances which, in turn, directly impede or alter neurological structures and connections. Toxic, unremitting stress literally changes the way the brain develops and the way the mind makes sense of relationships. In the long term, there is a significant risk of mental ill-health resulting from the chronic struggle to form mutually satisfying relationships with others, emanating from a deeply distorted view of oneself as entirely unlovable and unworthy of affection. Because the brain is a pattern-recognizing organism, familiar and predictable pathways are always selected, even if they are sometimes not optimal for the child's development.

If individuals go on to have children of their own, there is a significant risk that they will develop in the same way. This is far more complex and nuanced, however, than saying 'children who are abused usually become abusers'. There are many adults who were abused as children who, thankfully, do not go on to abuse a child of their own (or anyone else's). For example, more girls are sexually abused than boys... but the majority of adult sexual abusers are men, not women. Research on disorganized attachment now offers a powerful explanatory mechanism capable of clarifying with some precision why some children go on to abuse, while others do not.

Although the experience of 'fear without solution' leads to profound changes in neurochemistry, the effects can be reversed through the provision of warm, responsive, boundaried and predictable relationships. The consistent message is that early intervention is preferable. This need not necessarily mean removing children from their birth parents – it can often involve working with them to help increase 'sensitive and attuned parenting'. The aim is to offer the right kind of help, sooner rather than later. Therefore, in addition to outlining the complexity of disorganized attachment, we discuss the recent and, in the main, optimistic research findings about what can be done about it.

The effects of experiencing the persistent and chronic inability to find love and protection from a disconnected and neglectful caregiver can be lasting and damaging, especially when a child is frightened by an abusive parent. Consider the following extract from Graham Farmelo's 2009 biography of Paul Dirac – the Nobel Prize winner and pioneer of quantum physics – in his book *The Strangest Man*. Dirac's friend Kurt Hofer, himself an experimental physicist, is recalling the only time during their long relationship when Dirac spoke of his childhood. Farmelo describes how Hofer 'was ill-prepared when, one Friday evening in the spring of 1980, Dirac's vacuum-packed emotions burst into the open' (p.3). Hofer describes how Dirac's 'language remained simple and direct, but, as he began to talk about his childhood, his voice tightened...'

'I never knew love or affection when I was a child,' Dirac said, the normally neutral tone of his voice perceptibly tinged with sorrow... the family was dominated, Dirac recalled, by his father, a tyrant who bullied his wife, day in, day out, and insisted that their three children speak to him in his native French, never in English. At mealtimes, the family split into two: his mother and siblings would eat in the kitchen and speak in English, while Dirac sat in the dining room with his father, speaking only in French. This made every meal an ordeal for Dirac: he had no talent for languages, and his father was an unforgiving teacher. Whenever Dirac made a slip – a mispronunciation, a wrongly gendered noun, a botched subjunctive – his father made it a rule to refuse his next request. Even at that time, he had digestive problems and often felt sick when he was eating, but his father would refuse him permission to leave the table if he had made a linguistic error. Dirac would then have no option but to sit still and vomit. This did not happen just occasionally, but over and over again, for years. (p.5)

Dirac's monologue continued for over two hours when finally, exhausted,

he spelt out the conclusion he eventually reached about the extent of his debt to his father: 'I owe him absolutely nothing.' That final rasp made Hofer flinch; he could not help but grimace. Dirac hardly ever spoke an unkind word about anyone, but here he was, denouncing his own father with a vehemence most people reserve for the cruellest abusers. (p.6)

Kurt Hofer acknowledges that he 'simply could not conceive of any childhood as dreadful as Dirac's' (p.6) but 'could not help asking himself, over and again: "Why was Paul so bitter, so obsessed with father?"'. Readers are unlikely to be surprised why he was 'so obsessed with his father' and why he spoke, many years later, about him 'with a vehemence most people reserve for the cruellest abusers'. After all, what his father did *was* cruelly abusive.

In this book, we outline what disorganized attachment behaviour is and what happens when children are routinely afraid or wary of the people who they should see as their protectors, and as people who love, cherish and delight in them. We also outline and discuss contemporary, evidence-based interventions, aimed at helping family members. While disorganized attachment is a phenomenon affecting infants and young children, it re-emerges in adolescence and adulthood in different ways.

We have tried to write in an accessible, straightforward style because parts of the subject matter are complex and the research designs and findings sometimes dense. We have both noticed a look of horror slowly pass through an entire audience of practitioners and clinicians at recent conferences we have attended in this field, especially when neurological, biochemical and genetic research is presented. The common cry is 'This is very interesting, but I lost the plot when s/he talked about...' And when some of the newer forms of statistical analysis appear on the PowerPoint slides a palpable sense of panic mixed with frustration ripples through the lecture theatre. So we've also tried hard to present statistical information in an understandable and relevant form! Our aim in this book is that of explication and clarification to a readership eager to find out about the potential this field of research has for our understanding of abuse and maltreatment and how to work with adults to prevent its occurrence with both today's and tomorrow's children.

We are both experienced practitioners and managers, involved in working with children and families. Additionally, over the past 14 years, Yvonne has worked with a considerable number of professionals from all agencies on developing their knowledge and skills. David has been an academic for over 20 years, more recently as Professor of Social Work at Middlesex University, London, and then at the University of Kent, where he has also been Deputy Head of the School of Social Policy, Sociology and Social Research, one of the highest rated for its research excellence in the UK. His area of research expertise is in the field of child welfare and protection.

Child welfare and protection services and policies in the 21st century span a large number of organizations and professional groups. Consequently this book is relevant to social workers; doctors, paediatricians and health visitors; clinical and educational psychologists; police officers; and teachers. Their supervisors and managers will also find much in the book to interest them. Naturally, the book is of direct relevance to qualifying and post-qualifying practitioners, as well as post-graduate research students.

Layout of the book

In the first chapter we examine contemporary research into the various influences on, associations with and consequences of disorganized attachment (DA). Chapter 2 presents our *Pathway Model* summarizing the connections between what emerge as the main links between caregiver behaviours and DA. In Chapter 3 we look at how DA and the key caregiver behaviours can be assessed. Chapter 4 offers a review of the exciting research into affective neurology and biochemistry and how it links to disorganized attachment. Chapters 5, 6 and 7 focus on the caregiver behaviours identified in the Pathway Model described in Chapter 2 and which can begin to predict disorganized attachment relationships in young children, adolescents and adults. Chapter 8 considers the kinds of interventions able to help children and families. In Chapter 9 we outline a new project we began in three London boroughs in 2009, soon after the death of Peter Connelly. This book carries the subtitle 'Theory and Practice for Working with Children and Adults'. We consider the main practice-based implications of the theory and research in each chapter but we focus more specifically on interventions in Chapters 5 to 9. We conclude with some brief thoughts on the implications of what the research may tell us about trends in parenting more generally.

Part I

THEORETICAL AND RESEARCH BACKGROUND

Chapter 1

What is Disorganized Attachment?

Introduction

A brief historical context to John Bowlby's attachment theory

John Bowlby (1907–1990) is one of the most important theoretical psychologists in the past 50 years. His legacy is astonishing, and his ideas have revolutionized our understanding of close relationships, especially between carers and infants. His insights came at a personal cost as he was ostracized by the psychoanalytic fraternity for daring to contradict Sigmund Freud. Initially, too, his theory was met with derision by an incredulous public.

Bowlby believed that certain species – but most particularly humans and primates – demonstrate a need for proximity with an adult during infancy. Bowlby's insights as an ethologist were remarkably different from those of Freud's, who believed that an infant's affiliation to a carer was related primarily to the drive for food. Harry Harlow's controversial experiments with infant macaque monkeys were among the first to confirm Bowlby's perspective. Harlow separated infant monkeys from their mothers and placed them in an isolation cage for different periods of time. In the cage, which was maintained at a constant warm temperature, were two wire surrogate models. One of the wire surrogates had a bottle of milk placed at the breast area, while the other was wrapped in terry-towelling: a cuddly alternative to the 'milk-machine'. What would the separated infant do, and to 'whom' would it turn?

The answer was fascinating and overturned many of the received ideas about human motivation and drives, held it should be said by most people at the time. For a while, the infants showed clear indications that the experience of separation was visibly traumatic because the monkeys simply shivered in the corner, through fear, not the cold. When they became hungry they cautiously approached the wire 'milk-machine' and, realizing that it contained food, drank greedily…and then re-turned to the corner and shivered with fear again. After some time, the infant monkeys would fearfully touch the softer surrogate model. The feel of the towelling attracted them sufficiently for them to spend over 20 hours a day cuddling the 'soft' monkey (even though they were still petrified as a result of their loss). This unethical but astonishing experiment indicated to Bowlby that there was something else going on when an infant suckles its mother than simply food acquisition. He called this additional need, over and above the urge for milk, 'attachment'.

The evacuation of children during the Second World War

The seeds of Bowlby's ideas about attachment were sown during the Second World War, when hundreds of thousands of children were evacuated from UK cities to the countryside to avoid the consequences of German bombing raids. He studied what happened with two colleagues at Cambridge University – Melanie Klein and Susan Isaacs, both formidable pioneers in psychoanalysis and child psychology respectively. He noticed that, all other things being equal (i.e. not being placed in a receiving family in which the child was abused), the children who had been brought up in what we would now call 'secure parenting' – with parents who are loving, responsive and emotionally available, yet appropriately boundaried when necessary – coped and fared better than children who were brought up in the style of parenting almost universally assumed to be 'best' for a growing child. At this time the prevailing view was that a disciplined environment was best for all children. They should be 'seen and not heard' and 'know their place'. 'Big boys shouldn't cry'; if they *did* cry, then their tears would most often be met with a remarkably illogical and insensitive injunction: 'If you don't stop crying, I'll give you something to cry for.' Anything emotionally demonstrative, and any attempts to consider the child's feelings, were discouraged on the basis that it would 'spoil' the child; in fact, an oft-used phrase at the time was 'spare the rod and spoil the child' (which roughly translated means 'children need a good smack from time to time, otherwise they become disobedient and, if unchecked, increasingly belligerent and unlikable').

Bowlby's research with young offenders

John Bowlby also undertook research on young offenders – 'juvenile delinquents' as they were called at the time. Consistent with his abiding interest in how our past affects our present and future, he noticed that the most wayward youngsters had virtually all experienced chequered early caregiving histories. He found that these superficially 'tough' young offenders were at heart yearning for the attention, self-esteem and approval they had not experienced from their parents. He found in their and others' recollections of their early childhood numerous examples of all kinds of abuse, as well as neglect. But Bowlby was particularly struck by their memories of the emotional unavailability of their carers: at heart, these 'delinquents' either didn't know what they meant to their parents, or worse still they knew exactly what they meant to them; which wasn't very much at all. Criminal activity temporarily filled the gap, as it has for disaffected youth through the ages, and as it does today, but it never fully satiated the need for love and affection. Received wisdom reacted with incredulity to the suggestion that a young offender's behaviour could have anything to do with the way a child was brought up, except in the sense of the parents 'spoiling the child' through a lack of discipline. Criminals were simply the result of a 'bad seed' or because they were members of the 'poorer classes', a socio-political invention almost universally thought to equate with fecklessness and dishonesty, by definition. The idea that young offenders might have been brought up in ways which left them with a deep sense of anxiety over their sense of worth in their parents' minds was simply unheard of; and, when Bowlby began to articulate his thesis, it was ridiculed.

But it was this early series of observations and reflections – Harlow's work on separated infant macaques, the mass evacuation of British children in the 1940s and Bowlby's own research on the early relational biographies of young offenders – that formed the basis of his monumental trilogy centring on the processes of *attachment, separation* and *loss* (Bowlby 1969, 1973, 1980). Although a great deal of research has been undertaken since their publication, most notably more recently in the fields of neurology, biochemistry and genetics, Bowlby's underpinning theoretical ideas have proved remarkably robust and intact.

He proposed that the attachment behavioural system is responsible for regulating the infant's propensity to monitor physically and psychologically the accessibility of the attachment figure. Bowlby concluded that from a very early stage the attachment system acts initially to protect the child from harm, threat and, in particular, fear and danger, but later provides a 'secure base' from which the child can explore the environment. According to Bowlby (1969) the attachment system activates 'goal-corrected behaviour', a process of selecting from a range of possible behavioural responses certain specific, patterned actions to enable the individual to achieve physical and emotional closeness to the attachment figure as a 'safe haven' (Marvin and Britner 1999). Behaviours change as goal-proximity is reached, at which point the system is de-activated (but remains alert to additional environmental stressors and dangers). Attachment behaviours intended to increase proximity – such as crying, gazing and calling – are unconsciously selected if the child cannot reach his or her attachment figure, depending not just on the *physical* distance from the attachment figure but also his or her perceived *emotional availability*: the fact that a parent is nearby physically does not assuage attachment needs unless he or she is emotionally present. Perceived emotional closeness also determines how much hugging, clinging and smiling is required to ensure the caregiver stays near. When attachment is de-activated, it is replaced by exploration, feeding, etc.

Internal working models

As a result of these early experiences the growing infant develops 'internal working models' (Craik 1943), or 'representations', of relationships, reflecting internalized cognitive and affective schemata and incorporating positive or negative beliefs about the 'self', and about 'significant others' (Bowlby 1973). The accent on 'internal mental representations' – how we think about relationships – is important because, as Berlin and Cassidy (1999) point out, 'what distinguishes attachment theory from...other theories is the *specificity of its predictions about individual differences* and its arguments that mental representations...underlie the associations between early attachments and subsequent close relationships' (p.689, emphasis added). Internal working models 'reflect not an objective picture of the "parent", but rather the history of the caregiver's actions or intended actions with/toward the attachment figure' (Main, Kaplan and Cassidy 1985, p.85). During early childhood, internal working models are thought to be relatively flexible (hence the term 'working'). Bowlby (1979) maintained, however, that interactions of a similar kind strengthen the emerging working models, for better or worse, and in the process render them less susceptible to change.

Persistently rejecting, hostile, disconnected or frightening attachment figures usually lead to the development of an internal working model based upon an expectation that others are similarly unavailable or unpredictable (Bretherton and Mulholland 1999) or, worse still, that the self, deep at its core, is unlovable. This expectation, in turn, may lead the child to avoid others, attack others or deceive others, when distressed. These iterations often establish a vicious cycle.

The emergence of four pivotal attachment behaviours

From animal and human studies Bowlby observed that there were four components of attachment; first, we use a caregiver (or substitute) as a *secure base* when our attachment is activated; second, our 'home base' is where we *seek proximity* when we are afraid, hungry, ill, etc.; third, we use the secure base as *safe haven* from which to explore the external world which, when a child is very young, often comprises toys, co-lours, sounds, etc.; finally, we experience strong feelings of *separation protest* when key attachment figures are unavailable, either physically or emotionally. These behaviours operate throughout the lifespan, not just during infancy and childhood.

The following four questions, posed by Hazan and Zeifman (1994), arguably express the core dimensions of an attachment relationship:

> 'Whom do you like to spend time with?' (proximity seeking); 'Whom do you miss most during separations?' (separation protest); 'Whom do you feel you can always count on?' (secure base); and 'Whom do you turn to for comfort when you're feeling down?' (safe haven). (Hazan and Zeifman 1994, quoted in Feeney and Noller 1996, p.71)

To see secure base and safe haven activity at work, watch closely what happens on the return journey home on a crowded train after a day's work. Most commuters at some point will phone home or to a loved one, often stating 'I'm on the train!' There is more going on here than it might first seem because if the passenger is telling his or her partner in order to be picked up from the station, given that the commuter probably makes the same journey every day, he or she only needs to tell the partner if there is a delay (i.e. if he or she is *not* on the train!). What is actually being communicated 'below the surface' – and what might fascinate a social anthropologist – is something like 'Is everything OK, are you OK with me, do you still love me?' The person at the other end probably doesn't respond to any of these 'real' questions as 'I'm on the train' signifies a psychologically safe way for the commuter to gauge the reaction. An example of separation protest, at its most extreme and painful, begins with the death of a loved one and is expressed through the grieving process. A considerable amount of proximity-seeking is also apparent but, because the loved one can no longer be 'reached' physically, the person suffering bereavement usually experiences intense psychic pain and trauma.

Criticisms of attachment theory

As with any comprehensive psychosocial theory of human development, attachment theory has its critics. The first major critical perspective centred on 'mother blaming' and was perhaps best articulated in the early 1980s by Thomas and Chess (1977), and from within feminist critiques generally (e.g. Franzblau 2002). Their critique is also heavily predicated on what they termed the 'monotropic' focus of attachment theory, that is, the assumption that *one* adult was pivotal to the infant's subsequent development. Consequently, the thrust of their argument was that, by focusing upon the very earliest caregiving environment, attachment theory ended up criticizing mothers if optimal conditions did not prevail.

In his later writings, however, Bowlby himself recognized the limitations in over-emphasizing the *mother*–infant relationship. Consequently, in his later works he uses the term 'principal' or 'primary' caregiver (or 'attachment figure'), instead of 'mother'. He also revised his earlier thoughts about *maternal* deprivation (see Bowlby 1988). Most attachment researchers would now agree that children form attachment relationships with more than one adult and that the negative consequences of being separated from one attachment figure can, in many circumstances, be attenuated by another (Main and Weston 1981).

The more recent insights of Sarah Hrdy remind us that, until very recently in our evolutionary history, the average number of parents and 'allo-parents' in an infant's life was around four. Hence, 'mothers and others' (Hrdy 2009) have been the mainstay of a child's physical and emotional development. What attachment theory does is explain at a deep level the mechanisms by which such bonds are created and maintained as well as what happens if and when they are severed, either temporarily or permanently. It is less concerned with 'mothers' or 'fathers', more with universal explanatory processes by which we make lasting psychobiosocial connections with certain other 'special' humans. As we will see in Chapter 6 there are reasons connected with our evolutionary history why humans, with some exceptions, remain intersubjectively entwined in a 'delicate dance' (Y. Shemmings 1996) throughout our lives; no other species relates in the way humans relate to each other, and this is not primarily due to our facility for language acquisition. Reflect for a moment on the fact that it is only humans (along with some higher primates) who seek out another human being when frightened; most animals will seek out a *place*.

A second key critical perspective is that of 'infant determinism' (Goldberg 2000). This is 'the notion that phenomena occurring in infancy wield a special power over later years' (Goldberg 2000, p.246 – discussing the criticisms of Lewis 1997). In more recent attachment research, however, rather than speak of the whole of infancy as the *critical* period for development, the emphasis now is placed more upon *sensitive* periods or 'windows' (Schore 1994), during which key developmental accomplishments tend to be acquired. In this sense, and as Goldberg puts it, 'early attachment does not by any means "determine" later development, but rather it makes a unique contribution along with other influences' (p.247). She refers to Alan Sroufe's (1997) analogy, using the branches on a tree to depict the role of early development on subsequent maturation:

> One may arrive at many different end points from a given standing point and there are many opportunities to cross from one main limb to another via smaller branches. However, the further out one moves on a particular limb, the less likelihood there is of crossing over to other limbs. (Goldberg 2000, p.247)

Mary Ainsworth and the 'Strange Situation Procedure'

A crucial turning point in the development of attachment theory was the hugely influential and timely collaboration between John Bowlby and Mary Ainsworth in the late 1960s, during which period they developed the classic and elegant experiment known as the 'Strange Situation'. This is so called because the procedure mildly activates a toddler's attachment system when a stranger enters a room in which he or she is playing with toys accompanied by the child's primary carer. The Strange Situation Procedure (SSP) provides information about a child's trust in the physical and emotional availability and receptiveness of his or her primary caregiver.

Right from the beginning Bowlby and Ainsworth were interested in the extent to which attachment processes were culture-specific or whether they reflected a 'universal' phenomenon. This is partly why the first two experiments were conducted in Uganda and Baltimore. It is also important to bear in mind that their studies were not conducted in high-risk groups (the relevance of this sampling strategy will become apparent later in this chapter).

The SSP ends with the child being left on its own for a very short period, after which the carer returns. It was through the use of the SSP that the discovery of different attachment patterns first emerged, and it demonstrates powerfully the four components of attachment: secure base, safe haven, separation protest and proximity-seeking behaviours. And it was the SSP that first showed how some children organized attachment behaviour successfully when frightened or stressed. The full sequence used in the SSP is outlined in Box 1.1.

Box 1.1 The Strange Situation Procedure (SSP)

The experimental room contains toys and is often marked off into squares to assist observation. The procedure comprises seven steps or stages, as follows:

Preparation
The parent sits quietly in a chair and is asked not to participate while the toddler explores.

First appearance of the stranger
A stranger enters unannounced, chats to the parent and then approaches the infant with a toy.

First separation episode
The parent leaves quietly. The stranger leaves the child to play with the toys unless he or she stops, and then the stranger tries to interest the infant in them.

First reunion episode
The parent returns and waits for the infant to respond. The stranger leaves quietly.

Second separation episode
Once the infant is settled, the parent then leaves again, this time alone.

Second appearance of the stranger
The stranger re-enters and tries to interest the infant with a toy.

Second reunion episode
The parent comes back in, waits for the infant to respond and then picks up the child; the stranger leaves inconspicuously.

The SSP was designed originally to be used with toddlers aged between 12 and 36 months but it is sometimes used with older children (but the period of separation is extended). There is also an interesting variation by Steve Farnfield (2009), where the SSP is used to assess the nature of attachment between older siblings (who are left together in the room for much longer after the carer has left). He reports that this modification helps social workers decide whether to place siblings together in adoptive or foster homes (it may not be appropriate to place a younger sister with an older brother if there is a proven history of sexual abuse by the brother to his sister, for example).

Differences between secure and insecure attachment

It must have been fascinating to have observed the first SSP tapes because Bowlby and Ainsworth would have known they were travelling in uncharted territory. For example, it was not known whether there would be differences between securely and insecurely attached children when the parent left the room. Similarly, would securely and insecurely attached children be comforted by a stranger when left alone for a short time? And what would the child do when the stranger was in the room when the carer was there too: would the child approach the stranger? (After all, the carer talks to the stranger, so would this signal to the child that it's OK to go to them?) Finally, would differences emerge between securely and insecurely attached children upon the return of the carer after having been left alone?

Although the SSP coding system is complex[1] the early results indicated conclusively that most children reacted in the same way when the parent left the room (on either occasion): they cried and went to the door. Most children in other words displayed *separation protest* behaviour

---

1   See www.psychology.sunysb.edu/attachment/measures/content/ss_scoring.pdf.

(unless they showed an 'attachment disorder' – which, as we will see later, is not the same as disorganized attachment). Also, most children reacted in the same way when the stranger entered the room: with the carer present, the child looks to the carer for reassurance, but doesn't respond to the stranger directly; even with the carer absent, most children do not go to the stranger.

It was *upon the parent's return* that three differences were noted in the behaviour of the child. The first group of children would go to the parent, who typically would pick up and hug the child, soothing the child with reassuring tones. There were some gendered variations – fathers tend to ruffle hair, whereas mothers are more inclined to give pats and pecks or kisses – but the overall message is the same: 'I'm sorry I had to leave you; I know why you're upset, and it's OK to feel that way; let's make it better because I love you and I don't want you to be sad.' The child takes from this the message: 'It's OK to have feelings and I needn't be frightened to show them to my carer; I am loved and cherished.' Interestingly these children wanted to get down and play with the toys again, fairly quickly after being picked up and soothed, although they were seen to keep more of a watchful eye on their parents before being able to immerse themselves in their game. This was something they didn't tend to do at the start of the procedure, unlike insecure children who tend mindfully to watch their parents most of the time, irrespective of whether there is a real threat. Bowlby and Ainsworth referred to this group of children as *securely attached*.

The second group tended not to approach the parent on their return, even though they were visibly upset when their carer left the room. Instead they appeared relatively unmoved by the separation. We say 'appear' because, as will become apparent in Chapter 4, what is going on 'under the surface', especially with regard to levels of cortisol production and regulation, indicates a very different picture: these children are unconsciously repressing and suppressing anxiety. If the child does approach the carer, or looks as if he or she might cry, the parent tends to chide the toddler with a clear expectation that the child controls his or her emotion. The child is not usually picked up. The parental message here is: 'I will be cross with you if you get upset because there is no need to; you will only get my attention if you are behaving well, which for me means controlling yourself.' The child, in turn, takes away the message: 'I'm not sure how my parent thinks about me. If I show my feelings it annoys him/her, so it's not safe or a good idea to do so. My carer doesn't show physical or emotional affection towards me. I must try to be "good" at all times, otherwise s/he could reject me.' These children were referred to as *insecurely attached (anxious-avoidant)*.

The third group revealed a different pattern. When their parents returned, these children wanted to be picked up but they were not calmed or soothed by their experience, and almost immediately they wanted to get down...and then be picked up again. They were fractious and were unable to be soothed by the parents who, in their turn, seemed to find the experience of their child being upset very confusing...but unable – as opposed to unwilling – to do much about it constructively. Their efforts to calm their child seemed rather haphazard and usually misplaced (or 'misattuned', the term used in more recent attachment research. The message from the parent was: 'I find all of this distressing but I don't know what to do about it. I don't know what s/he wants or how to stop the crying so I just give up or get more flustered.' The child takes away the idea that 'I don't really know what to do to get my carer's attention: sometimes s/he feeds me when I'm hungry, another time it'll be when s/he's hungry; sometimes s/he plays rough when I need to be calm, yet at other times, when I need to be fired up, s/he goes all quiet. I just can't work my parent out and I don't know how she sees me and whether s/he really loves me – s/he says s/he does often...but...' These children were called *insecurely attached (resistant-ambivalent)*.

No doubt for the sake of brevity, the word 'anxiety' is now routinely omitted, so we talk about 'avoidantly' or 'ambivalently' attached children, but it is important not to forget that it is *anxiety* that lies at the heart of the experience of the insecurely attached child. At the core, children can only achieve proximity by markedly downplaying or excessively over-accentuating affect when they are frightened, hungry, angry, tired or in pain and, later on, as they develop more complex emotions, such as feeling lonely, sad, jealous, frustrated, etc.

The main point about each of these three different attachment organizations is precisely that: they represent an *organized* way for the child to maintain proximity to his or her caregiver. Securely attached children learn intuitively that the expression of their needs, whatever they are and however strong, can be expressed safely in their caregiver's presence who, in turn, will strive to understand and regulate those needs. Insecure avoidant children learn that the best way to keep their parent available – physically, rather than emotionally – is not to display their feelings. The insecurely ambivalent toddler 'knows' that he or she has to adopt a strategy which involves behaving more randomly and unpredictably than his or her caregiver.

Most people intuitively think that security is the optimal behaviour but Patricia Crittenden stresses that insecure attachment is not per se to be avoided:

> Anxious patterns [but she means 'organized' attachment patterns] are often thought of as undesirable…anxious attachment is good, it is the child's contribution to his or her own survival…anxious attachment is not the problem; danger is the problem, and that is what we, as professionals, should focus on. Change the danger, not the child. (Crittenden 2008, p.21)

You might like to try the exercise in Box 1.2 to check out your understanding of the secure and insecure attachment organizations. You will find the answer at the end of the chapter.

Box 1.2 An exploratory exercise on child security
Items taken from the Attachment Q-Set (Vaughn and Waters 1990)

Which of the following behaviours do you think are indicative of security?

1. Child is careful and gentle with toys and pets

2. Child is more interested in people than things

3. Child laughs and smiles easily with a lot of different people

4. Child quickly gets used to people or things that initially made him or her shy or frightened

5. Child prefers toys that are modelled after living things

6. Child readily shares with carer or lets carer hold things if he or she asks

7. When child is near carer and sees something he or she wants to play with, child doesn't fuss or try to drag carer over to it

8. Child is willing to talk to new people, show them toys, or show them what he or she can do, if carer asks him or her to

9. Child clearly shows a pattern of using carer as a base from which to explore

10. Child recognizes when carer is upset and becomes quiet and upset him or herself

Prevalence and culture

There is a remarkably reliable 60/40 split between securely and inse-curely attached children respectively. As Marinus van IJzendoorn and Abraham Sagi put it, the three basic attachment patterns have been 'found in every culture in which attachment studies have been con-ducted so far' (van IJzendoorn and Sagi 1999). The largest study to date, using a rigorous sampling frame across the US by Philip Shaver and his colleagues (see Mickelson, Kessler and Shaver 1997), eventually comprising 8098 adults, found, like most of the smaller preceding stud-ies, 59.0 per cent of adults, as 'secure', 25.2 per cent as 'avoidant' and 11.3 per cent as 'ambivalent' (leaving 4.5 per cent unclassified). This ratio holds across cultures, as do the four basic attachment behaviours of proximity seeking, secure base effect, safe haven and separation protest. There are observable cultural differences when it comes to the amount of time a carer (typically the mother) spends with new-born and very young babies, with Japanese mothers in Sapporo (Behrens, Main and Hesse 2007) tending to spend longer holding their babies in close proximity than (say) northern European mothers (Grossmann *et al.* 1985). The implication for the SSP is that the procedure is not used until later; but when it is, Japanese toddlers react in the same way as other children.

The four basic attachment behaviours can therefore be viewed in a similar way to Paul Ekman's work on how our facial expressions univer-sally display powerful clues to our internal emotional state and that, with at least six of our primary emotions – happiness, sadness, anger, fear, surprise and disgust – all cultures tend to use the same combinations of facial muscles when experiencing these emotions (Ekman 2007). So, for example, in the case of happiness, all cultures studied so far display subtle micro-movements of muscles at the corner of the eyes, which it is virtually impossible to control (except from a local anaesthetic…or from Botox injections!) and also very difficult to move at will. Notice that 'smiling' is not a good indicator of happiness, as the mouth *can* be made to smile deliberately. There is, of course, a huge cultural contribution to our displays of happiness but it concerns *what makes us laugh and what we find funny*: when we do, we all show our emotion in the same way, irrespective of where we were born or where we live.

It is important to remember that we are only referring here to attachment-specific behaviour and culture. Participants on educational and training programmes regularly point out that in some cultures 'stranger-danger' is not promoted; indeed, children are encouraged *not* to be wary of strangers. This difference might manifest itself in such children talking to a stranger in a supermarket, airport or on a train if accompanied by their parent or trusted carer...but they would tend not to allow the stranger to comfort and reassure them when they are on their own in the SSP, unless they are displaying an 'attachment disorder'.

There is more of a cultural variation when it comes to the split between the two insecure attachment organizations. In the US and northern Europe studies regularly find around 25 per cent avoidant attachment compared with around 15 per cent ambivalent attachment. Move south, towards north Africa and southern Europe, and we find almost complete reversal, with more individuals assessed as ambivalent than avoidant. This may explain some of the national stereotypes when describing people from different countries (for example, the British 'stiff upper lip' compared to the more emotional, 'hot-blooded' Italian).

Attachment in adulthood

Internal working models are thought to begin at around 12 months, and then continue developing throughout the lifespan into complex mental representations of how 'self' and 'other' interrelate. This is often depicted geometrically by two orthogonal axes. Positive and negative views of self and other produce four quadrants constituting different attachment 'styles'. The concept and number of attachment 'styles' (which suggests innate traits) tends now to be rejected in favour of the term 'organization' to describe the enduring lifespan aspects of attachment behaviour.

By focusing on the child's internal world Ainsworth *et al.* (1978) proposed a dynamic, internal representational model from their study of the behaviour of infants in the SSP that reflected their *expectations* of the caregiver's availability and responsiveness – what Howard Steele refers to as our ability to know that we are 'heard, seen, held and understood'. Such expectations are derived from the child's experience of how he or she has been responded to in the past, based upon the growing infant's 'self–other' geometry.

Adult attachment theory grew as a consequence out of the early pioneering work on infant development into adolescence and then naturally on to the study of close relationships in adulthood. In general, most attachment theorists maintain that, although there is only one secure style, as in childhood there exist different ways of being insecure. There is also the concept of an 'earned secure' (Hesse 1999) attachment organization which refers to adults who, whilst not being securely attached as children, have 'acquired' an ability to relate to others more securely, usually as a result of meeting a person who has offered model-disconfirming behaviour, such as a partner, teacher or therapist. Most childhood attachment researchers continue to refer to Ainsworth's 'avoidant' and 'ambivalent' styles.

Instead of the axial descriptors 'self' and 'other' the psychometric work of Chris Fraley and colleagues consistently report the robustness, reliability and validity of 'attachment-related avoidance' and 'attachment-related anxiety' (Fraley and Phillips 2009). In addition to the *balanced* (secure) and *preoccupied* styles, their model sub-divides the avoidant style: the *dismissing* style reflects a positive view of 'self' combined with a negative view of 'others', whereas the *fearful* style combines negative views of both 'self' and 'others'. Childhood 'ambivalent' attachment becomes the 'preoccupied' pattern in adulthood and, in a similar vein, avoidant attachment maps to the 'dismissing' organization. But the 'fearful' attachment pattern in adulthood is thought to include aspects of both insecure infant attachment organizations (Klohnen and John 1998).

Attachment theory as a 'theory of emotion regulation'

Theoretical and empirical studies suggest that anger, sadness (or depression) and anxiety (or fear) form the basic negative emotions (Feeney 1995). (This is different to Paul Ekman's work on emotion, which refers merely to facial expression.) Judy Feeney goes on to link anger, sadness and anxiety with the three types of emotional expression – protest, despair and detachment – which, as we have already seen, John Bowlby saw as connected to the disruption of attachment relationships. However, not all emotions are experienced subjectively in the same ways. Often, powerful cultural forces inhibit their expression. Thus,

> while anger, sadness, and anxiety are all rated as negative in hedonic tone (i.e. low in pleasantness…) there are important differences among these emotions. The subjective experience of anger is associated with tension and impulsiveness and with a tendency for active and destructive behaviour: for this reason, the expression of anger is often discouraged by social norms… By contrast, the experience of sadness, which is associated with perceptions of deprivation, is characterised

by less tension than most negative emotions and is generally regarded as more tolerable; the experience of anxiety is associated with uncertainty, insecurity, and lack of control, and is marked by high tension but low impulsiveness... (Feeney 1995, p.145)

From an attachment perspective, emotion regulation develops as a result of the way early caregivers responded to the infant's distress signals. This in turn leads to different learned and internalized strategies to organize emotional experience and to deal primarily with negative feelings. Through a 'process of generalisation, these strategies come to be applied to any distressing situation' (Feeney and Noller 1996, p.37).

Our emotional states are often moderated with the help of others – through their empathy, support and sometimes humour – or by the use of mood-altering substances such as cigarettes, alcohol and other narcotics (Magai 1999) as well as by over- or under-eating. The term 'affect regulation', however, most typically refers to 'acquired strategies of emotion *self*-management' (Thompson 1994, p.28, emphasis added). It is these *internal* strategies of emotion regulation which are now a key area of attachment research; indeed, some attachment writers now argue that 'attachment theory can be described as a theory of affect regulation; that is, a theory about how people handle negative emotion' (Feeney and Noller 1996, p.36; and see also Mikulincer and Shaver 2007). Patricia Crittenden, for example, sees attachment behaviours as a direct result of the way the child learns to deal with fear and danger (Crittenden 2008).

In the main, affect regulation strategies are only needed in stressful situations – humans do not usually become overwrought when blissfully happy! – and they constitute an important feature of all attachments, but especially those concerned with disorganization. A significant area of recent research is the operation of the hypothalamic-pituitary-adrenal (HPA) axis, an important mechanism for regulating our neuroaffective biochemistry and which is seriously disrupted in children exhibiting disorganized attachment behaviour.

The discovery of disorganized attachment behaviour

We now return to the early experiments by Bowlby and Ainsworth because they found a number of children whose behaviour did not fit the three categories that seemed to accommodate all the other children they encountered. Their original studies using the SSP consistently identified a group of children whose behaviour could not be subsumed under the three categories of secure, avoidant and ambivalent attachment behaviour. Whilst these children tended, in the main, to behave like other children both when the carer left the room *and* in the stranger's presence – although a few, as we have mentioned already, exhibited what would later be termed 'attachment disorders' – the researchers noticed that some children behaved oddly when their carer returned. They saw children who, on reunion with the parent, would begin to approach the carer, but then stop suddenly in their tracks and not move for 15–20 seconds; or they would hold up their hands in front of their face. One child was observed to walk towards the carer while turning his or her head the other way; quite a few sank to the floor and remained there for some time, motionless and 'frozen'. Karlen Lyons-Ruth offers more recent examples:

> One unclassifiable infant, for example, cried loudly while attempting to gain her mother's lap, then suddenly fell silent and stopped moving for several seconds. Others were observed: moving away from the parent to the wall when apparently frightened by the stranger; screaming by the door upon separation from the parent and then moving silently away upon reunion; raising hand to mouth in an apprehensive gesture immediately upon seeing the parent; and, while in an apparently good mood, swiping at the parent's face with a trancelike expression. (Lyons-Ruth and Jacobvitz 2008, p.676)

Bowlby and Ainsworth recorded these behaviours as 'unclassified' and enquired into their early histories. They noticed that many of the children had been abused and/or neglected (or there were unproven or unsubstantiated concerns about maltreatment). But it wasn't until the early 1990s that Mary Main and Judith Solomon began to analyse the behaviour more systematically from an empirical and theoretical perspective. The kinds of behaviours seen in children exhibiting DA were categorized by Main and Solomon in 1990 after re-classifying 200 'anomalous' SSP videotapes. Lyons-Ruth and Jacobvitz (2008) describe the behaviours as follows (note the 'shutting down' quality of each, denoting 'fear without solution'):

> unclassified infants were observed approaching the parent with head averted; rocking on hands and knees following an abortive approach; or screaming by the door for the parent, then moving away on

reunion. What unclassified infants appeared to have in common were contradictory intentions (approaching a parent with head averted), or behaviours that involved apprehension, either directly (fearful facial expressions, oblique approaches), or indirectly (e.g. disoriented behaviours, including dazed or trance-like expressions; or freezing of all movement at the parent's entrance). (p.676)

Such behaviour was demonstrated in about 10–15 per cent of the children, a figure which we will see has appeared regularly in replications or in studies using similar methods (see Out, Bakermans-Kranenburg and van IJzendoorn 2009).

Mary Main and the notion of 'fear without solution'

Mary Main is thought to have first coined the evocative phrase 'fear without solution' to capture the central paradox underpinning disorganized attachment, which is an overwhelming sense of *fear* that cannot be resolved in either the short or the medium term. The powerful emotion at the root of DA is, however, somewhat different from our usual experience of fear. Consider, for example, encountering a maze and then gradually realizing that there is no way out. One can imagine the growing panic as one's fate unfolds. Alternatively, imagine entering a supposedly haunted room and accepting a bet to stay the night on your own there. Even the toughest and most hardened sceptic is likely to become troubled by fearful thoughts. But this is not like the fear experienced by the very young child. His or her fear is characterized by a lack of preparedness, even an absence of foreboding, with a shocking immediacy that neither of two options is going to provide any respite from an avalanche of fear that envelops him or her when the carer re-enters the room in the SSP.

A large number of studies on the developmental origins of DA behaviour followed swiftly after the observations made by Mary Main and various associates (Main and Solomon 1990; Main and Weston 1981) as well as a number of systematic reviews by Marinus van IJzendoorn and his colleagues at the University of Leiden. These studies also include a growing and reliable index of key correlates and consequences of disorganized attachment.

Disorganized attachment behaviour is only observed in infants and toddlers for a short time, after which the child's behaviour resolves to a more organized attachment pattern (Lyons-Ruth and Jacobvitz 2008), including occasionally even to a secure pattern. By early adolescence disorganized attachment behaviour tends to become more controlling in one of two ways. School-age children and early adolescents will either act 'punitively' towards the parent, by showing hostile or directive behaviour, typically by the use of harsh commands, verbal threats and physical aggression (Moss, Cyr and Dubois-Comtois 2004), or by a more apparently 'caring' approach. Such children appear excessively cheery, polite or helpful toward the caregiver but the behaviour is actually geared to controlling the parent, as a result of their chronic unpredictability or malevolence (and often both).

We have seen that our state of mind with regard to close relationships – our internal working model of attachment – is a critical factor influencing the kind of parenting given to a child: how we were parented has a powerful influence on the way we parent our own and other people's children (think of adopters, foster carers and those involved in group care). Things may appear to proceed relatively smoothly until there is a trauma of some kind that isn't 'made sense of' in the mind of the person to whom it is happening. And it's not always the obvious traumas such as death and divorce, for example, which become unresolved. What seems to be fairly incontrovertible is that the way we deal with the 'big' problems life throws at us is heavily dependent upon the way we learned to deal with them as a child. Fascinatingly, it tends not to be *events* in themselves that cause problems for us, rather it is the *sense we make* of the events that determines whether eventually they become integrated, and 'dealt with', so that we can 'move on' instead of becoming emotionally stuck. An example is given in Case study 1.1 as it powerfully illustrates the point (the case comes from our experience working in social services some years ago).

Case study 1.1 An example of a child developing a view of self as unlovable

Two girls aged 12 were admitted to the accident and emergency department on a Friday afternoon. The orthopedic surgeon and the nursing team were struck by the almost identical nature of the fractures to their arms. But the circumstances which led to their admission to hospital were remarkably different. The first girl had been riding her bike when she skidded into the path of a car which clipped her back wheel and sent her crashing into the kerb, shattering her arm. The second girl – whom one of us was visiting – had been told by her father the day before that if she didn't improve her mark in the maths test the next day, he would break her arm. Not surprisingly, she did badly. True to his word he went into the garage, grabbed a hammer and proceeded to hit her with it, just once – not ferociously, but in a cold and calculating manner to do what he said he would do: break her arm.

To the hospital team, these are virtually the same physiological events, and so the procedure for treatment and post-operative care will be the same. To the social worker, the psychologist or the foster carer, on the other hand, these are radically different *psychosocial* events. Over and above the injury itself, the first girl's ability to get back on a bike with confidence will likely depend on two things: the patience, encourage-ment and kindness of the close people in her life – parents, siblings, friends, teachers, etc. – alongside her temperament, that is, whether she is timid or outgoing, tenacious or reticent, etc. The second girl's chance of 'recovery' is very different because she has to contend with and make sense of questions about how could her father hate and loathe her so much that he could inflict such terrible injuries; and over so very little. She is unlikely, however, to hold her father responsible for what hap-pened. She is far more likely to develop the internal belief that *she* is to blame, because *she* is naughty – even wicked – and almost certainly unlikable, unlovable, even despicable. After all, he didn't harm her in a fit of temper (which she might *just* have understood and been able to make sense of, with some help).

If someone comes along in her life, now or in the future – a teacher, a boy/girl friend – who genuinely does like or love her, this will be ex-perienced as extremely threatening. Her mind will be screaming at her: 'How can someone possibly love me? My own father didn't – it's only a matter of time before this person sees the real me.' And it is at this point that something awful happens: if the person doesn't reject her, she is very likely to make herself as unlikable and unlovable as she can, to 'get it over with'. It is as if her mind cannot tolerate the idea that someone *might* possibly love her – 'Daddy doesn't, so why would you?' It is this phe-nomenon, similar to breaking one's toys and smashing up one's room, seen when we begin to get close to children who are deeply hurting, that so often throws unsuspecting workers off the scent and upsets them, precisely because it always seems to happen just at point when they thought they were getting somewhere.

But if we can think it through from the point view of an internal working model of attachment, it begins to make a lot more sense. Of course she rejects us when we think we are getting through. Keep things superficial and it's OK; get closer emotionally, show her we really care, and that can be devastating and terrifying because the chance of further rejection, in her mind at any rate, is inevitable. She is – to herself, that is – a loathsome creature…that's why her daddy broke her arm. If the first girl was brought up in a secure environment (or even a moderately in-secure avoidant and ambivalent one) she probably will not have thought that the accident happened because of anything to do with her – except if she had been careless on the bike. So she can resolve it (re-'solve', i.e. 'work out again') by, in the main, simply getting on the bike again.

This example is a powerful illustration of the following point made by David Howe:

> Abused children are likely to deny the hostile, negative feelings and the mental representations that their attachment figures hold of them as children. To accept such feelings and representations is to have to face the...fact that your carer, whom you love and on whom you depend, has malevolent intentions towards you. (Howe *et al.* 1999)

Before moving on to look at contemporary research into disorganized attachment we need to distinguish *disorganized attachment* from *Reactive Attachment Disorder* (RAD). RAD comprises a set of contradictory at-tachment behaviours when the child is presented with two different scenarios: (i) with strangers and (ii) when in distress. A distinction is made between *inhibited RAD* (e.g. presenting as uncommunicative, not accepting comfort at times of threat, alarm or distress), on the one hand, and *disinhibited RAD* (e.g. non-selective, random intimacy-seeking; showing a lack of appropriate stranger-wariness; indiscriminate and superficial closeness to any adult), on the other.

The problem with the construct and operational conceptualization of RAD is that the behaviours have not been subjected to the rigorous theoretical and psychometric analysis applied to DA. There are consid-erable overlaps between the inhibited RAD and avoidant (organized) at-tachment strategies, for example. This conceptual confusion is sufficient to leave a number of authors perplexed. For example, 'according to the experts, there are only a few empirical studies on the validity of the RAD... In fact, it is astonishing that a widely used diagnostic system for attachment disorders seems almost not to be informed by attachment theory' (van IJzendoorn and Bakermans-Kranenburg 2003, p.315).

How contemporary research into disorganized attachment is conducted

We focus on specific findings from research into disorganized attach-ment in the next chapter but we conclude Chapter 1 by illustrating how observationally based research is designed and undertaken. In contemporary studies with very young children (e.g. Abrams, Rifkin and Hesse 2006; Hesse and Main 2006; Lyons-Ruth 2003; Out *et al.* 2009), rather than run the SSP in full, carers are asked to interact and play with their child; and in many studies the carer is asked to engage in different kinds of tasks designed progressively to 'challenge' the parent. For example, the session might start with free play with toys; then the parent might be asked to play with his or her child without the toys (e.g. by telling a story – but the parent is not prompted to do so unless he or she is stuck for ideas); after this, the parent might be asked to initiate co-operative activity, such as painting a picture together with his or her child, and then after a set period of time to ask the child to clear up.

These orchestrated observations have added considerably to our knowledge of the kinds of caregiver behaviours associated with DA than is possible using the SSP, which necessarily focuses primarily on carer separations and reunions alongside the appearance of the 'stranger'. The SSP is not designed specifically to explore other interactions between parent and child. And, unlike the SSP which is age-restricted, guided parent–child interactions can be used with older children. For example, in Nancy Kaplan's 1987 study, six-year-olds were shown a picture of a parent–child separation and asked to talk about what the child might do next. One child quickly replied: 'Probably gonna lock himself up. *[Lock himself up?]* Yeah, probably in his closet. *[Then what will he do?]* Probably kill himself' (Kaplan 1987, pp.109–111).

This type of study revealed that parents whose children were classified as disorganized in the SSP exhibited very 'frightening' and 'bizarre' behaviours when playing with their children. And, worryingly, such behaviours occur at the level of around 15 per cent in 'low-risk' populations – the figure that Bowlby and Ainsworth found in their early SSP research which, as mentioned earlier, was also undertaken within low-risk groups. We now know from a number of studies, including the meta-analysis undertaken by Marinus van IJzendoorn and his colleagues at Leiden University, that the proportion of disorganized infants in such low-risk samples is 'disturbingly high, averaging fifteen percent, but ranging to above thirty percent' (Hesse and Main 2000, p.1102). They continue, 'Although a subset of these infants will have been maltreated, it is likely that other factors are involved as well. Intriguingly, about equal percentages of marked lapses in the monitoring of reasoning or discourse during the discussion of loss or abuse within the AAI have also been reported in low-risk populations' (p.1009).

Before we turn in the next chapter to an exploration of research findings we wish to stress that disorganized attachment cannot be inferred from behaviours such as a child's room being a mess, or that he or she appears to be clumsy. 'Disorganized attachment' is a precise term that must involve a situation which mildly activates the child's attachment system *and* into which a carer is 'introduced', either physically as in the SSP, or by asking the child to think about that carer.

Answer to the exercise in Box 1.2

The first five items are not related to attachment security or insecurity, whereas the last five are very closely related, with Item 9 being the most predictive because it captures the essence of what attachment processes are ultimately directed towards: when an individual is secure he or she can find the emotional space to *explore*. The first five items relate more to the child's temperament, which is connected to attachment but in quite complex ways which we consider in more detail later. The final point to note is that the items related closely to attachment (6–10) are different to the first five in one obvious way: they all refer to how the child behaves *in the vicinity of the carer*. This is an important point for child welfare professionals who are often expected to refer to the child's attachment in their assessments.

Chapter 2

Key Pathways to Disorganized Attachment and its Consequences

Introduction

So far we have outlined the key dimensions of disorganized attachment behaviour and how to begin to recognize it. We now present and discuss contemporary research findings to examine other variables with which DA is associated, along with ideas about what might affect its occurrence. A series of questions immediately spring to mind: Are boys more likely to develop DA than girls? Is its occurrence related to temperament, or even genetics? Do children exhibit DA in the presence of one parent or both (or, indeed, other individuals in general)? Are children more likely to show DA behaviour if their parent is depressed, or a substance misuser? Does family violence increase the likelihood of DA? And what of maltreatment itself: does it always lead to DA? We conclude the chapter with a brief review of the consequences of disorganized attachment in adolescence and adulthood.

Forgive us for starting though with a short section on statistics but it is necessary in order to make sense of the findings covered. On the other hand, if you know about the difference between correlation and causation, and mediator and moderator variables, and you're familiar with the concept of 'effect sizes', then you could skip the next section; alternatively, if your knowledge of statistics is a little rusty and you would like a quick refresher, try Chapter 6 in Orme and Shemmings (2010).

Some statistical points

The first point to clarify is the nature of causation itself. This is the idea that one event leads to another and must be distinguished from correlation, which simply means that two events are *related* in some way.

Take the example of smoking and lung cancer. The two are positively correlated as it is consistently the case that a high level of smoking is associated with a greater risk of lung cancer and vice versa: *not* having smoked (or having given up for some years) is associated with a *lower* likelihood of developing lung cancer. But this is not the same as saying that smoking *causes* lung cancer, because there are many people who smoke who don't go on to develop the condition and, conversely, there are people who get lung cancer who have never smoked a cigarette. In respect of disorganized attachment, we are still far from being able to say much, directly and unequivocally, about causal relationships; but there are some clearer pathways of influence emerging between variables.

There will, of course, be circumstances when smoking *is* the direct cause of the cancer, but in other circumstances a connection will be made to an independent variable (known variously as 'predictor' or 'focal' variables – such as genetic predisposition, age, gender, lifestyle, etc.). When independent variables operate together they produce an *interaction* effect on the dependent variable (sometimes referred to as 'target', 'outcome' or 'criterion' variables). So, for example, one individual's genetic predisposition on its own (called a 'main effect') may not lead to lung cancer, yet another person's lifestyle, on its own, may not cause lung cancer. But for a third individual, if *both* factors are present, he or she may well develop the disease. Interacting variables are often called 'moderator' and 'mediator' variables in contemporary research.

Research needs to be based upon experimentation to reveal more about moderator effects; without experimental design, research is 'underpowered' to explore underlying influential mechanisms. But moderator effects reveal little about *why* differential effects emerge between predictor and outcome variables. To bridge this gap requires an exploration of *mediator* variables. A mediator variable explains *why* two or more variables are connected whereas a moderator variable simply tells us that they *are* related. Here is an example from another field:

> As an example, let's consider the relation between social class (SES) and frequency of breast self-exams (BSE). Age might be a moderator variable, in that the relation between SES and BSE could be stronger for older women and less strong or nonexistent for younger women. Education might be a mediator variable in that it explains why there is a relation between SES and BSE. When you remove the effect of education, the relation between SES and BSE disappears. (University of Wisconsin – Madison 1999)

There are four conditions that need to be satisfied to establish whether a variable has a mediating effect (we do not need to explain them here but if you are interested refer to Baron and Kenny 1986 or visit David Kenny's website at http://davidakenny.net).

To relate these points to our review of the correlates and pathways towards disorganized attachment, typical predictor variables include: the parent's gender, the level of substance misuse, level of family violence, genetic predispositions, the level and nature of unresolved loss and trauma in the caregiver, etc. As we shall see, some but not all of these predictor variables are associated with DA to different degrees, but the main effects do not always operate directly on the outcome variable. Some of these predictors interact with each other; in other words, they moderate or mediate the effect on DA. As will be shown, it is only when likely mediator variables are purposefully included into the design of the study that we can begin to see possible pathways of influence.

We want to stress the difference between 'significance levels' and 'effect size' and why the latter has tended to eclipse the former in contemporary research. The following excerpt from a recent book co-authored by one of us (David) explains this point:

> A word about the use of 'significant' as there is often misunderstanding about what it means. Just because a set of results is statistically significant doesn't necessarily mean that they are particularly important in terms of their impact, or 'effect size' as statisticians call it. This can often occur when very large samples are drawn from a given population. Significant findings can emerge but they may not reveal much by way of information about the phenomenon under consideration. This is why a current trend in quantitative research is to concentrate more upon choosing an 'accurate' sample, rather than adopting a 'blunderbuss' approach. An illustrative example is seen in a large European study which looked at, among other things, differences between attachment styles according to gender (Schmitt and 130 members of the *International Sexuality Description Project*; n = 17,804 in 62 cultural regions, 2003). Although some significant results were found, they were often in the order of little more than 0.1 or 0.2 on a scale continuum of 1–6, hence it was the sheer size of the sample that had produced the results. This is why in contemporary research the 'effect size' is measured… (Orme and Shemmings 2010, p.69)

Finally, newer statistical procedures such as path analysis, structural equation modelling and Bayesian analysis are being used more frequently in attachment-based research because they offer greater potential for understanding the effect of intervening variables than do methods relying exclusively on multi-variate analyses.

Some special features of attachment-based research into disorganization

We sometimes refer in what follows to differences in the results depending on whether the Main and Solomon coding is used to classify DA behaviour. The reason is because it includes more index behaviours than other classifications available when most of the research was undertaken.

A number of developments have taken place since the early 1990s: we now have the Atypical Maternal Behaviour Instrument for Assessment and Classification (AMBIANCE; Lyons-Ruth, Bronfman and Parsons 1999) which measures a broad spectrum of disrupted caregiver behaviour and, even more recently, the Disconnected and extremely Insensitive Parenting measure (DIP; Out et al. 2009), which offers the prospect of overcoming what some consider to be a certain lack of discriminant validity in the AMBIANCE measure (see Madigan et al. 2006).

Disorganized attachment is not an attachment 'style' in its own right: children display DA behaviours under specific conditions of activation but their overall attachment pattern resolves into one of the other three organizations as soon as the specific threat that led to their disorganized behaviour disappears. Researchers need to take account of its fleeting nature, which usually means undertaking painstaking observations of parent–child interactions to carefully, reliably and accurately identify DA. This results in small samples, which is not a problem if participants are selected in accordance with psychometrically sound sampling criteria; indeed when this occurs, effect size and statistical power are both increased. (Effect sizes are rated as follows: small effect size, $r = 0.1–0.23$; medium, $r = 0.24–0.36$; large, $r = 0.37$ or larger).

If you are wondering how a child who displays DA might later exhibit secure attachment behaviour then consider the case of asylum-seeking children. They may well have been securely parented until their world was turned upside down by war, or by having witnessed or been the victim of torture. Such experiences may produce DA behaviour in situations which consciously or unconsciously remind the child of earlier trauma but, at other times – for example when with new foster carers – the child may experience genuine or felt security.

In much of the research a 'D' child's *non*-DA behaviour is categorized into one of two classifications: when the child is *not* showing DA, does his or her attachment appear secure or insecure? Karlen Lyons-Ruth changed this coding to that of a more precise *disorganized-approaching* (D-approach) and *disorganized-avoiding/resisting* (D-avoid/resist). The results were fascinating:

> Statistically, the two corresponding subgroups of mothers differed more from each other than from mothers whose infants were not disorganized. Mothers of D-avoid/resist infants displayed significantly higher rates of both role-confusion (self-referential behaviour) and negative intrusive behaviour than did mothers of D-approach infants. Negative intrusive and role-confused behaviours were strongly correlated as well, so these mothers were displaying toward their infants a contradictory mix of rejecting and attention-seeking behaviours. We termed this parenting profile hostile/self-referential regarding attachment. In contrast, mothers of D-approach infants exhibited significantly higher rates of withdrawal than did mothers of D-avoid/resist infants, as well as higher rates of fearful behaviour. Mothers in this subgroup were more fearful, withdrawing, and inhibited and at times appeared particularly sweet or fragile. They were very unlikely to be overtly hostile or intrusive and they usually gave in to the infant's concerted bids for contact. However, they often failed to take the initiative in greeting or approaching the infant, and they often hesitated, moved away, or tried to deflect the infant's requests for close contact before giving in... We termed this group helpless/fearful regarding attachment. Infants of helpless/fearful mothers looked different from infants of hostile/self-referential mothers in that they all continued to express their distress, approach their mothers, and gain some physical contact with them, even though they also displayed disorganized behaviours, including signs of conflict, apprehension, uncertainty, helplessness, or dysphoria. (Lyons-Ruth 2003, p.892)

Carlo Schuengel and his colleagues also discovered the partially protective role of 'alternate' secure parenting. Referring to this study, Marian Bakermans-Kranenburg and her colleagues concluded that 'unresolved, but (alternate) secure mothers showed significantly less-frightening behaviour towards their babies than did unresolved insecure mothers. Moreover, the link between unresolved loss and disorganized infant attachment was only apparent in the group with mothers who were both unresolved and (alternate) insecure' (Bakermans-Kranenburg, van IJzendoorn and Juffer 2005, p.194).

In their latest chapter on disorganized attachment in the revised (2008) *Handbook of Attachment*, Karlen Lyons-Ruth and Deborah Jacobvitz refer to a Leiden University meta-analysis conducted in 1999 – alongside other studies – and point to the following results:

> In 20 studies across 25 samples (N = 1,219) van IJzendoorn and colleagues found that disorganised attachment was accompanied by a secondary classification of ambivalent in 46% of cases, avoidant in 34% of cases and secure in 14% of cases. However, these subtypes may be differentially distributed in low- and high-social risk environments. (Lyons-Ruth and Jacobvitz 2008, p.668)

They go on to indicate that, in middle-income samples, more disorganized infants have been reported to be classified as disorganized-secure and quote a range of 52 per cent to 62 per cent. They also point to studies showing that 'less stable and less supportive family contexts have been associated with instability in attachment classifications across all categories' and that other studies 'found that disruptive family events were specifically related to change to a disorganised classification from 12 to 18 months of age' (p.670).

How does research into disorganized attachment tend to be designed and conducted?

Meta-analytic techniques

Due to the intensity of the observational procedures adopted, by necessity much attachment research relies on relatively small samples. If experimental conditions, sampling techniques and variable control mechanisms adhere to strict protocols, researchers are able to combine the results of a number of smaller studies, in effect, into one large study using a complex statistical procedure called 'meta-analysis'. Marinus van IJzendoorn and his colleagues at Leiden University have become the leaders in this field of statistical research in attachment theory, some of which has concentrated upon DA. Their meta-analysis of DA comprised a statistical combination of nearly 80 studies involving more than 6000 infant–parent pairs. It permitted a series of questions to be considered, each of which we discuss briefly. (A small point about convention to note in what follows is that the combined sample size is denoted by the upper case 'N', with lower case 'n' used to record the size of each composite sample in the meta-analysis.)

An example of the design of a recent study

We first present an outline of a well-designed contemporary study into DA research by Dorothee Out, Marian Bakermans-Kranenburg and Marinus van IJzendoorn at Leiden who developed a new measure of *Disconnected and extremely Insensitive Parenting* (Out *et al.* 2009). The methodological processes of sample selection and assessment procedure reflect elements of other attachment-based research into DA. We provide this outline to 'bring to life' the sections which follow, where we analyse key correlates and pathways of disorganized attachment.

Three samples totalling 202 mothers and their infants were studied. The first sample (n = 71) comprised mothers and their 16-month-old infants; the second consisted of a twin study (n = 68); the third sample included mothers (n = 63) who had experienced a loss through death. This design permitted the comparison between two 'normal', low-risk samples (1 and 2) with a third sample chosen to reflect mothers who were statistically more likely to be experiencing unresolved loss and/ or trauma.

The next step was to investigate the distribution of certain contextual variables (such as the mother's educational level, number of hours she worked out of home, the child's gender and age, number of siblings, etc.). Attachment classifications of the infants were undertaken at the university. Observations were video-taped to enable coding to be completed by more than one rater (to check inter-rater reliability – which was high in this study). Raters had been trained personally by Erik Hesse and Mary Main *and* had attended training on the use of the AMBIANCE measure.

The Strange Situation Procedure (SSP) was used with all mothers. This brings us to a problem with the SSP, expressed by Marinus van IJzendoorn and members of the Leiden team:

> The Strange Situation procedure may offer too small a window on infants' behaviour under stress to exclude the possibility of false negatives. For research, as well as for diagnostic purposes, two ways of improving the assessment of disorganized attachment may be considered. First, naturally occurring stressful situations may be observed for additional signs of disorganized attachment…[but]…the attachment figure may not always show the behaviour that triggers a disorganized response of the infant. Second, because disorganization of attachment is expressed in problematic management of stress and in problematic regulation of negative emotions, salivary cortisol

levels or heart rate may be used as additional markers of disorganized attachments. (van IJzendoorn, Schuengel and Bakermans-Kranenburg 1999, p.242)

In the first two sub-samples, the mothers had a short break during which they were asked to complete a brief questionnaire while their children played. (This request acted as what is known as a 'competing demand' task, and is a way of gauging both organized and disorganized attachment behaviour.) Disconnected and extremely insensitive behaviours were coded at three points: during the break, during the competing demand task, and during a 'free-play' period of about 10 minutes at the end of the SSP. The procedure for the third sample was slightly different because no questionnaire was administered. Instead, after the SSP, mothers were interviewed about their experiences of loss; they were then asked to play with their child for about 15 minutes.

To test the validity of the new instrument and to complete the measures needed to undertake the validation, each parent–child interaction was classified using SSP coding procedures. Children coded as 'D' were re-coded to see which style their behaviour returned to, after disorganization episodes. We now reproduce a longer section from the article, to show the attention to detail needed:

Disconnected parental behaviour

For the first dimension, all items from Main and Hesse's (1998) coding instrument for frightening, frightened, dissociated, sexualized and disorganized parental behaviour were adapted and rearranged, which resulted in five categories of parental behaviour: (1) frightening and threatening behaviour, (2) behaviours indicating fear of the child, (3) dissociative behaviours indicative of absorption (stilling, freezing or handling as though the child is an inanimate object) or intrusion of an altered state of awareness (such as inexplicable shifts in mood or sudden fear regarding the environment), (4) interacting with the child in a timid, submissive and/or deferential manner, sexualized/romantic behaviours, and (5) disoriented/disorganized behaviours (such as contradictions in behaviour or vocalizations, disorientation and other anomalous movements and postures). Initially, very few adjustments were made compared to the original FR [Frightened/Frightening] system. However, it appeared that the coders differed considerably in their scores on the disconnected dimension. During discussion of the tapes, it became clear that each coder had formed her own assumptions on what constitutes (severe) disconnected behaviour. Therefore, several adjustments were made compared to the original FR system because of the complexity of coding disconnected behaviours and in order to further clarify the distinction between these behaviours and extreme insensitivity. In the current DIP coding system, each behaviour is accompanied by specific criteria that need to be fulfilled before a score can be assigned. For disconnected behaviour, lack of meta-signals indicating play or affection (such as smiling), the absence of any explanation or justification for these behaviours and their sudden occurrence are important considerations. Furthermore, behavioural descriptions are presented, specifying different components of parental behaviour such as facial expression, vocalizations, posture and movements… Important factors are the severity (for example, fear manifested in facial expressions, movements and vocalizations), the duration and frequency of occurrence, and the timing (whether it occurs when the child is in distress or displaying attachment behaviour)…clarification of the behavioural aspects of disconnected behaviours (e.g., lack of meta-signals indicating play) clearly distinguishes these parental behaviours from extreme insensitivity.

Extreme insensitivity

The second dimension covers two forms of extreme parental insensitivity: (1) parental withdrawal and neglect; and (2) intrusive, negative, aggressive or otherwise harsh parental behaviours. The distinction between extreme insensitivity and mere insensitive responses lies in the duration, frequency, quality and severity of the behaviours (e.g., aggressive behaviours) as well as the context in which the behaviour occurs (e.g., when the child is in distress). This dimension is an adaptation of a selection of items from the AMBIANCE (Bronfman, Parsons and Lyons-Ruth 2004). The items that referred to extremely insensitive behaviour were selected and combined into more general categories of parental behaviours. Similar to the disconnected dimension, specific criteria were formulated that need to be fulfilled for the behaviour to be counted as extremely insensitive (and not disconnected or merely insensitive), and coding instructions for assigning a score were added. Parental withdrawal and neglect is scored when the parent (repeatedly) fails to show responsive behaviour when the child is in distress, seeks contact or approaches the parent. For example, the parent ignores a crying child, does not respond to the child's repeated vocalizations, or does not intervene when the child engages in dangerous behaviour. Physical intrusiveness is scored when the parent gets too close to the child and intrusively overrides the child's cues, resulting in too intense and vigorous interactions. Finally, rough behaviour and physical aggression are also included…as well as hostile, rejecting comments in which the parent expresses his or her anger, frustration, contempt or disgust. If any of the extremely insensitive behaviours fulfils the criteria for disconnected behaviour, they are scored only under the first dimension of the system. For example, when the parent suddenly displays threatening behaviours and voice alterations, unaccompanied by meta-signals of affection or play and unrelated to the context, these behaviours are coded as disconnected. In contrast, when aggressive behaviour does not fit this description and is clearly embedded in the context (for example, the parent hits the child because the child does not comply) it is coded as extremely insensitive. (Out *et al.* 2009, pp.428–429)

The newly devised behaviours were then coded on a 9-point scale and a final score given along each dimension together with a final, overall classification – automatically coded 'D' if the highest score was over 6, but with coders using their discretion if the score was 5.

Ethical challenges in attachment-based research

Ethical questions have always been raised about the SSP – visit relevant YouTube sites and read some of the 'posts', and you will see what we mean! – because it is thought by some to be unethical to activate a child's attachment system by subjecting him or her to two separations. It upsets most people to see the reaction of the child when the caregiver leaves the room. The counter argument is that a child experiences many short separations in a day, in naturally occurring situations: when mum or dad has to leave the room to make a drink, go to the bathroom, etc. Certainly concerns were expressed in the early days of the experiments using the SSP because the separations were too long and children captured on video became too distressed; and we saw in the previous chapter that in some cultures the procedure is postponed until he or she is a little older, to respect different traditions.

The purpose of the SSP is to mildly challenge the child, by *gently* activating his or her attachment system. The aim should never be to cause the child unnecessary distress. In the future, however, due to a significant increase in attachment-based research focused on neuroaffective, biochemical and genetic indices, we are likely to see an increase in techniques to induce or even prime attachment behaviour, such as: presenting 'still-faces' of adults, including caregivers, expressing different emotional states to gauge a child's reaction; using an uncommunicative clown as the stranger (because doing so increases the level of unfamiliarity and 'strangeness'); and using subliminal priming techniques (but only with adults). These developments will test the ability of ethics committees to weigh up intrusions into privacy with the quest to understand problems such as child maltreatment, with the promise of genuine breakthroughs in our ability to assess, diagnose and, more importantly, intervene to help children, and adults.

Disorganized attachment and its key correlates

General prevalence and stability over time

Marinus van IJzendoorn's (1999) meta-analysis of disorganized attachment found that 14 per cent of children from middle-class, non-clinical samples (N = 1882) were classified 'D'. Demographic variations were also discovered. For example, the proportion of D children rose to 24 per cent within lower socio-economic status (SES) groups (N = 493). In older children the percentage only rose to 15 per cent (N = 492). In low socio-economic status samples (N = 586) disorganization levels rose to 25 per cent and this difference (compared to 14 per cent) was significant, as indicated by moderate effect sizes. When only the Main and Solomon (1990) classifications were included, the percentage of DA in low SES samples rose to 34 per cent (n = 338).

Despite disorganized attachment behaviour being, by definition, strongly influenced by the child's immediate caregiving environment, theoretically we would be fairly confident that observed DA behaviour would remain constant over time (assuming there was no significant change in caregivers). This hypothesis was confirmed in the Leiden meta-analysis, where DA was found to be remarkably stable (from 1 to 60 months, with an average of 29 months) and, in terms of short-term stability, was even higher. In lower SES samples stability went down marginally, whereas the reverse was true with higher SES samples; but these between-SES differences were marginal and non-significant.

Child-specific characteristics

The next question is whether disorganized attachment behaviour could be a function of certain characteristics of the child – for example, the child's gender or temperament. Also, could the presence of particular illnesses lead to DA? And is there any evidence of a link between the genetic make-up of the child and the level of disorganized attachment behaviour?

GENDER

In general there are few studies on gender differences in respect of attachment organization. There is some evidence from Shelley Taylor and her colleagues' work with primates that maternal caregiving activates certain hormones, especially oxytocin. This, in turn, leads to a higher level of affiliative – or 'tend and befriend' (Taylor *et al.* 2000) – behaviour; and under certain stressful conditions females *approach* when anxious, whereas males are more likely to *retreat*. In other words, there would be a gendered 'fight–flight' response to threat and there is some evidence for this assertion, although the sample size was small. These differences are, however, likely to be culturally determined, as it remains the case that women undertake most caregiving during the very early stages of an infant's life; if fathers did more, then it is possible that they would similarly experience increased oxytocin levels. In terms of DA, however, the Leiden meta-analysis found no gender differences.

TEMPERAMENT

When a child develops DA patterns, are they specific to one or more carers and does the behaviour eventually generalize to most close relationships? This raises questions about the effect of temperament on disorganized attachment behaviour. If temperament is a significant factor, one would expect to find evidence of disorganized attachment behaviour, irrespective of the carer present, but indications are that infants are 'unlikely to be classified as disorganized with more than one carer' (Lyons-Ruth and Jacobvitz 2008, p.668). Lyons-Ruth and Jacobvitz (2008) refer to the 1990 study by Main and Solomon in which 31 out of 34 infants were classified as disorganized with only one carer. They also point out that van IJzendoorn *et al.*'s (1999) meta-analysis (N = 1877) found no significant associations between infant DA and 'temperamental' variables. Furthermore, of the eight studies (N = 1639) meta-analysed by van IJzendoorn *et al.* (1999), no significant association was found between infants with 'difficult' temperament and DA. From their analysis, the combined effect size across 13 samples (N = 2028) was non-significant (r = .0008). Even when the Main and Solomon (1990) classifications were included, the combined effect size was still non-significant (r = .005). Hence, as the authors conclude, 'there is no reason to assume that disorganized attachment is the consequence of the infant's difficult temperament' (van IJzendoorn *et al.* 1999, p.233).

NEUROLOGICAL AND COGNITIVE FACTORS: AUTISM, CEREBRAL PALSY AND DOWN'S SYNDROME

The Leiden meta-analysis also considered neurological features of a child's make-up (N = 248). The percentage of children displaying DA with autism, cerebral palsy or Down's syndrome was higher (around 35 per cent) than in non-clinical or low-risk samples. Professionals working with children where there are concerns about developmental delays and/or maltreatment need to take account of such predisposing factors if they have reason to believe that a child is exhibiting DA behaviours. But Marinus van IJzendoorn concludes that more research is needed to investigate more fully the possibility of neurological antecedents of DA.

To investigate whether children with certain physical conditions might show signs of DA due to the condition itself, rather than as a result of the immediate caregiving environment, studies which had included conditions such as congenital heart disease and cleft palate appear in the meta-analysis. As predicted, such children were no more likely to exhibit DA than other groups (20 per cent compared to 14 per cent, but this was non-significant).

RELATIONSHIP OF DISORGANIZED ATTACHMENT TO ADHD

On the surface there might appear to be a similarity between DA and ADHD (attention deficit hyperactivity disorder) but disorganized attachment behaviour is not the same as *disturbed* behaviour. Evidence showed no association between DA and established cases of ADHD in a unique sample of mother–child dyads, followed up to seven years of age. Furthermore, the rate of the likely number of assessed cases of ADHD was similar to that of the general population rate (Faraone *et al.* 1998). There does, however, appear be a genetic link with ADHD but which operates in a different way to DA, as we now discuss.

GENETICS

At first sight it appears that hereditary factors do indeed contribute but, as we shall see in Chapter 4, it is more complicated than initial studies suggested. What emerges is a complex interaction between genetics and caregiving risk. For example, as Lyons-Ruth and Jacobvitz (2008) argue, temperamental differences operate differently among high- and low-risk samples and they conclude: 'the findings accrued to date indicate that attachment disorganisation emerges *within a particular relationship*; they do not support the notion of attachment disorganisation as an individual trait or inborn characteristic of the child' (Lyons-Ruth and Jacobvitz 2008, p.699, emphasis added). It is interesting to compare these findings about DA to other studies concerned with secure attachment. In an earlier meta-analytic study looking at the distribution of attachment organization in both clinical and non-clinical samples (N = 1624 children) Femmie Juffer and her colleagues at Leiden University remind us that 'problems on the child's side were not associated with a decrease in the percentage of secure attachment' (Juffer, Bakermans-Kranenburg and van IJzendoorn 2008a, p.98).

Parent-specific characteristics

We now consider the likely influence of parent-specific features: are we more likely to see DA in children when a parent is depressed, or who misuse alcohol and/or drugs? And if so, what are the explanatory mechanisms? What about children who live in caregiving environments where there is family violence or in dangerous neighbourhoods: are they more likely to exhibit DA?

SUBSTANCE MISUSE AND PARENTAL DEPRESSION

We return to van IJzendoorn *et al.*'s meta-analysis to explore the effect of a number of parent-specific factors. Children of parents with alcohol or drugs problems were more likely to display DA (43 per cent) when contrasted with comparators (14 per cent). Only 19 per cent of children whose parents were depressed show DA behaviours and a low correlation overall was obtained in situations when children witness marital/relational disharmony (effect size r = .05 – non sig).

It is perhaps at first sight surprising that, with the full sample of depressed parents (n = 340), the percentage of disorganized children was only 21 per cent and that when the Main and Solomon classifications (n = 212) were deployed it actually falls to 19 per cent (van IJzendoorn *et al.* 1999). These were no significant differences compared to the normative 14 per cent, but from an attachment perspective the result is not as odd as it may seem: many parents experience depression but it does not necessarily impair their ability to provide secure, or even organized *in*secure, caregiving for a child. Because the results on depression, especially in its chronic and bipolar forms, are surprising, researchers urge that more tightly designed studies are undertaken. Interestingly the 1999 meta-analysis made no reference to the absence of studies at the time on parental mental illnesses because, theoretically at any rate, paranoid and delusional states are as likely (if not more so) to produce disorganized attachment behaviours in some children.

What these studies show consistently is that DA is related to the *quality of protective behaviour* from carers, so we now consider aspects of parenting variables in more detail.

Parent and caregiver behaviours
THE PREVALENCE AND SIGNIFICANCE OF MALTREATMENT BY CARERS

We now turn our attention to the question of maltreatment because 'parental maltreatment is probably one of the most frightening behaviours a child may be exposed to' (van IJzendoorn and Bakermans-Kranenburg 2009, pp.2–3). It should come as no surprise that the predisposing factor most likely to be associated with DA is maltreatment by a carer. The abuse and neglect of a child is far more likely than any other single factor to lead to disorganized attachment behaviour because it is at the heart of what DA means: the paradox for the child is that the very person who should be able to protect him or her is at one and the same time the source of danger.

From the very start of their work on attachment theory, when Bowlby and Ainsworth first began to use the SSP, it was predicted theoretically that child maltreatment was a key determinant of disorganized attachment behaviour. More recently, the combined effect size across the five studies focusing on child maltreatment and DA in the Leiden meta-analysis was impressive ($r = .41$) and thus confirmed their predictions. In groups of maltreating parents ($n = 165$) 48 per cent of children were found to be disorganized compared to the normative 14 per cent in low-risk groups, but this percentage rose to 77 per cent when only the Main and Solomon codings were used (van IJzendoorn *et al.* 1999). The 1999 meta-analysis also reports on Dante Cicchetti and his colleagues' research (Barnett, Ganiban and Cicchetti 1997; Beeghly and Cicchetti 1994) who found over 80 per cent of children who had been maltreated also displayed DA behaviours. The authors refer to the effect sizes as 'impressive' (p.236) with greater associations, again when the

Main and Solomon coding system was used. Referring to a more recent study by Cicchetti and Curtis (2006), Lyons-Ruth and Jacobvitz (2008) add that '90% of maltreated infants were disorganised, compared to 43% of low income controls' (p.668) (where there may also have been instances of maltreatment).

It is now relatively clear that disorganized attachment is a 'relationship-specific phenomenon' (van IJzendoorn *et al.* 1999, p.235). In the main, therefore, it is not characteristics of the parent per se – for example, whether parents are depressed, use alcohol or drugs to excess or are engaged in or experience family violence – that is most predictive of DA; nor (with the exception of a recently discovered genetic link) is DA more likely to occur given certain characteristics of the child – for example, the emergence of DA is not related significantly to gender or temperament.

We now explore the relationship between three key intervening variables – unresolved loss, insensitive parenting and frightening parenting. It is rather complex. We unravel the confusion by examining each variable separately and then we review research findings exploring their interrelationship as co-determinants of maltreatment. We conclude by exploring a missing link in the pathway connecting these three variables to disorganized attachment.

UNRESOLVED LOSS AND TRAUMA

The early studies by Mary Main and Erik Hesse concluded that unresolved memories of trauma, abuse or unexplained loss, along with attendant repressed feelings, can lead to serious disruptions in caregiving behaviour which can be unconsciously distressing, frightening and confusing for infants and young children. It is now fairly well established that parents of 'disorganized infants tend to show momentary lapses in the monitoring of their reasoning or discourse such as extreme attention to minor details, incompatible beliefs, or sudden visual sensory images' (Out *et al.* 2009, p.420). A consistent relationship has been found between parental unresolved loss and trauma, and infant disorganized attachment, using meta-analytic techniques. For example, a meta-analysis of 10 studies involving 548 participants in 1995 produced a combined effect size of $r = .31$ (van IJzendoorn 1995).

The phenomenon of unresolved loss has similarities with the symptoms of post-traumatic stress disorder (PTSD) symptoms (although the research to date has been conducted using self-reported data, with all its attendant weaknesses as a measure of dissociation). The primary explanation for how unresolved loss leads to DA is that parents' attempts 'to defend themselves against re-experiencing the fear, helplessness and anger associated with the trauma may result in repeated failure to comfort and sooth children when their attachment system is activated' (Out *et al.* 2009, pp.420–421).

Precisely how unresolved loss re-emerges later on, when a survivor becomes a parent or caregiver, is not straightforward. Karlen Lyons-Ruth suggests that

> mothers with a history of physical abuse or witnessed violence were more likely to display the hostile profile of behaviour at home, while mothers with a history of sexual abuse or parental loss (but not physical abuse) were more likely to withdraw from interaction with their infants. Clinical treatment of sexual abuse survivors clearly reveals the underlying fear and rage of those who have been sexually victimized. However, sexually abused mothers appeared more likely to manage their negative affects by moving away from interaction with the infant, while mothers who had witnessed violence or been physically abused appeared to handle their underlying fear by identifying with an aggressive style of interaction... (Lyons-Ruth 2003, p.893)

But the connections are more complex when we consider the relationship between unresolved loss and trauma alongside the emergence of subsequent frightening behaviour. To return to the terminology discussed at the beginning of this chapter, we can now begin the process of unravelling the effects of mediator variables.

Mediator variables in the pathways to disorganized attachment

Parental insensitivity

Depressed carers, parents using drugs and alcohol to excess, carers experiencing relational disharmony; none of these adults are necessarily acting in ways *toward their children* to cause them harm. Witnessing domestic violence, seeing a parent desperately sad (but without knowing why) and watching a carer progressively 'lose it' with drink or drugs are never optimal for a child's development, but these behaviours in themselves do not necessarily lead children to lack an organized strategy to seek and maintain proximity when their attachment system is activated.

This kind of parental behaviour may result in insensitive responses to a child's demands but 'parental insensitivity' is not found to be a significant determinant of DA. The van IJzendoorn *et al.* 1999 meta-analysis established a non-significant effect size (r = .10) when investigating associations between DA and parental insensitivity among the studies considered (N = 1951). As Karlen Lyons-Ruth put it, 'surprisingly, parental behaviour that is coded as insensitive...has only been weakly correlated with infant disorganised attachment behaviour' (Lyons-Ruth 2003, p.889). Not surprisingly, parental insensitivity was correlated with attachment *in*security, but not *disorganization*.

In a research review on gene–environment interaction, Marian Bakermans-Kranenburg and Marinus van IJzendoorn (2007) remind us that, while parental (in)sensitivity is widely regarded as the key influence in attachment, it still 'accounts for only a third of the association between parental attachment security, leaving a transmission gap of unexplained variance in infant attachment security' (Bakermans-Kranenburg and van IJzendoorn 2007, p.1160). The problem with the concept of insensitive parenting is that it is too multi-dimensional to predict DA accurately. One of its dimensions – *frightening* behaviour – has, however, proved more reliable as a determinant of disorganized attachment behaviour.

Frightening parental behaviour

Studies of non-maltreated samples 'have demonstrated that anomalous parenting, involving (often only brief episodes of) parental dissociative behaviour, rough handling, or withdrawn behaviour, is related to the development of attachment disorganization' (van IJzendoorn and Bakermans-Kranenburg 2009, p.2). But there is still some equivocation over connections between frightening behaviour and disorganized attachment. For example, a meta-analysis conducted in 2006 by Sherry Madigan and her colleagues obtained a link between frightening and extremely insensitive caregiving as a key determinant of DA. But when unresolved loss was entered into the equation, things become more complicated. So although robust associations have been found between parental unresolved loss and trauma, frightening behaviour and DA in the 12 studies reviewed by Madigan *et al.* (2006), 'less than half of the association between unresolved loss or trauma was explained by mediation of frightening parental behaviour' (Bakermans-Kranenburg and van IJzendoorn 2007, p.1161).

Rejecting a simplistic relationship, Madigan *et al.* (2006) posit the following alternative way of conceptualizing the association: 'the interplay between genetic vulnerability and experiences with anomalous parenting may be important in explaining why some children are affected by anomalous parenting and others remain resilient' (Madigan *et al.* 2006, p.102). Referring to the research within low-risk groups, Dorothee Out and colleagues argue that

> subtly frightening, frightened and dissociative parental behaviour might be the primary determinants of infant attachment disorganization in these samples. Similar to abusive parenting, these FR parental behaviours may place infants in an irresolvable and disorganizing paradox: their parents are the only potential source of comfort and protection while at the same time they frighten their children through their behaviour. (Out *et al.* 2009, p.420)

Discovering a missing link between unresolved loss and insensitive and frightening parenting

We conclude with an attempt to connect this still rather confusing relationship between mediating caregiver variables – frightening parental behaviour, insensitive parenting behaviour and unresolved loss – and their effect on disorganized attachment. To summarize: until recently, initially promising connections have uncovered discontinuity between anomalous parenting, especially 'frightening, threatening and dissociative' (Main and Hesse 1992) carer behaviour and the presence of unresolved states of mind. But what we have also seen is that each of these variables is only partially associated with DA. To confuse matters more, insensitive parenting can sometimes (but certainly not always) lead to evidence of DA in infants.

Put as simply as possible: *some* parents who experience unresolved loss and/or trauma may develop dissociative states, *some* of whom may display insensitive caregiving, but which does not necessarily always lead to disorganized attachment behaviour in their children. *Some* parents experiencing dissociative states may unintentionally display disconnected caregiving responses to their children, *some* of whom will develop disorganized attachment, while others do not (although they will almost always develop an organized insecure attachment pattern and it is never optimal for a child's development to be frightened by a carer's reactions to him or her).

The question of whether unresolved states of mind lead inevitably to infant DA was explored in 2003 by Abraham Sagi-Schwartz and colleagues who studied the level of 'unresolved state of mind' in women survivors from the Holocaust (Sagi-Schwartz *et al.* 2003). Not surprisingly, they found a significantly higher level of unresolved loss in the Holocaust survivors when contrasted with a comparison group *but their trauma was not always transmitted to their children.* As Lyons-Ruth and Jacobvitz (2008) explain:

> The authors noted that it may be important that the traumatic events were not created by attachment figures but emerged from an outside destructive force (i.e. the Nazis). The basic trust the survivors had developed with their parents prior to the Holocaust may have empowered them to cope with the war, adapt to normal life after the war, and become attachment figures themselves. (p.673)

It is also interesting to compare these findings with Daniel Schechter's Columbia Trauma Study (Schechter 2003) where, similarly, it was found that interpersonal violent trauma among a group of mainly Hispanic women was not necessarily associated with seeing their own child in a negative light, nor did it predict their capacity to appreciate their child as having hopes, intentions and thoughts independently of their own: what Peter Fonagy termed 'mentalization' and 'reflective function' (RF). Peter Fonagy and Mary Target note that in the Columbia Trauma Study maternal RF was highly associated with either negativity or distortion of maternal attributions concerning the infant. The study used the Working Model of the Child Interview (WMCI; Zeanah and Benoit 1995) which distinguishes between 'distorted' and 'disengaged' maternal representations – ways of internally depicting and thinking about their child. As the authors conclude: 'the results imply that the severity of interpersonal violent trauma does not predict the way a mother will perceive her child as measured by the WMCI. However, the mother's capacity to see the child in a balanced (secure) way is related to the extent to which she depicts her child as intentional' (Fonagy and Target 2005, p.337).

So it was the 'disengaged' mothers who had experienced significant trauma who were more likely than the 'distorted' mothers to show low RF. This finding is remarkably similar to the recent insights by Dorothee Out, who also found that it was disengaged carers who were more likely to produce disorganized attachment behaviour in their children. What Peter Fonagy and Mary Target then argue persuasively is that the intervening explanatory mechanism is RF. Why might this be the case and how might the mechanism work? Peter Fonagy and Mary Target explain: 'Secure attachment history of the mother permits and enhances her capacity to explore her own mind and liberates and promotes a similar enquiring stance towards the mental state of the new human being who has just joined her social world' (Fonagy and Target 2005, p.335).

They claim to have discovered a missing link to connect some of the loose ends identified at the beginning of this section. How can we begin to tell which 'unresolved' parents are more likely to exhibit insensitive and/or frightening behaviour? It appears that it might be those who display low RF.

The study by Sherry Madigan and colleagues in 2006 included the diagram shown in Figure 2.1 to illustrate how three key variables are interrelated. The researchers report that the model satisfies all four of Baron and Kenny's (1986) conditions for mediation.

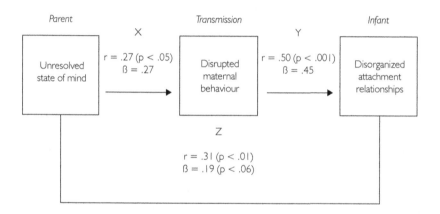

Figure 2.1 Madigan et al.'s (2006) mediator diagram

We now, very tentatively, offer a revised pathway diagram in Figure 2.2 to show the connections between all the currently identified mediator variables. It builds on Madigan *et al.*'s empirically derived path diagram by sub-dividing *Disrupted Maternal Behaviour* into *Disconnected* and *Extremely Insensitive Parenting* and includes *Low Mentalization/RF* as a mediator to *Disorganized Attachment*. Further research is required to shed light on the strength and direction of influence between all four predictors and disorganized attachment behaviour. We again stress that this is not a diagram of firm causal connections.

Maltreatment Pathway Model

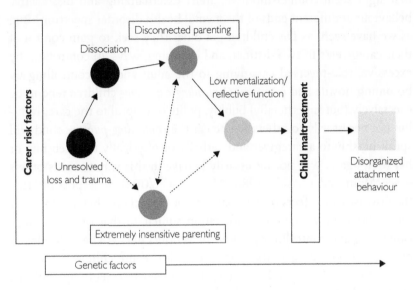

Figure 2.2 Modified pathway diagram connecting parental behaviour to DA

Infant disorganized attachment and subsequent mental health problems

We conclude this chapter by considering what happens in adolescence and adulthood to infants and younger children who consistently lack organized attachment experiences. The 1999 meta-analysis by Marinus van IJzendoorn and his colleagues formed the conclusion that disorganized attachment is 'an early sign of psychopathology' (van IJzendoorn *et al.* 1999, p.244). The authors draw attention to the fact that the 12 studies reviewed on 734 children were all correlational studies, so the usual caveats about problems interpreting causation apply. Nevertheless, they found more externalizing behaviour among those children assessed as showing DA behaviour. Elevated externalizing behaviour, assessed by parents, teachers or observer, was also found in a more recent meta-analysis by Pasco Fearon and colleagues. They reviewed 69 samples

(N = 5947) and also found significantly elevated risk of externalizing behaviour problems in DA children (Fearon *et al.* 2010).

The Leiden researchers also found evidence of elevated rates of dissociation too, and were quick to point out that this finding may at first sight seem counter-intuitive: aren't externalizing and dissociative behaviour at different ends of the mental health disorder spectrum? But, as we have seen, as DA children get older they seek to gain control of their caregiver/s in two distinct, and opposing, ways: (i) controlling by excessive, role-reversed caregiving to the adult and (ii) controlling by becoming hostile and punitive. *Controlling-caregiving* children tend to be excessively (but superficially) bubbly, polite or helpful to the caregiver – but not necessarily to others – whereas the *controlling-punitive* child will speak harshly to a caregiver and verbally or physically threaten him or her (but, again, will not necessarily behave in this way towards others – see Main and Cassidy 1988; Moss *et al.* 2004). It is possible that the downstream effects of externalizing or dissociative behaviours after toddlerhood may suggest a bifurcation similar to that of controlling-caregiving and controlling-punitive behaviours likely to have developed during the preceding years. Compared with secure children, 'punitive and hostile' children tend to 'externalize', whereas 'caregiving' children are more likely to 'internalize'.

Consequences of disorganized attachment

In the 2008 *Handbook of Attachment* Michelle Deklyen and Mark Greenberg undertook an evidence-based review of the links between early attachment and the development of later mental health disorders in childhood. Refreshingly, they comment early on that the 'enthusiasm to utilize attachment theory has at times led to overinterpretation of findings and a fruitless search for a "Holy Grail" of psychopathology' (Deklyen and Greenberg 2008, p.638). Whilst they conclude by questioning whether *attachment insecurity alone* would lead to mental health disorders, they are in little doubt that it is 'the absence of a coherent strategy (*i.e. disorganisation*) rather than insecurity *per se* that is linked to maladaptation' (p.649). Similarly, in the next chapter of the *Handbook*, Mary Dozier and her colleagues contend that 'the only clear connections between infant attachment and adult psychopathology are between disorganized attachment and dissociative symptoms in adolescence and early adulthood' (Dozier, Chase Stovall-McClough and Albus 2008, p.736). They conclude that part of the reason is that the child quickly develops a 'sensitized neurobiology' (p.736).

So-called 'disruptive' behaviours in young children, of course, are often unconscious ways to regulate unpredictable, frightening and abusive caregiving patterns. This is especially so with later role-reversing behaviours. Gaining some control, direction and predictability over a maltreating parent by becoming aggressive, sly or powerful are, of course, the very behaviours in a school-age child that if pronounced and regular will signal maladjustment and 'disorder' to teachers.

The review by Mary Dozier and her colleagues looked at whether early and later childhood attachment predicted mental health problems in adulthood. They relate all the findings to a clearly explicated, theoretical discussion rather than simply produce a catalogue of interesting but de-contextualized research findings. Again, they find convincing evidence linking 'attachment-related trauma to later dissociative symptoms' (Dozier *et al.* 2008, p.720). They then analyse the research for the main types of mental disorder.

Evidence of early attachment links to types of mental disorder

With *depression*, whilst there are clear differences between unipolar and bipolar forms, both are highly heritable, with severe unipolar depression more heritable than less severe forms. Consequently, unless there is accompanying unresolved loss or trauma, there are few reliable links between depression and DA. The evidence for *anxiety disorders* also finds few links with disorganized attachment specifically (but it does establish consistent patterns of association with infants with ambivalent attachments even after differences in temperament were controlled for). Similarly, with *eating disorders*, no direct links to DA are found. While it may have been assumed that infant DA and *schizophrenia* would be linked to earlier DA, due to the high heritability of the condition it has so far proved impossible to isolate a specific connection. The authors also point to another problem: research doesn't always take account of the fact that lack of coherence within Adult Attachment Interview (AAI) transcripts – the main index of insecurity and/or disorganization – is also one of the markers of schizophrenia; hence, contamination of results is a persistent problem.

It is when considering dissociative disorders, borderline personality disorders (BPD) and antisocial personality disorders that stronger connections emerge, both empirically and theoretically. Studies have shown conclusively that *dissociative disorders* are strongly connected to DA (see Carlson 1998; Liotti 2004; Sroufe *et al.* 2005). It would be surprising if this were not the case, as 'dissociation' is one of the key intervening variables to emerge from the retrospective research reviewed above. Notably, the incidence of abuse in people with dissociative disorders is very high too, almost reaching 100 per cent in some studies. No 'associations emerged between disorganized attachment and any variables assessing endogenous vulnerability, such as prenatal difficulties, difficulties during childbirth, or maternal drug or alcohol use' (Dozier *et al.* 2008, p.729). Finally the authors note that 62 per cent of adults diagnosed with dissociative disorders had mothers who had lost a close relative within two years of their children's birth (p.730).

The word 'border' in *borderline personality disorder* indicates that the condition contains neurotic and psychotic behaviour; but, in the main, BPD is recognized by negative emotion and symptom exaggeration. Consequently, there are correlations with infant and early childhood DA, which may possibly reflect more of the externalizing form in which DA becomes transformed as children get older when they need to inject predictability into their experience of being parented. Similarly, with *antisocial personality disorder* – often referred to as 'conduct disorder' in early adolescence – there are connections with unresolved states of mind, typically revealed in the AAI.

In this chapter we have explored links between parenting and disorganized attachment as well as mental health conditions resulting *from* disorganized attachment. With *organized* secure and insecure attachment, the research is far more equivocal, but some robust patterns have begun to develop with regard to disorganized attachment; robust enough, we feel, to permit us to develop our Pathway Model to represent the key influences from parenting variables to DA and maltreatment. In summary, in a paper written in 2003 for the journal *Attachment and Human Development*, Marinus van IJzendoorn and Marian Bakermans-Kranenburg are clear when they state: 'Disorganised attachment has been shown to be indexed with clear-cut behavioural markers...and have serious developmental consequences... Extreme indications of disorganisation may be regarded as psychiatric disturbance with more or less severe symptoms and consequences' (van IJzendoorn and Bakermans-Kranenburg 2003, p.317).

Chapter 3

Identification and Assessment of Disorganized Attachment

Introduction

We begin with a short background section on attachment measures generally and then we outline the methods available to assess and identify each of the variables identified in the Pathway Model at the end of the last chapter.

Child behaviours

(measures of *disorganized attachment* in children of different ages)

Measures

Toddlers	*Strange Situation Procedure coding for 'D' behaviours*
Younger children	*Story Stem Completion*
Pre/young adolescents	*Child Attachment Interview*

Caregiver behaviours

Unresolved loss	*Adult Attachment Interview*
Dissociation	*Tellegen's Absorption Scale; Dissociative Experiences Scale*
Frightening/frightened	*Frightened/Frightening coding; Atypical Maternal Behaviour Instrument for Assessment and Classification*
Disconnected/insensitive	*Disconnected and extremely Insensitive Parenting Measure, Assessment of Parental Sensitivity*
Reflective functioning	*Parent Development Interview; Working Model of the Child Interview; Reading the Mind in the Eyes Test*

By presenting examples of measures, we could give the impression that they can be used as check-lists; nothing could be further from the truth and we wish to stress that, apart from the two self-report measures of *Dissociation* (and to some extent the *Mind in the Eyes* test), each measure requires intensive training before they can be implemented and scored. Much of the training is provided at the Anna Freud Centre in London, at Leiden University and at various universities in the US and usually takes place in a block of between three and five days with a follow-up day to enable participants to practise the skills learned and/or code excerpts and transcripts. To become accredited coders, participants are required to achieve a high level of concordance (usually 80–90 per cent) with an expert rater. *It is important not to attempt to use these measures without such training.* Furthermore, it will become obvious that the ability to 'read' and understand child and carer attachment behaviour requires knowledge and experience, along with a certain flair for noticing what one is observing.

Calibrating attachment

At first sight, there exists a baffling array of over 80 measures of attachment, incorporating psychometric scales, interview schedules and observation manuals, each claiming to partition, calibrate and enumerate different attachment phenomena. But they can be divided into *self-report* measures and *developmentally based* measures, each originating from different psychological traditions and each with different foci and research interests. At times the two traditions have ploughed their own furrow. To achieve a working rapprochement, a special edition of the journal *Attachment and Human Development* in 2002 (Vol. 4) explored the similarities and differences between the two traditions. The conclusion reached was that much of the discord could be overcome if the two groups accepted that they were measuring different aspects of attachment dynamics and organization (see Shaver and Mikulincer 2002).

Self-report questionnaires directly assess adults' views of contemporary attachment figures (often a romantic partner or other close adult relationship), whereas *developmentally based* interviews, observations and projective measures seek to capture an individual's 'state of mind with respect to attachment' (Shaver and Mikulincer 2002, p.134), often about *past* relationships. The important point is that,

> even though over half the questions in the Adult Attachment Interview dwell on the interviewee's past recollections of childhood and experiences of being parented, the result is a detailed understanding of current representations of attachment organisation: it is how the past and present are made sense of now that determines attachment classification. This explains why a person can score differently on two separate occasions, even though their temporal 'past' remains constant. But it is the way the past is cognitively processed and contemporaneously experienced, not the content of past events per se, that forms the basis of [developmentally based] ratings. (Shemmings 2004, p.306)

Self-report measures of attachment

Self-report scales and inventories have largely been developed by social psychologists, who tend to use them on account of their convenience, low cost and capacity for surveying large samples (Shaver and Mikulincer 2002). One of the first attempts to capture different adult attachment 'styles' is the forced-choice measure by Cindy Hazan and Philip Shaver (1987). Respondents *rank* the following three descriptions in respect of a romantic partner; the highest is their attachment classification (a 5-point Likert scale is used to further distinguish responses):

Secure

I find it relatively easy to get close to others and am comfortable depending on them and having them depend on me. I don't often worry about being abandoned or about someone getting too close to me.

Ambivalent

I find that others are reluctant to get as close as I would like. I often worry that my partner doesn't really love me or won't want to stay with me. I want to merge completely with another person, and this desire sometimes scares people away.

Avoidant

I am somewhat uncomfortable being close to others; I find it difficult to trust them completely, difficult to allow myself to depend on them. I am nervous when anyone gets too close, and often, love partners want me to be more intimate than I feel comfortable being. (p.512)

This measure is based on the three 'child-derived' classifications emerging from the *Strange Situation*. Kim Bartholomew and colleagues went on to align the three descriptors with adult attachment labels. As we have already seen, she called the first two *Balanced* and *Preoccupied* respectively (Bartholomew and Horowitz 1991, p.227) but subdivided the 'avoidant' attachment organization into *Dismissing* and *Fearful*. The statement for 'Dismissing' became 'I am comfortable without close emotional relationships. It is very important to me to feel independent and self-sufficient and I prefer not to depend on others or have others depend on me', while the 'Fearful' descriptor was 'I am somewhat uncomfortable getting close to others. I want emotionally close relationships but I find it difficult to trust others completely, or to depend on them. I sometimes worry that I will be hurt if I allow myself to become too close to others.' The 'Fearful' adult self-report classification is not the same as disorganized attachment, because, as we have seen, the latter is not a stable pattern but a temporary constellation of a *child's* attachment behaviour.

Bartholomew also introduced a 5-point Likert-type scale (from 1 = 'least like me' to 5 = 'most like me') and this enabled subsequent researchers to work statistically with dimensional data and thus permitting certain kinds of analyses to be performed which are not possible with categorical or discrete data (e.g. 'secure', 'avoidant', 'ambivalent').

The Attachment Style Questionnaire (ASQ) was devised by Judy Feeney and colleagues in 1994 to preclude the requirement that respondents needed to reflect upon (or even be in) a romantic relationship (Feeney, Noller and Hanrahan 1994). It consists of 40 items to which participants indicate their level of agreement on a 6-point Likert-type scale (1= *totally disagree*; 6 = *totally agree*). It is loosely based on the Hazan–Shaver and Bartholomew–Horowitz measures but it incorporates other items.

Today's 'gold standard' among self-reports of attachment is considered by many social psychologists to be Chris Fraley's 36-item Experiences in Close Relationships – Revised (ECR-R) as it possesses robust psychometric properties.

Later versions of self-report measures continued the shift away from individual classification (which is not always reliable) to the study of the distribution of the key dimensions tapped into by the instrument. The ECR-R, for example, is known to reflect the two orthogonally intersecting axes *attachment-related anxiety* and *attachment-related avoidance* outlined in Chapter 1, and has led to an explosion of research aimed at studying the connections between variables thought to be associated with attachment processes.

Developmentally based measures of attachment

In this book we are concerned specifically with *disorganized* attachment and this focus reduces the psychometric landscape considerably, restricting us to the use of developmentally based measures. Adult participants are asked a series of questions focusing on their *representations* of attachment experiences and, if they are parents, how those representations influence or predict the attachment organization of their children (Belsky 2002). Infants, toddlers and younger children are observed or asked to complete attachment-based stories designed to mildly activate attachment behaviour, either with a caregiver directly or by asking the child to reflect on experiences with the caregiver.

Developmentally based measures probe non-conscious processes to explore internal working models of attachment and use in-depth interviews and observation-based methods; consequently, these measures use controlled, so-called 'manualized' procedures. They are undertaken in a laboratory, in the child's home (or family/day centre) or within 'naturally occurring situations' (for example, in a nursery). They may be child- or parent-focused, depending on the aims of the study and the design of the instrument. The reliability of DA raters is crucial and this is why both *intra*-rater reliability (i.e. how consistent an individual rater is over a series of observations) and *inter*-rater reliability (i.e. how well an individual rater compares with other, accurate raters) are important. The levels of reliability achieved in studies using these measures are now impressive (see van IJzendoorn *et al.* 1999).

We consider each of the measures outlined at the start of this chapter.

Child behaviours (measures of *disorganized attachment* in children of different ages)

Toddlers – Strange Situation Procedure coding for 'D' behaviours

The kinds of behaviours seen in children exhibiting disorganized attachment were categorized by Main and Solomon in 1990 after re-classifying 200 'anomalous' Strange Situation Procedure (SSP) videotapes. Lyons-Ruth and Jacobvitz (2008) describe the behaviours as follows (note the 'shutting down' quality of each, denoting 'fear without solution'):

unclassified infants were observed approaching the parent with head averted; rocking on hands and knees following an abortive approach; or screaming by the door for the parent, then moving away on reunion. What unclassified infants appeared to have in common were contradictory intentions (approaching a parent with head averted), or behaviours that involved apprehension, either directly (fearful facial expressions, oblique approaches), or indirectly, e.g. disoriented behaviours, including dazed or trance-like expressions; or freezing of all movement at the parent's entrance. (p.667)

It is essential to remember, however, that these behaviours are only in-dicative of DA in the very precise circumstances of the SSP (or another very similar way of activating the attachment system). For example, children will sometimes display 'dazed' behaviour when playing a make-believe game. But one would not expect to see such behaviour when a child is frightened by something and while he or she avoids seeking a reassuring cuddle with the carer. In infants and very young children, DA behaviour markers are observable *when the carer is present*; this is the key to understanding disorganized attachment. Main and Solomon (1990) went on to propose specific behaviours now used to classify children's behaviour as DA within SSP, including: alternating between strong attachment and freezing; contradictory behaviours, such as lots of contact followed, or even accompanied, by avoidance; marked and unusually clumsy behaviour when the carer is present; unexplained movements in slow motion; fearful movements in the presence of the carer; and significantly odd and unexplained changes of emotion.

Again, some of these indicators can be seen when children are in-volved in 'pretend' play, so they must be interpreted very carefully if they occur within 'naturally occurring' situations.

Younger children – Story Stem Completion

Story Stem Completion tasks are used with children between the ages of four and nine years. Methods include the MacArthur Story Stem Battery (MSSB; Bretherton, Ridgeway and Cassidy 1990); the Story Stem Assessment Profile (SSAP; Hodges *et al.* 2003); and the Manchester Child Attachment Story Task (MCAST; Green *et al.* 2000). The SSAP consists of 13 short 'beginnings' (i.e. stems) of stories which the child is asked to complete with the request 'Can you *Show Me* and *Tell Me* what happens next?' (the use of *both* verbs is important). The stories are 'brought to life' by means of *Play People*, animals and other 'props' to help make them more concrete, given the age of the child. Each story activates the attachment process for different reasons. The child's responses are gauged in respect of: separation, ability to seek comfort, conflict, external threats, minor accidents and losses, frustration, injury, exclusion and jealousy. So, for example, one of the stories begins with one of two 'adult' *Play People* saying 'You've lost my keys!' The other 'adult' replies 'I *haven't* lost your keys'. Adult 1 says 'You *always* lose my keys'; Adult 2 replies 'Well, I haven't lost them this time'. It is at this point that the child is asked to show *and* tell what then happens. There are strict 'rules' governing what an interviewer can and cannot say by way of prompts and what many people learning these methods find difficult is that they mustn't praise the child excessively or be too encouraging; they have to remain neutral.

Using another example, the first story begins with a child who lives with his or her mother, father and brother or sister. The child is told that they are all sitting in their house. A doll (of the same gender as the child) is taken by the interviewer round the back of the house, so that 'no-one can see them anymore'. The interviewer asks the child to listen, then makes a loud crying sound, and then asks the child to 'show and tell' what happens next.

The point of this remarkably creative and powerful measure is the children who are secure, ambivalent and avoidant – but especially children who experience disorganized attachment – produce markedly different accounts, especially in the way they develop and end their stories. This occurs simply as a result of the mild activation of their attachment system (which demonstrates how near the surface is the behaviour). Children displaying DA quickly describe quite frightening events; they often become very quiet or they will whisper a somewhat garbled account; their language may become confused and even bizarre. The task itself, by design, has produced in their verbal behaviour some-thing akin to the physical reaction they would likely have shown earlier as a toddler in their responses to the SSP (had it been conducted). As Nancy Kaplan put it, they become 'inexplicably afraid and unable to do anything about it' (Kaplan 1987, p.109).

One of us (Yvonne) is accredited to undertake Story Stem Completion but, understandably, the Training Manual accompanying Story Stem Completion is restricted and so there are limits to what we can publish as examples. But Erik Hesse and Mary Main, referring to work undertaken in 1987 by Nancy Kaplan, illustrate the kind of behaviour that typifies the responses of a child completing the Story Stem tasks. In her study, Kaplan showed children aged six a series of parent–child separations. Here is an example:

> *Direct descriptions of fearful events.* These included markedly catastrophic fantasies, such as suggestions that family members might come to great bodily harm, or that the parents or child would die. One child said:
>
>> She's afraid. *[Why is she afraid?]* Her dad might die and then she'll be by herself. *[Why is she afraid of that?]* Because her mom died and if her mom died, she thinks that her dad might die. (Kaplan 1987, pp.109–110)

Hesse and Main then draw on similarly designed research by Carol George and Judith Solomon in 1999. Here a six-year-old has been asked to talk about a doll-play separation:

> And see, and then, you know what happens? Their whole house blows up. See…they get destroyed and not even their bones are left. Nobody can even get their bones. Look. I'm jumping on a rock. This rock feels rocky… And then the rocks tumbled down and smashed everyone. And they all died. (George and Solomon 1999, p.17)

Returning to Kaplan's study, Hesse and Main illustrate 'disorganisation in language and behaviour' by 'using nonsense language ("yes-no-yes-no-yes-no"), making illogical statements, or becoming markedly behaviourally disorganized' (p.1109) with the following example:

> Happy. *[What's he happy about?]* 'Cause he likes his grandfather coming. *(Child jumps on back of stuffed animal in the playroom and hits it.)* Bad lion! *(Hits it more.)* Bad lion! (Kaplan 1987, pp.110–111)

To standardize the way in which the tasks are introduced (and to reduce the length of part of the training) there is now a computerized version of Story Stem tasks designed by Helen Minnis and her colleagues (Minnis *et al.* 2006). The child performs the tasks on a laptop or PC with an in-built camera so that the responses can subsequently be coded and rated.

Using the SSAP, developed by researchers at the Anna Freud Centre in London, three clear markers of disorganized attachment are regularly and consistently found within the narratives of children completing Story Stems: (i) catastrophic fantasy, (ii) bizarre/atypical responses and (iii) 'good/bad' shift. We now give examples of each.

STORY STEM DA MARKER 1 – CATASTROPHIC FANTASY

In the 1990s the BBC documentary series *Panorama* produced a programme entitled 'Children Behaving Badly'. A couple's four-year-old son had been excluded from nursery and behaves aggressively and he is disruptive and clearly a cause of concern to them both. They attend parenting classes and while initially there appears to be some improvement, both in his behaviour and their ability to deal with him, the progress soon evaporates and they are back to square one. At the BBC's request, the family agreed to have cameras installed downstairs in their house in order to show his difficult behaviour during 'naturally occurring' daily-living events. What we see is a little boy who is shouted at regularly, and who is sworn at and criticized over very minor events (e.g. spilling porridge on his pyjamas, dropping some peas on to the floor when opening the fridge). He is told 'you're horrible'; he hears someone say to his mother 'he needs sorting', to which she replies 'you try and be nice to him and he treats you like a bit of shit'.

During a therapy session with the little boy, Story Stem was used and *Panorama* showed the 'Lost Keys' stem. As soon as the researcher asked him to 'Show me and tell me what happens next' he immediately picked up the 'accuser' and proceeded to stab the other doll, saying 'I'll kill you, don't you dare talk to me like that…don't you DARE talk like that'. He then laughed, got down and began to walk off (but not in a defiant or truculent way). The researcher asked him what had happened and he replied 'They're dead, they can't get up – they're dead' in a rather matter-of-fact way. The point here is that the meaning should not be interpreted literally: he has not seen an adult killing another. His reaction is a representation of his lived experience in his family, where he is frightened of both parents and feels desperately unloved and unlovable, maybe even hated. When the 'story' begins with conflict, he reacts the way he does because, in his mind, minor disagreements soon escalate and end up with him being derogated and emotionally annihilated. Interestingly, when the mother was asked what she hoped to gain from attending the parenting classes she replied saying that she wanted *him* to appreciate *her* more. Given that he was aged four at the time, this suggests the strong possibility of low reflective function (RF) on her part.

STORY STEM DA MARKER 2 – BIZARRE/ATYPICAL RESPONSES

A child will sometimes simply just say things which make no overall sense; there is barely a thread through the excerpt, as in this example, where the story involves the protagonist's hand being mildly burned on the side of a pan: he replies, singing the words in a rhythmic way, 'Oh the walls are pink, and the pan is blue, and the sky is yellow, and I love you...I love you and I love me and we're all gonna do a great big wee'. At no other point was such a tone adopted and no reference was made to it again; neither was the child 'fooling around', nor did he seem distressed.

STORY STEM DA MARKER 3 – 'GOOD/BAD' SHIFT

Here there is a marked tendency for the child's narrative to become disjointed but in such a way that there is no monitoring, correction or reflection, such as 'Hang on, what I just said doesn't make sense; what I meant was...' (This is why the interviewer must *not* include questions about unmonitored inconsistencies, e.g. 'A little while ago you said X and now you've said Y so I wonder, can you help me make sense of this please?') One of the Stems starts with a piglet getting lost. One child oscillated wildly between describing the pig as a defenceless 'baby' and the next as a predatory animal, likely to kill and eat other figures in the story (including the 'child' doll). No attempt was made to explain the 'line' of the story; it is as if there are two different tales being told: one 'good' and one 'bad'. There is usually an accompanying feeling of incoherence, which is unscrutinized and which usually stands in marked contrast to other, less troublesome prompts for the child.

Pre/young adolescents – Child Attachment Interview

The Child Attachment Interview (CAI) was devised in 2003 by Mary Target, Peter Fonagy and Yael Schmueli-Goetz for children aged 7 to 11. The principles underpinning it are the same as those informing the innovative Adult Attachment Interview, created in 1985 by Carol George, Nancy Kaplan and Mary Main. We concentrate later on the AAI but in essence it asks adults a series of around 20 questions. One of the key questions, which is introduced early on, is the request for them to choose five words or short phrases to describe their relationship to their mother and father *as far back as they remember.* This reflective question comes after a couple of introductory questions which are relatively innocuous (for example, 'Can you tell me who's who in your family?'). The shift in narrative and discourse is quite often dramatic – referred to by George *et al.* (1985) as 'surprising the unconscious' – and, again, it soon distinguishes between the three organized attachment patterns. They are then asked to think of five words or short phrases to capture their earliest memories of their relationship with their mother and father (or whoever they consider to have been their caregiver).

Questions that follow seek to gauge interviewees' memories about: what happened when they were ill as a child; their recollections about who they went to if distressed; whether they remember ever feeling rejected; their memories about separations and losses; and whether they were ever threatened or frightened. The interview concludes with some questions that give interviewees a chance to reflect on their childhood.

Because the CAI is for children it is not possible for them to reflect back on their childhood because they are clearly still firmly situated *in* their childhood. But, as with the AAI, the CAI is centrally concerned to explore the child's representations of relationships. The questions posed follow a similar pattern to the AAI, except that children are asked to think of three words instead of five to describe their relationship to their parent. Time is always available at the end for the child to wind down (and be thanked). As the interviewer is often a psychologist or social worker, he or she can return to any aspects of the interview that worry him or her (or the child).

As with narratives of children indicating disorganized attachment in the Story Stems, there are clear DA markers in the CAI. We now give a brief example of each.

CHILD ATTACHMENT INTERVIEW DA MARKER 1 – SUDDEN EMOTIONAL SWITCHING IN RESPONSE TO LOSS, TRAUMA AND/OR FRIGHTENING EVENTS

A child may swing violently between opposing emotions, which are often unconnected to the story being narrated. So we may see and hear 'fascination amidst repulsion' and 'excitement mixed with fear'; but the contradictions are not monitored, reflected upon or rationalized. It is the almost seamless 'running' of one feeling into another, like watercolour and oil paint mixing together, that is striking. There can also be energy and vigour in one part of the narrative and yet, at another point, an alarming stillness. There is usually a feeling that separation – and particularly loss – get ratcheted up and intensified. Sometimes the child makes faces or sounds that seem random and unconnected to what he or she is trying to communicate. Often, if emotions *are* expressed, they can appear artificial, simulated and almost theatrically manufactured.

CHILD ATTACHMENT INTERVIEW DA MARKER 2 – FREEZING AND VERY LONG PAUSES

As the marker suggests, here the child drifts into lengthy and unpredictable breaks in the narrative. There is usually an awkwardness to them. They are not temporary halts or breaks to give the child time to think or develop ideas. The experience tends to give an impression of time being suspended, rather than a break; it is a discontinuity rarely revisited.

CHILD ATTACHMENT INTERVIEW DA MARKER 3 – MAGIC/OMNIPOTENCE

Alternatively, some children – or the *same* child within the *same* interview – will suddenly seem to be magically in control of what they are describing, especially if it is frightening. This is not the same as a child becoming a 'superhero' to escape a dangerous situation – the normal 'make believe' of a child exploring and having fun. With the child exhibiting disorganized attachment, we see responses unfold in inexplicable, frightening and sometimes supernatural ways.

CHILD ATTACHMENT INTERVIEW DA MARKER 4 – EXAMPLES OF CONTROLLING- OR PUNITIVE-CAREGIVING RESPONSES (INCLUDING TO THE INTERVIEWER)

There are times when the child will be abusive to the interviewer, which is far beyond normal adolescent truculence or a lack of co-operation; interviewers are likely to feel uncomfortable themselves – as they will with any of these behaviours – but here the controlling behaviour feels somewhat menacing. Alternatively the child may be more taunting, spiteful or punitive by saying things such as 'I might tell you about this or I might not; I might not answer any more questions because people like you make me sick' ('people like you' is unlikely to be explained or amplified). But a few minutes later, the interviewer might be told he or she is a lovely person and that the child likes him or her and wants to talk more.

CHILD ATTACHMENT INTERVIEW DA MARKER 5 – GOOD/BAD SWITCH
CHILD ATTACHMENT INTERVIEW DA MARKER 6 – CATASTROPHIZING

These two markers are very similar to those we saw with the Story Stem indices but are more linguistically developed, as a result of the child's age. So, 'aliens' may intrude and take the child away and torture him or her; the child may be imprisoned, and often abandoned. Children who have been abused or emotionally maltreated are likely to represent their experiences in an incoherent and jumbled manner. They won't be able to talk about them in such a way as to make sense of them.

Caregiver behaviours

As we saw in the previous chapter, there are three key caregiver behaviours now thought to influence, separately and in combination, the development of disorganized attachment: (i) unresolved loss and dissociation, (ii) extremely insensitive and disconnected caregiving and (iii) low RF. We offer an overview of each at this point, leaving the detail to Part 2.

Unresolved loss – Adult Attachment Interview

The narrative approach to elicit working models of attachment used in the Adult Attachment Interview (AAI) gives participants a number of opportunities to reflect upon loss and trauma. As with Story Stems and the CAI, unresolved loss and trauma are marked by inconsistencies and lapses in discourse. Hesse and Main (2000) give the following two examples:

> 'We went to the hospital in, let's see, I think it was the grey Buick, and I sat in the back to the right of my mother, I was wearing jeans and polo shirt, well not jeans but, you know, khakis, and we turned first down West Street and then, there was kind of a lot of traffic, so we took...'

> In other instances the speaker may shift abruptly into eulogistic ('funereal') speech: 'She was young, she was lovely, and she was torn from us by that most dreaded of diseases, tuberculosis. And then, I remember, time and time again, the sounds of the weeping, the smell of the flowers, the mother torn from where she lay weeping upon her daughter's coffin...' (p.1113)

Dissociation – Tellegen's Absorption Scale

It is possible to gauge levels of unresolved loss by using different measures than those emanating from attachment research (but which, nevertheless, correlate well with existing psychometrically robust attachment measures). The Tellegen Absorption Scale (TAS) first appeared in 1974. The items measure the overall tendency for an individual to become 'absorbed' so that focal attention is increased and, consequently, peripheral awareness is diminished. Because of this it is often used as an indication of 'hypnotizability'. The TAS (Tellegen and Atkinson 1974) is the one used most frequently and it correlates positively with the AAI (Hesse and van IJzendoorn 1998). The instructions for completion are:

> This questionnaire consists of questions about experiences that you may have had in your life. We are interested in how often you have these experiences. It is important, however, that your answers show how often these experiences happen to you when you are not under the influence of alcohol or drugs.

The psychometric structure of the TAS comprises six factors: (i) responses to engaging stimuli, (ii) synaesthesia, (iii) enhanced cognition, (iv) vivid reminiscence, (v) enhanced awareness and, finally, (vi) oblivious/dissociated involvement. It is interesting to note that some of these factors have a positive connotation too, as they reflect what might be loosely termed 'heightened awareness'.

Dissociation – Dissociative Experiences Scale

The 28-item Dissociative Experiences Scale (DES) was devised by Eve Bernstein and Frank Putnam in 1986. It has become the most widely used self-report measure of dissociation, especially in studies of dissociative disorders. The DES consists of three factor scales which represent two pathological types of dissociative experiences ('amnesic experiences' and 'depersonalization/de-realization') and one referring to 'normal', dissociative-like experiences (e.g. absorption). Therefore, in some respects, the TAS measures in more detail the third scale in the DES. There is a modified 'adolescent' version of the DES called the A-DES (Armstrong et al. 1997), which consists of 30 items.

Finally, the DES, A-DES and TAS have robust and impressive psychometric properties and data are available on their validity and reliability. Consequently, they are used more frequently in attachment-based studies, in combination with the developmentally based measures (e.g. Hesse and van IJzendoorn 1998).

Frightening/frightened – Frightened/Frightening coding

Main and Hesse developed five Frightening or Frightened (FR) scales in 1992 to which a sixth item was added by 2006 to produce a coding system which is now often used in research into disorganized attachment. The augmented FR scale comprises the following:

1. Threatening behaviours – e.g. suddenly looming into the child's face, especially his or her eyes; taking up various threatening poses; creeping silently towards the child and pretending to maul by, say, baring one's teeth (remember: to an *infant*; and not playfully).

2. Frightened parental behaviours – e.g. backing away from the baby. For example, in Hesse and Main (2000), they describe a child pushing a toy car when, unexpectedly, the mother screams… 'OH NO, they're gonna have an accident; everyone's gonna get KILLED'.

3. Dissociative or trance-like behaviours – e.g. using a ghostly, haunted voice; 'backing away while stammering in an unusual and frightening voice… *D-don't follow me, d-don't…*' (Hesse and Main 2000, p.1115).

4. Timid or deferential parental behaviours – e.g. speaking to their baby with simpering voice.

5. Sexual/spousal behaviours toward child – e.g. extended 'sexualized' kissing or fondling.

6. Disorganized parental behaviour – i.e. behaviour similar to Main and Solomon's (1990) seven-fold descriptors of disorganized behaviour.[1]

---

1   *Source*: Hesse and Main, 'Frightened, threatening, and dissociative parental behavior in low-risk samples: Description, discussion and interpretations.' *Development and Psychopathology 18*, 2, 309–343, 2006 © Cambridge Journals, reproduced with permission.

Frightening/frightened – Atypical Maternal Behaviour Instrument for Assessment and Classification

Karlen Lyons-Ruth and her colleagues (Bronfman *et al.* 2004) developed the Atypical Maternal Behaviour Instrument for Assessment and Classification (AMBIANCE) which comprises scales addressing: 'affective errors', 'disorientation', 'negative-intrusive behaviour', 'role confusion' (including 'role reversal', but not when it involves a child needing to care for a parent as a result of, for example, disability) and significant and chronic 'withdrawal'.

Disconnected/insensitive – Disconnected and extremely Insensitive Parenting Measure

The next development was the extension of the FR system to include a 'broader range of disrupted parental behaviours, including extreme insensitivity' (Out *et al.* 2009, p.422). The measurement of caregiving behaviours is constantly developing and the latest extension comes from Dorothee Out and her colleagues at Leiden University in the form of the Disconnected and extremely Insensitive Parenting (DIP) Measure. The DIP genuinely builds upon the FR and AMBIANCE because they were aware of a need to distinguish more clearly, as the name of the full title of the DIP indicates, between *Disconnected Parenting* and *Extremely Insensitive Parenting*. And as we saw in the previous chapter, their hypotheses were confirmed by the differential effects each had on disorganized attachment as well as the influence of unresolved loss and trauma on them respectively.

Reflective functioning – Parent Development Interview

RF is measured largely using the AAI, and we give examples of how this is achieved in more detail in Chapter 6, but we now look briefly at two specific measures of RF in respect of parenting behaviour: the Parent Development Interview (PDI) and the WMCI.

One of the key findings from research into (mis)attuned caregiving is that 'significantly reduced sensitivity is associated with a tendency to attribute *negative intentionality* to the baby from a very early age' (Bakermans-Kranenburg and van IJzendoorn 2007, p.143). Negative intentionality, or attributing intentions to a child which he or she could not or is most unlikely to possess, is a feature of maltreating parents. It also indicates a strong tendency to demonstrate low RF on the part of such parents towards their children.

The PDI was devised in 1994 by Arieta Slade and colleagues and, as with the AAI, it is not based on an observed interaction; rather, it assesses the representational models the parent has of – and towards – the child. It focuses on three areas: (i) the parent's overall awareness of the parent–child relationship, (ii) the carer's perspective on that relationship and (iii) what the parent thinks is the *child's* view of that relationship. With that focus it taps into RF which, as we saw in the previous chapter, is a key mediator variable in the pathway leading to disorganized attachment. The main scales include:

> *compliance* (the extent to which the content of the response involves the mother's role as a socialization agent and the child's compliance with expectations and requests); *achievement* (the response describes the parent as teacher and monitor of developmental progress); *comfort/ safety* (how the parent comforts and provides a secure base); *enmeshment* (scored when the parent's report reveals a lack of appropriate parent–child boundaries due either to role reversal or the parent's needs taking precedence over the needs of the child, e.g., 'I go to him for a hug when I am down'; 'He's my best friend') and the *emotions, pain and worry about the future*. (Sayre *et al.* 2001, p.378)

The Anna Freud Centre in London runs courses on how to code the PDI, specifically for RF. Carers who score highly on the PDI-RF scale are demonstrably aware of the way their child functions mentally and can both understand and appreciate how their own mental state interacts with their child's. They comprehend their child's experiences as unique, rather than being congruent or mirrored with their own experiences. They comprehend and welcome the intentionality of the child. Low RF parents are markedly different and 'parents of disorganized infants are almost a standard deviation higher on this measure than parents of secure ones' (Fonagy and Target 2005, p.336). Furthermore, 'there is a substantial correlation between AMBIANCE codings and RF' and, given the very different bases to these measures, there is a strong connection 'between the observed frequency of behaviours (such as demanding a show of affection from the infant), fearful behaviour or intrusive or negative behaviours (such as mocking or criticizing) and narratives that…show little appreciation that the infant's mind cannot be directly read, or depict her as having no feelings, thoughts or wishes' (p.336).

Reflective functioning – Working Model of the Child Interview

The AAI ends with opportunities to integrate experiences coherently (which securely attached adults are able to do). For example: 'Looking back, do you think your mother/father loved you?', 'Do you think your childhood experiences have affected your adult personality, and in what ways?', 'Are there aspects of your childhood that you think were a setback or hindered your development?' and, finally, 'Why do you think your mother/father acted as s/he did during your childhood?'

The WMCI was developed in 1986 and revised in 1993 by Charles Zeanah and colleagues (see Zeanah, Benoit and Barton 1993). The WMCI comprises 19 main questions, each sub-divided into a number of prompts and sub-questions. As with the PDI, it includes a scale to measure RF; and like the AAI, CAI and PDI, the WMCI is a structured interview focusing on a carer's representations or working model of his or her relationship to a specific child. Here is Question 6, which mines the rich seam of RF more specifically (from Zeanah *et al.* 1993):

> What about your child's behaviour now is the most difficult to handle? Give a typical example.
>
> • How often does this occur? What do you feel like doing when your child reacts that way? How do you feel when your child reacts that way? What do you actually do?
>
> • Does he/she know you don't like it? Why do you think he/she does it?
>
> • What does the child do after you respond to the difficult behaviour in the way you described? How do you imagine the child feels when you respond this way?
>
> • What do you imagine will happen to this behaviour as your child grows older? Why do you think so/what makes you feel that way?

Reflective functioning – Reading the Mind in the Eyes Test

The Reading the Mind in the Eyes Test was devised by Simon Baron-Cohen. The user is presented with 36 photographs of faces cropped to the eye region. The rubric for each of the 36 questions is: 'For each pair of eyes, choose which word best describes what the person in the picture is thinking or feeling.' The options for the first image are 'Playful',

'Comforting', 'Irritated' or 'Bored'. This test is also increasingly being used as a complementary measure in attachment-based research focusing on RF and its connection to disorganized attachment.

Accessible websites devoted to specific measures

Adult Attachment Interview (AAI): www.psychology.sunysb.edu/attachment/measures/content/aai_interview.pdf

Dissociative Experiences Scale (DES): http://counsellingresource.com/quizzes/des/index.html

Experiences in Close Relationships – Revised (ECR-R): www.psych.uiuc.edu/~rcfraley/measures/ecrr.htm

Reading the Mind in the Eyes Test: www.glennrowe.net/BaronCohen/Faces/EyesTest.aspx

Tellegen's Absorption Scale (TAS): http://socrates.berkeley.edu/~kihlstrm/TAS.htm

Working Model of the Child Interview (WMCI-RF): www.oaimh.org/newsFiles/Working_Model_of_the_Child_Interview.pdf

Chapter 4

Neurological, Biochemical and Genetic Explanations

Neurobiological processes and attachment

Organized attachment

Recent discoveries in neurology, biochemistry and genetics now add weight to what Bowlby and the early attachment pioneers hypothesized and subsequently began to confirm through detailed observation. Using sophisticated scans of blood-flow and electrical activity to and around the brain, neurobiological activity mirroring their theoretical insights can now be observed. Again, using the Strange Situation Procedure (SSP), scans show that, at around 36 months and beyond, neural blood flow of *securely* attached children is evenly distributed across both hemi-spheres, whereas in *ambivalent* children it is concentrated in the right hemisphere (a key affective area in the brain), and in the left hemisphere (a key cognitive region) for *avoidant* children (Schore 1994, 2000). As we will see, with children who display DA, whose parents experienced unresolved loss and trauma and/or exhibit extremely insensitive and disconnected parenting and/or low reflective function (RF), there are now clearly observable consequences taking place in brain structure and function as well as measurable differences resulting from biochemical processes involved in regulating stress and anxiety.

EARLY NEUROBIOLOGY

During the early weeks post-delivery, the infant's immediate social environment impacts directly upon the organization of the early de-veloping right cortex which undergoes a growth spurt during the first 18–36 months (Tucker 1992). Allan Schore outlined in detail what takes place during the initial development of the brain, concluding that the early social environment, especially experiences mediated by the primary caregiver, directly influences the wiring of the neural circuitry responsible for the child's socio-emotional development (Schore 1994). It is the orbitofrontal cortex (OFC) that is uniquely involved in the regulation of emotion and motivational states (Schore 1994). Because the OFC is the primary site of brain functioning at birth (Murray and Andrews 2000), face-to-face interactions at approximately two months are 'short, highly arousing, affect-laden, interpersonal events that expose infants to high levels of cognitive and social information' (Feldman, Greenbaum and Yirmiya 1999, p.233). As the adult and infant resonantly match each other's temporal and affective patterns, each recreates a synchronized inner neurobiological state. Consequently, optimal psychobiological attunement histories are more likely to lead to secure attachment behaviours while misattuned affect transactions produce insecure attachments (Schore 1994).

Infants' affective experiences are stored more densely in the right hemisphere during the very early stages of neural and structural expansion. The child's brain 'uses' the output from the primary caregiver's right cortex to mirror the developing neural circuits in its own right cortex. This eventually leads to an increase in affect-regulating abilities. It is as though the OFC is 'downloading' the software – babies are born with the 'hardware' – that it needs in order to grow; but the software it gets comes from the immediate caregiver, which may be incomplete or even 'damaged', to continue with the IT metaphor.

Bidirectional 'synchrony' of right hemispheric cortices is now thought to develop as a consequence of the infant and primary caregiver mirroring each other's affective states, mainly through eye-gazing because the OFC is situated behind the eyes, close to the brain stem. It is responsible in the early days of life for the infant's more instinctual reactions (Schore 1994). Because the 'right hemisphere is dominant for the production of cortisol, and immune, neuroendocrine, and cardiovascular functions, synchronised and psychobiologically attuned caregiver–child interactions are thought also to be highly conducive to physical health' (Schore 1994, p.446). The right brain therefore is centrally involved in the vital functions that support survival and enable the organism to cope, actively and passively, with stress. The early attachment relationship thus directly shapes the infant's right brain stress-coping systems.

In order to enter into this communication, the primary caregiver needs to become 'psychobiologically attuned' (Schore 1994) not so much to the child's overt behaviour as to the reflections of his or her internal state. Significantly, therefore, it is the *emotional*, far more than the *physical*, availability of the caregiver that constitutes the central growth-promoting feature of early rearing experience (Ader and Cohen 1993).

Allan Schore reports that brain development is at its most active during early growth-spurt periods. But internal working models can change at any point during the lifespan when previously under- (or un-) used neural pathways will repair or even start to grow (Schore 2000). In other words, certain types of intervention can interrupt the intergenerational transmission of maltreatment, disorganized attachment and relational trauma (as we will see in Chapter 8).

Our developing understanding of the neurobiology of maltreatment and disorganization

How is neurobiological research undertaken?

Research into the structure and operation of the brain is undertaken with sophisticated and expensive equipment, such as Magnetic Resonance Imaging (MRI) scanners which measure the structure and function (fMRI) of the brain. A structural scan involves taking pictures of 'slices of the brain', particularly what is known as 'grey matter'. Other types and variants of scanning provide different neural information; for example, Diffusion Tensor Imaging (DTI) produces data on 'white matter'. Resultant images can be two-dimensional or three-dimensional. Because the 100 billion or so neurons in the human brain 'communicate' through minute electro-chemical signals it is possible to measure the electrical activity in the brain using high-density electroencephalographs (EEGs). High-density EEG 'nets' – which look rather like hair nets, with 0.5-inch diameter 'suckers' placed onto the relevant areas of the person's head – are also less expensive and (usually!) less 'troublesome' for participants.

Such scanning provides a powerful and accurate measure of how the brain has developed in a way that behavioural and other outcome measures cannot match (although they are still needed to complement the neurological data, to show the outward manifestation of structural neurological damage, for example). Structural MRI scans can map differences between maltreated and non-maltreated children in areas of the brain known to govern particular emotional, physiological and cognitive activity.

MRI scanning is non-invasive as it deploys magnetic and radio waves; there is no use of X-rays or any other form of radiation. Some people, however, find the experience of being enclosed in the 'tunnel' rather claustrophobic, but there are now more 'open' versions of MRI scanners and, to varying degrees, they can ameliorate the unpleasant effects.

Functional MRI scans measure the amount and location of blood in different areas of the brain to reveal precisely the areas that are active when an individual undertakes a task (such as looking at a photo expressing different emotions). For example, Pollak *et al.* (2001) asked maltreated individuals and controls to look at different facial expressions of anger, fear and happiness. They found that differences between the two groups emerged only for fear, an emotion highly associated with threat, which, again, strongly suggested attributional and attentional differences between maltreated and non-maltreated children, especially over assumptions of others' hostile intentions. Such studies are of considerable relevance to the study of disorganized attachment.

Neurological studies into disorganized attachment are difficult to design because it is virtually impossible to scan a child's brain at the precise point when he or she experiences 'fear without solution'. What researchers have done, therefore, is to study *maltreated* individuals and this can provide information by proxy on DA as a result of the high correlation between maltreatment and disorganized attachment. As a result of difficulties gathering a sample of maltreated *children*, to date most studies have recruited adults who were abused as children. An exception is research recently begun by Eamon McCrory at University College London. Together with colleagues at the Anna Freud Centre he is using fMRI scans with maltreated children known to social workers in London.

To develop our understanding of disorganized attachment, eventually we need neurobiological information on each of the key variables in our Pathway Model. It is important to explore any differences between organized and disorganized children within the architecture and wiring of the brain when such children have experienced significantly traumatic parenting. We also need to know more about the neurobiology of parents who exhibit low RF and extremely insensitive and disconnected parenting, and who themselves have experienced unresolved trauma and loss. Similarly, as yet, we have no neurological data on what happens in the brain before, during and after different interventions.

The hypothalamic-pituitary-adrenal axis stress response

Growing interest has developed during recent years over the role played by the hypothalamic-pituitary-adrenal (HPA) axis stress response. The

HPA axis refers to the complex series of biochemical interconnections between the hypothalamus and the pituitary gland and the adrenal or suprarenal glands near the apex of each kidney. Each component 'communicates' to the others to ensure that the correct level of cortisol, for example, is produced when the body experiences fear and danger. The HPA axis also helps regulate temperature, digestion and the immune system, and is a major part of the system controlling our reaction to stress, trauma and injury; hence the connection to the biopsychosocial mechanisms underlying DA.

The way the HPA axis works is complex. Cells in the paraventricular nucleus (PVN) of the hypothalamus produce the corticotropin-releasing hormone (CRH) and arginine vasopressin (AVP) into the pituitary stalk. These changes are needed when we face physical or emotional stress. The hypothalamus secretes CRH which, in turn, binds to specific receptors on the pituitary cells to produce the adrenocorticotropic hormone (ACTH). These and other hormones coordinate our behavioural, autonomic and immune responses to stress. Thus, the HPA axis is involved centrally in cortisol production which activates stored glucose for secretion into the blood.

The HPA axis aims to produce the *optimal* amount of cortisol: too much or too little can cause problems. For example, blood sugar levels can rise or fall outside safe limits. If the under- or over-production of cortisol becomes chronic – so-called 'toxic stress' (National Scientific Council on the Developing Child 2005) – the consequences can be severe and lead to psychopathological conditions and psychiatric vulnerability in adulthood. Put simply, chronic excess of cortisol damages the brain.

Compared with the cost and complexity of undertaking neurological studies, measuring cortisol levels is relatively straightforward as they only require the taking of saliva samples. In relation to disorganized attachment, two earlier studies (Hertsgaard *et al.* 1995; Spangler and Grossmann 1993) established a connection between infants with insecure or disorganized attachment patterns and raised cortisol levels. Thus, as Karlen Lyons-Ruth and Deborah Jacobvitz (2008) remind us, these studies confirm Main and Solomon's (1990) contention that 'disorganised infant behaviour reflects the lack of an effective strategy for coping with stress' (Lyons-Ruth and Jacobvitz 2008, p.670).

The neurobiological role of oxytocin and dopamine

Using blood, saliva or urine samples as part of research into the bio-chemistry of maltreatment and disorganized attachment is proving to be interesting and has already confirmed a number of theoretically consistent hypotheses. Most studies have focused on the role of two neurotransmitters: oxytocin and dopamine. Oxytocin plays a role in attachment due to its known connection to social recognition, trust, love, generosity and caregiving behaviours (especially mothers with new-born infants) – it is present in huge quantities immediately after childbirth, for example. Fascinatingly, being given a sniff of oxytocin before doing the Reading the Mind in the Eyes Test increases both accuracy and speed of response (Domes *et al.* 2007). Oxytocin levels increase in response to massage, light stroking and pleasant sounds and smells; they are also linked to enhanced composure and calm in a crisis due to reduced anxiety, and even physical pain. Conversely, low oxy-tocin levels are strongly related to emotional abuse (Heim *et al.* 2009).

Dopamine, on the other hand, is a neurotransmitter that regulates reward and attentional strategies. Parenting brings into play a series of neural circuits involved in reward-seeking and stress regulation. As we will see, research into the effects of dopamine is building up a profile of a particular variant of a receptor which is related specifically to children who have exhibited disorganized attachment.

'Switching' between the executive and subcortical parts of the brain

An increase in dopaminergic circuitry occurs when we are under stress. Our prefrontal cortex (PFC) – the executive part of the brain that helps us be logical, measured and to defer gratification – becomes 'disconnected' and sub-cortical areas take over, resulting in increased impulsivity. The process is similar to what happens when we eat chocolate for comfort under stress (sub-cortical activity), even though our more rational mind – the executive role of the PFC – tells us that it will only give temporary relief, make us feel bad afterwards by increasing our craving next time and make us put on weight. All of that we 'know', but that doesn't stop us eating chocolate! Other sub-cortical demons are *excessive* alcohol con-sumption and drug-taking, gambling, eating disorders and buying things we don't need; we all do different things when our PFC is hijacked.

The HPA axis contains accelerators and brakes to moderate and control the way the entire system works when we are stressed. Under optimal conditions, feedback-looping operates to ensure that a steady-state is maintained after the stress has subsided; under such optimal conditions a set of control mechanisms link to the higher order 'executive functions' located in the PFC and the amygdala, one of two almond-shaped structures near the PFC ('amygdala' is the Greek word for 'almond'). The problem for the child exhibiting disorganized attachment is that the HPA axis is always on red-alert: even though there may *actually* be no real threat, the body stays on permanent 'look-out' and remains in an almost permanent state of hypervigilance and anxiety. It is this state that can eventually impair or impede the structure, function and neural circuitry of the brain. Mild cognitive impairments can also follow, as a result of the brain and body being in a chronic state of over-attentiveness and hypervigilance. Significant interruptions and disturbances to parental care can alter the way the HPA axis operates, either by amplifying or weakening its effect; the timing and duration of periods of separation, for example, are both crucial factors in determining the effect on HPA activity.

Patrick Luyten refers to this phenomenon as a 'bio-behavioural switch' (Luyten, Kempke and Van Houdenhove 2009). When there is early adversity, the switch point kicks in sooner than it should, leading to impulsivity, poor decision-making, impaired appraisal of consequences and a compulsion to seek immediate reward. At a neurological level, both scanning and imaging show a reduction in dendritic branching, which means that fewer neural connections are made, resulting in decreased volume in the PFC along with reduced hippocampal volume. The effect on parenting is that the carer cannot bear to be with his or her child when he or she is distressed, so the child ends up rejected or shouted at (and often both). The emotional state of the other person is either of no interest or is feared; either way the effect is what Peter Fonagy refers to as a *vicious mentalizing cycle* resulting in reduced mentalizing capacity, leading to emotional dysregulation and thereby impeding further mentalizing.

People with chronic substance addiction illustrate these dynamics very clearly. The biochemistry of close personal relationships and drug addiction are very similar. Indeed Peter Fonagy and Linda Mayes coined the phrase 'attachment is an addiction'.[1] Their evidence-informed argu-

---

1   Referred to at the *Child Abuse: Neuroscience and Intervention* conference in London in November 2009.

ment is that substance abuse and drug addiction are attempts to replace the opiates normally provided by social attachments. But as the latter are more difficult to establish and maintain, for some individuals it is easier to replace the deficit 'on the street'. With substance mis-users the 'bio-behavioural switch' cuts in too early, leaving the individual vulnerable to impulsive responses because his or her PFC has 'switched' off its executive function.

What we are talking about when we consider the effects of maltreatment and disorganized attachment, therefore, is not the same as a 'naughty' bout of chocolate eating, which we all need to do from time to time and which, in moderation, does no lasting damage. Chronically impaired neurobiology of the HPA axis, on the other hand, which is especially vulnerable to early adversity, caused when a child experiences maltreatment and prolonged fear of his or her secure base, can be lasting if left unaddressed.

Specific findings in maltreated/disorganized children and later as adults

The few contemporary studies on the neurobiology of maltreated children have produced mixed findings, even though the design of the studies has been sound. An article in 2010 by Eamon McCrory, Stephane De Brito and Essi Viding in the *Journal of Child Psychology and Psychiatry* offers the best summary of these findings to date. Contradictory findings in otherwise well-designed studies are often an indication of the presence of confounding and interacting variables, and in which genetics play a role too. For example, it appears that the presence of a parallel affective disorder (for example, depression) muddles results, so that an over-activation of HPA functions may have depended on whether another child, say, was depressed *and* maltreated. But it appears that the presence or not of a chronically threatening environment is a key factor determining impaired HPA functioning. So, for example, being abused at home *and* bullied at school can have an effect on a child's neurochemistry. Antisocial behaviour also moderates the effect on HPA functioning, along with maltreatment.

With adults who have been maltreated as children, studies using the Trier Social Stress Test (Kirschbaum, Pirke and Hellhammer 1993) – in which the participant has to make an unprepared speech in public and perform mental arithmetic in front of an audience – found that depression in women moderated pathways to HPA axis stress modulation (McCrory *et al.* 2010).

There is some evidence that abused or neglected children have smaller cranial and cerebral volume, as well as reduced white matter in key parts of the brain, irrespective of moderating variables. No apparent reduction in hippocampal volume – an important sub-cortical area responsible for long-term memory and special navigation – has yet been found in children (McCrory *et al.* 2010) but it *has* been noted in adults maltreated as children and who also exhibited PTSD or experienced chronic stress (McCrory *et al.* 2010).

There are two possible explanations for this finding. First, the *neurotoxicity hypothesis* posits that some harmful effects only become visible over a longer time period; second, the *vulnerability hypothesis* contends that there may be predisposing factors in existence prior to the abuse (McCrory *et al.* 2010). To explore the second explanation studies are beginning to focus on adults maltreated as children who have *not* gone on to develop mental illnesses, because they may reveal information about innate or acquired resilience (McCrory *et al.* 2010).

The corpus callosum is the largest white matter structure in the brain and is responsible for the communication between hemispheres of (among others) arousal, emotion and higher cognitive abilities. Maltreated children were noted to have smaller corpus callosa, using a measure of the direction and thickness of the white fibre area (McCrory *et al.* 2010). Always known by experienced social and health visitors to be particularly insidious, studies show that a parent who regularly mocks and humiliates a child leads to reduced white matter connectivity (which may explain why such children lose confidence in the use of language and show impaired affect regulation).

The quality of carer behaviour on reunion is one factor that, in animals at any rate, can moderate the experience of stress (there is no reason to suppose human and primate neurobiology is any different, especially given Bowlby's theoretical insights and observational discoveries from the SSP). This also explains why proximity-seeking 'down regulates' emotion, which has been demonstrated in neurobiological research. Michael Meaney's work with rodents and their offspring demonstrates the way maternal care results in structural changes in the amygdala, hypothalamus and hippocampus resulting in losses of branches and spines in neurons during and following stress (Diorio and Meaney 2007). Studies with rat pups and mothers showed that the more the mother licked and groomed the pup, the more attuned was the HPA axis response to stress, possibly even producing stress-resilience (Diorio and Meaney 2007). Bear in mind too that

> in rats one day of maternal deprivation was sufficient to decrease brain-derived neurotropic factor in the hippocampus and initiate pre-programmed cell death… Although the results aren't quite so dramatic in humans, where one day in the life of a newborn rat is equivalent to approximately six months of deprivation in human infants…it does make it clear that sustained neglect has far more detrimental consequences than child abuse. (Crittenden 2008, p.177)

Genetic explanations

Susan Hart (2008) reminds us that the 'genes are the basis for the development of an individual, and they ensure continuity as well as variation from generation to generation. Some genes take effect from the first cell division or at certain times during the foetal period, while others take effect late in life' (p.22). Unfortunately, genetic research needs large samples to overcome the problem of tracking a single pathway from a specific genotype to something as complex as 'maltreatment'. Karlen Lyons-Ruth and Deborah Jacobvitz (2008) also point out that considerable 'statistical power is needed to detect differences between correlations' (p.669).

Until relatively recently, the preferred way to explore the effect of genetics was to compare monozygotic (identical) with dizygotic (non-identical) twins. But when disorganized attachment is entered into the equation, not surprisingly there are few studies available to compare DA in identical and non-identical twins! Fortunately, complementary methods are now available to study the possibility of DA being partly heritable. They involve analysing the structure of genes at the molecular level. This is achieved by taking 'buccal swabs' – a saliva sample taken from inside the cheek.

Research on genetics and its connection to disorganized attachment is inevitably complicated because, first, it assumes some knowledge of genes and chromosomes and, second, as a direct result of the unfamiliar language. We suspect that many people in the helping professions (even some health professionals) will struggle with some of the papers referred to in this chapter; we certainly did! Nevertheless, we urge readers to persevere as their efforts will be rewarded with a much deeper understanding of disorganized attachment than is possible from psychosocial research alone. As with much research it is not necessary to understand all of the technical or statistical bases behind the study. It would be difficult, however, to appreciate the findings in this area without a basic appreciation of two key ideas within genetic research: the 'allele' and the 'promoter polymorphism'. (Sometimes a distinction is made between 'receptor genes' and 'transmitter genes' but, for the most part, the difference is obvious.)

An *allele* is one member of a pair or series of genes occupying a specific position on a specific chromosome. Genes either have two, three or four alleles (and they usually have two). When referring to articles about DA and genetics it is only necessary to appreciate that the word 'allele' can in some respects be replaced by the phrase 'gene location'. With our aim of keeping things as simple as possible, a 'promoter polymorphism' simply means the 'root of a genetic connection'. (A polymorphism is a small gene variant.) Take, for example, the following short excerpt from Lyons-Ruth and Jacobvitz (2008) – 'The dopamine D4 receptor (DRD4) gene has been considered a candidate gene for infant attachment behaviour' (p.669). At its simplest, this tells us that dopamine (a neurotransmitter that can lead to increases in blood pressure and heart rate) might be connected to infant attachment. The authors go on to inform us that, in one study by a team of Hungarian geneticists, led by Krisztina Lakatos (Lakatos *et al.* 2000, 2002), they 'found associations between the DRD4 7-repeat genotype and disorganised attachment in a low risk sample' (p.669). Analysis of a second polymorphism affecting dopamine efficiency (the −521 C/T promoter polymorphism) revealed that 'the association between the 7-repeat allele and disorganised attachment was observed only in the presence of the −521T allele' (p.669).

If you are feeling put off by such language, try not to be as, for the most part, you can ignore it! All you need to appreciate is that dopamine was thought to be connected at a molecular genetic level to DA. When both alleles were present – the DRD4 receptor *and* the −521T promoter – Lakatos *et al.* (2002) established that the connection with DA was 40 per cent, compared to 11 per cent for the rest of the sample. The important point to consider, however, is that when two subsequent studies – one of them by two key members of the Leiden team and one by Gottfried Spangler and Peter Zimmermann – replicated the earlier research by Lakatos *et al.* they did not find the same connections (see Bakermans-Kranenburg and van IJzendoorn 2004; Spangler and

Zimmermann 2007), because it was felt the Hungarian team did not take account fully of gene–environment interactions.

Gene–environment interaction

Many researchers in this field appear now to conclude that what is confounding the findings is the connection between genes and environment – referred to in this and other research into molecular genetics as 'G×E interactions'. As Susan Hart (2008) reminds us, 'interaction between genes and the environment begins during gestation when the foetus develops sensory organs and the beginnings of motor control' (p.21). Contemporary understandings of the connection between genes and environment strongly indicate a complex relationship between the two. For example, children might inherit the tendency to be overweight, but if there is very little food around for them to eat, and they end up poorly nourished, they will be underweight for their age. Similarly, it is thought that there is a G×E contribution to schizophrenia in that particular kinds of stressful environments during adolescence (especially around excessive pressure to achieve academic success) may in ways not yet fully understood 'activate' a genetic predisposition in some people, but not others, to develop the condition. Another environmental factor thought by some to lead to gene expression is cannabis use (Caspi *et al.* 2003).

Certain polymorphisms that produce (some) resilience to maltreatment in one person can lead to vulnerability in another which, in due course, may lead to a variety of psychological and psychiatric disorders. But it gets more complicated in that the same genes are not related exclusively to specific disorders. For example, the serotonin transporter 5-HTT gene has been linked to PTSD, depression *and* antisocial behaviour (Feder *et al.* 2009). Minor genetic differences can produce huge variation later; but how? The metaphor of a giant oil tanker sailing an infinite sea has been used to capture the notion that an infinitesimally small change of course at the beginning will, if uncorrected, nevertheless lead to appreciable variations soon afterwards; a few years later the variation in overall direction will have become enormous.

Finally, there is 'gene–gene' as well as 'gene–environment' interaction. For example, there are now thought to be nine genes which help us 'pick up the baby' soon after its birth (and not do much else): if all goes well 'your ticket is punched when you hold your baby'[2]...or at least it is for most parents; for others, it can be a time of unbearable emotional pain, full of regular reminders of insensitive parenting provided during their own childhood.

Differential susceptibility and diathesis-stress models of G×E interaction

The fundamental idea behind *gene–environment (G×E) interaction* applied to the potential heritability of disorganized attachment would be that some infants may be more defenceless in the face of insensitive parenting than others. In the field of genetics research this is known as 'differential susceptibility', elaborated by Jay Belsky (see, for example, Belsky 2005). This is different from an alternative model known as the 'diathesis-stress' hypothesis ('diathesis' means 'vulnerability'). The 'diathesis-stress' model assumes negative outcomes may result from unfavourable environments only, whereas Belsky's differential susceptibility hypothesis allows for the possibility of negative outcomes in unfavourable environments *and* for more positive outcomes in favourable environments.

We will illustrate this difference by returning to the example of dopamine. Remember that there are two forms of the dopamine D4 receptor allele: the short one and the long one, called the 'DRD4 7+' (or 7-repeat). Remember too that the −521 C/T variant of the DRD4 allele is also known to be involved at the molecular level. In summarizing the results of a number of studies, Marian Bakermans-Kranenburg and Marinus van IJzendoorn (2007) begin by reporting the study by Lakatos *et al.* (2002) which produced a ten-fold increase in DA in infants where both the long form of the DRD4 receptor *and* the −521 C/T variant were present. Using the same sample, Gervai *et al.* (2005) wanted to know whether the parent's DNA also contained elements of the two polymorphisms. (They didn't, but the absence was related to secure attachment, not to the presence of disorganized attachment.)

At first reading, these findings are frustrating because they *appear* to produce contradictory results; but Bakermans-Kranenburg and van IJzendoorn (2007) explain why. The problem surrounds the age-old

---

2   A phrase used by Linda Mayes from Yale University at the *Child Abuse: Neuroscience and Intervention* conference in London in November 2009.

problem in statistics of the need to consider interaction effects. We looked at interaction in Chapter 2 but here is a frivolous example. In the US, marshmallow figures – called *Peeps* – are very popular with children (and adults apparently). They are eaten with ice-cream, toasted, etc. – in fact there are whole websites devoted to Marshmallow Peeps. Apparently, if you put one in a glass jar and introduce cigarette smoke to it, nothing happens; neither does anything happen if you introduce alcohol. But if the Peep is introduced to both simultaneously, it darkens and eventually disintegrates (there is a specific website demonstrating this too at www.saynotocrack.com/index.php/2007/04/06/marshmallow-peep-research).

Bakermans-Kranenburg and van IJzendoorn (2007) summarized the way G×E interactions appear to work with regard to infants' development of DA. They go some way to closing a second 'transmission gap' which is:

> Why do certain key theoretical and empirically derived aspects of parenting, which are known links to DA – typically anomalous frightening and dissociative behaviours – still leave a large amount of the variance in infant DA unaccounted for? Why doesn't this kind of 'poor parenting' tell the whole story; what else might be going on?

One of the most fascinating and challenging findings to have emerged is that an interaction effect may be at work between favourable and unfavourable caregiving environments *and* the long form of the DRD4 gene. This means that, although it can't yet be claimed that secure parenting with children with the long form of the allele will lead to them becoming *more* secure than children with the short form, we can say that it is likely to lead to far less disorganized attachment behaviour within secure caregiving environments. (Remember that some secure parents at times display frightening behaviour due, it is thought, to temporary dissociation as a result of their own unresolved loss or trauma.) There are, however, some results available from a similar study into children displaying aggressive behaviours (often referred to as 'externalizing', or 'oppositional', behaviours) who also have the long form of the DRD4 allele (Mills-Koonce *et al.* 2007). It has now been shown experimentally that such children do much worse under adverse parenting but, fascinatingly, they also do much better under supportive conditions. Similar studies have yet to be completed in respect of DA.

Professionals working with children and parents are often sceptical about genetically based research, partly because they feel that there is little they can do to affect matters. This is true to some extent but consider for a moment the use of these findings in the following scenario. A child protection team manager is faced with a situation in which an 18-month-old child showing clear signs of disorganized attachment is being considered for short-term fostering because the birth parents are not able to cope at present due to their chronic dependence on Class A drugs. The research findings would indicate that an intervention programme should be provided to offer the toddler consistently secure parenting, and that this will be even more effective if the child has a genetic susceptibility towards DA (and maybe aggression too). If the child is eventually returned to the birth parents it will be important to address any unresolved loss as well as reduce, on the one hand, frightening/frightened, hostile or helpless parenting behaviours, alongside a plan to replace harsh, intrusive and insensitive approaches to discipline with gentle but firm 'positive discipline', on the other. This will need to form the key components of direct work with the carer/s (and we stress the need to work with *all* primary carers). The results of the research could be used in a court to give a greater indication of the success of the intervention as well as reassure the team manager that the parenting intervention is designed well, based upon an evidence-informed approach. Irrespective of the genetic predisposition of the child, the outcome is promising; in terms of aggression, if the child has the long form of the DRD4 allele then it tells us that if we get the intervention wrong it is likely to make matters worse – but if we get it right, things will get a lot better, and probably quicker.

Developments in genetic research offer promising possibilities in extending our understanding of the nature and causes of DA. One of the problems, however, is that reading the reports of findings can prove daunting and off-putting. We conclude this chapter with a few tips on making sense of genetics-based articles.

Try your hand at making sense of the following extract from a paper written in 2008 by Marinus van IJzendoorn, Marian Bakermans-Kranenburg and Judi Mesman entitled 'Dopamine system genes associated with parenting in the context of daily hassles' published in the journal *Genes, Brain and Behavior*. Remember: the trick is to ignore much of the technical detail around the biochemical and molecular genetic information.

Box 4.1 'Dopamine system genes associated with parenting in the context of daily hassles' – van IJzendoorn, Bakermans-Kranenburg and Mesman (2008) *Genes, Brain and Behavior*

Abstract

The current study examined the molecular genetic foundations of sensitive parenting in humans and is the first to test the interaction between genes and environment in modulating parental sensitive responses to children. In a community sample of 176 Caucasian, middle class mothers with their 23-month-old toddlers at risk for externalizing behaviour problems, the association between daily hassles and sensitive parenting was investigated. We tested whether two dopamine-related genes, dopamine D4 receptor (DRD4) and catechol-O-methyltransferase (COMT) gene polymorphisms, modulate parents' vulnerability to the negative influence of daily hassles on sensitive parenting behaviour to their offspring. Sensitive parenting was observed in structured settings, and parents reported on their daily hassles through a standard questionnaire. In parents with the combination of genes leading to the least efficient dopaminergic system functioning (COMT..., DRD4, 7 Repeat), more daily hassles were associated with less sensitive parenting, and lower levels of daily hassles were associated with more sensitive parenting ($d = 1.12$). The other combinations of COMT and DRD4 polymorphisms did not show significant associations between daily hassles and maternal sensitivity, suggesting differential susceptibility to hassles depending on parents' dopaminergic system genes. It is concluded that the study of (multiple) gene–environment interactions (in the current case: gene by gene by environment interaction, G x G x E) may explain why some parents are more and others less impacted by daily stresses in responding sensitively to their offspring's signals.

If all the biochemistry is removed what emerges is actually quite a straightforward summary headline message:

OUR SUMMARY

A low-risk sample of 176 mothers showed 'differential susceptibility' to daily hassles when bringing up their children, depending on the efficiency of their dopamine system. Specifically, the more hassles experienced, the less sensitive the parenting in those mothers with the least efficient dopamine system (i.e. levels remain relatively high). These results partly explain why the 'same' environment can affect people differently, in this case with respect to parenting skills.

The reason for the technical detail is because studies need to be replicable and this often means specifying precisely how the study was carried out.

The way serotonin operates is also of interest to genetic researchers in the field of disorganized attachment. Dopamine levels affect heart beat and blood pressure whereas serotonin regulates fear and anxiety; and, as one would predict, they are closely connected. Here's one final example from two of the same authors, this time entitled 'Oxytocin receptor (OXTR) and serotonin transporter (5-HTT) genes associated with observed parenting', published in 2008 in the journal *Social Cognition and Affective Neuroscience*. You might like to have a try at creating a short headline summary.

Box 4.2 'Oxytocin receptor (OXTR) and serotonin transporter (5-HTT) genes associated with observed parenting' – Bakermans-Kranenburg and van IJzendoorn (2008) *Social Cognition and Affective Neuroscience*

Abstract
Both oxytocin and serotonin modulate affiliative responses to partners and offspring. Animal studies suggest a crucial role of oxytocin in mammalian parturition and lactation but also in parenting and social interactions with offspring. The serotonergic system may also be important through its influence on mood and the release of oxytocin. We examined the role of serotonin transporter (5-HTT) and oxytocin receptor (OXTR) genes in explaining differences in sensitive parenting in a community sample of 159 Caucasian, middle-class mothers with their 2-year-old toddlers at risk for externalizing behaviour problems, taking into account maternal educational level, maternal depression and the quality of the marital relationship. Independent genetic effects of 5-HTTLPR SCL6A4 and OXTR rs53576 on observed maternal sensitivity were found. Controlling for differences in maternal education, depression and marital discord, parents with the possibly less efficient variants of the serotonergic (5-HTT ss) and oxytonergic (AA/AG) system genes showed lower levels of sensitive responsiveness to their toddlers. Two-way and three-way interactions

with marital discord or depression were not significant. This first study on the role of both OXTR and 5-HTT genes in human parenting points to molecular genetic differences that may be implicated in the production of oxytocin explaining differences in sensitive parenting.

Here's a short headline summary:

OUR SUMMARY

In a low-risk sample of 159 mothers, those who had less efficient ways of regulating oxytocin, through the production of serotonin, showed less sensitive parenting behaviour. This appeared to be the case irrespective of their levels of education, their levels of depression or the amount of marital disharmony they said they experienced.

Part 2

INTERVENING FACTORS LEADING TO DISORGANIZED ATTACHMENT

Chapter 5

Unresolved Loss and Trauma

Introduction

Most people reading this book will have experienced some sort of loss or trauma. Some may have been involved in a car crash; others may have lost a parent or a partner, even a child (before or after birth); some may have witnessed things that were deeply troubling. This chapter focuses on *unresolved* loss and trauma which is different because, as the first word indicates, it centres upon whether we can now make sense of what happened or, to use the more modern idiom, 'achieve some degree of closure and move on'. Unfortunately, however, the mere passage of time does not always resolve matters. Trauma resolution, without help from a trained counsellor or therapist, depends on four factors: (i) the severity of the event and the circumstances surrounding it, (ii) whether or not a close, intimate person to the survivor was involved in the trauma as a 'persecutor', (iii) the state of the person's circumstances, especially his or her close relationships, both at the time and currently, and (iv) the level of security within the person's attachment history. Moreover, the second two factors act as buffers against the first two: if we have a relatively secure childhood and the 'state' of our current relationships and circumstances feel solid and supportive, then we are likely to survive emotionally almost any loss or trauma.

In 1996 when one of us (Yvonne) was a manager of adult services in a large county council social services department, she was concerned about older people's experience of dying in the department's residential homes. As a result she undertook research which was subsequently published in *Death, Dying and Residential Care* (Y. Shemmings 1996). She was particularly interested in the responses of residential care staff to the seemingly constant exposure to death in the homes due to the residents' age and extreme frailty. During interviews it emerged that some carers seemed to suffer the loss disproportionately. It was noticeable that those with unresolved personal loss seemed to experience the death of residents with what seemed to be rather surprising reactions. When returning to manage children's services, she was able to use this awareness to explore the effects of unresolved loss on parents involved with social care services as well as foster carers and residential workers. Loss in itself does not necessarily affect parenting; rather, it is the sense which is made of the loss that determines whether an appropriate level of resolution is possible. Similarly, unresolved trauma can have lasting effects, and it is the sense children make of what has happened to them which is key to 'processing' and therefore resolving the loss.

Loss, grief and attachment theory

John Bowlby's interest in loss emerged out of his research into separation. From an evolutionary perspective, because infant humans are developmentally immature and highly dependent for so long, insistent protest during the early phases of caregiver absence was a sound strategy to promote survival. Although Bowlby's ideas about loss changed and developed over the course of his career, he continued to view the loss of an attachment figure as a major factor in personality development.

Resolving loss and trauma is connected to the way we handle grief. Bowlby's (1980) primary interest centred upon the suppression of grief, which he saw as inhibiting a natural sequence of painful emotional reactions. Unless allowed to run its full course, grief suppression would lead to psychological and physical ill health (Bowlby 1980). His theoretical position initially produced contradictory empirical findings but, like much research into bereavement – even from an attachment perspective – people's experiences, reactions and displays of grief were treated in an undifferentiated way with regard to attachment organization. This is because, as with the attachment system behaviours of *secure base behaviour, proximity-seeking, safe haven* and *exploration*, 'bereavement' was viewed initially by most researchers as a universal construct. This led to confusing results until Fraley and Shaver (1997) demonstrated how the experience and expression of grief reactions were functions of attachment organization. Thus it can be expected that people will experience and express grief differently, depending on their attachment style and internal working models of relationships.

Critical perspectives on the 'grief discourse'

Wortman and Silver (1989) explicate and define the 'grief discourse' in the following extract from their article:

individuals who encounter a loss are expected to go through a period of intense distress; failure to experience such distress is thought to be indicative of a problem. Moreover, it is assumed that successful adjustment to loss requires that individuals 'work through' or deal with their feelings of grief rather than 'denying' or 'repressing' them. Within a relatively brief period of time, however, people are expected to resolve their loss and recover their earlier level of functioning. (p.349)

They point out that the grief discourse has remained intact, unscathed and free from critical analysis despite, as they then attempt to show, there having been almost no empirical evidence. On the contrary, Wortman and Silver (1989) cite countervailing evidence to buttress these assertions. They point to an unfortunate consequence of this in that professional practice based upon these assumptions defines those who do not react in these ways as 'reacting abnormally and inappropriately' (Wortman and Silver 1989, p.349) and thus people are denied what might be more effective and sensitive forms of support and intervention.

Chris Fraley and Philip Shaver accused these authors of tactically 'distorting' Bowlby's theory 'in an attempt to formulate a position that "competes" with their own' (Fraley and Shaver 1999, p.749) and, 'because they want to criticise what they regard as Bowlby's advocacy of "broken bonds", they uncritically celebrate all continuing bonds'. Fraley and Shaver (1999) take this strident position because they argue that, as Bowlby later changed the third stage from 'detachment' to that of 're-organisation', consequently he 'did not believe that an individual must "detach" from the partner in order to recover from the loss' (p.750).

Resolving the tensions

So does it matter if we 'bottle things up'? In essence Wortman and Silver's critique centres on whether the suppression of intense emotions following loss is necessarily damaging. Bowlby (1980) reasoned that an absence of conscious grief would result in individuals experiencing negative affect but Fraley and Shaver (1999) point to contradictory evidence from Bonanno et al.'s (1995) research in emotionally repressing individuals who, it was claimed, were more likely to have relatively low clinical ratings of grief at 6 months and 14 months after loss. Furthermore, 'in a follow-up at 25 months after loss, they were no more likely than less defensive people to have developed health problems or delayed onset of grief' (Fraley and Shaver 1999, p.745). As already stated, this led Bonanno *et al.* (1995) to conclude that mild or even moderate levels of emotional dissociation or detachment during the bereavement process led more often to subsequent healthier recovery than the more outward expression of grief.

At first sight, these findings are hard to reconcile with Bowlby's contention that the repression of grief would lead to subsequent problems with psychological adjustment. But Bowlby (1980, 1988) always maintained that a true absence of grief would be an appropriate response in people who were relatively emotionally detached from the deceased person. He also recognized that some people who were emotionally close to the deceased person could nevertheless appear to close off affect relatively successfully. But the question remains, 'What is "successful"?' It was precisely in situations when 'grief is the price paid for love'[1] that Bowlby maintained his belief that the repression or suppression of affect would lead later on to emotional turmoil and psychological problems. Thus Bowlby was always more interested in why those who had reason to grieve failed to recognize or express such feelings. Because Bonanno *et al.* (1995) did not select their sample by exploring the level of emotional closeness between the grieving survivor and the deceased person it is difficult to interpret their results when claims are made about whether suppression and denial are 'successful' strategies.

With regard to the sample *as a whole*, it was found that suppression did *not* lead to a substantial increase or decrease in loss-related thoughts and feelings during the early phases of the experiment. But when participants were divided into three attachment groups significant differences were noted, especially during the later stages of the experiment: 'Ambivalent...adults suppressing loss-related thoughts led to an increase (a rebound) in such thoughts in later phases of the experiment.' In contrast, for (avoidant) adults 'suppressing loss-related thoughts led to a decrease in these thoughts and feelings later on' (Fraley and Shaver 1999, p.747). Regarding the avoidant group, these authors also noted that 'it was as if the dismissing defences, once activated, continued to do their work even when it was no longer called for by experimental instructions' (Fraley and Shaver 1999, p.747).

It appears that suppression may help avoidant adults because their defences are 'so well organised that they can shut off feelings in the

---

1   Part of Prime Minister Tony Blair's message to relatives of those killed in the Twin Towers in New York on 11 September 2001.

context of loss. In contrast, suppression appears to be harmful for (ambivalent) adults' (Fraley and Shaver 1999, p.747). Fraley and Shaver (1999) point out that 'Bowlby himself recognised that some exceptionally self-reliant individuals can weather losses without showing much grief and without suffering later breakdowns or episodes of serious depression' (p.754). But, of course, this does not mean that such suppression is not harmful; although it is interesting that Fraley and Shaver (1999) add that 'we agree with Bowlby's critics, however, that he probably overestimated the extent to which suppression of grief is harmful' (p.754). As Fraley and Shaver (1999) conclude, 'there is no one way to experience a loss' (p.755).

What is 'unresolved' loss and trauma?

When a physical injury is sustained, for example a broken leg or fractured skull, it is described as a 'trauma' (to the body). Similarly, an emotional shock, especially one that has a lasting effect, is also described as a 'trauma'. As in the UK, in the United States it is considered that 'childhood trauma including abuse and neglect is probably the single most important public health challenge' (Benamer and White 2008, p.45). Furthermore, 'children can also be traumatised by medical and surgical interventions, and may be victims of accidents and of community violence' (Spinazzola et al. 2005, p.433). However, there is an objective difference in the experience for the child if the trauma is caused by a person who is meant to care, protect and nurture the child.

If loss and trauma are 'resolved', the original memory is eventually integrated within its original context in such a way that makes sense in the present. If the original memory remains disjointed and partitioned from the present, intrusive half-remembered images may return unannounced, often as a result of sights, smells and sounds alongside thoughts and emotions accompanied by physiological responses (Fearon and Mansell 2001). When these different fragments of our memory system remain disconnected, loss and trauma are said to be 'unresolved'. It is what we have called 'repeating what we can't remember', to suggest that we don't control unresolved loss and trauma: it controls us, in the sense that the memories will return, unannounced and usually unwanted. As one might expect, there are some similarities between loss and trauma which aren't resolved and PTSD.

ꓑl losses and traumas are the same. Attachment-related traumas ꓱrent from event-based traumas, such as accidents. Depending ꓱe severity of event-based traumas they are generally thought more ꓱely to be straightforward to resolve, in the sense that they don't leave intrusive memories and flashbacks. People seem to recover *emotionally* from a car crash quicker than if a loved one acts treacherously or deserts him or her for another person.

The Adult Attachment Interview (AAI) reveals at a number of points whether an individual is likely to have unresolved losses. An example is a woman in Eric Hesse and Mary Main's study of frightening behaviour – whose son was coded as 'Disorganized' – who referred to an incident when she was very young. A workman at her house had said teasingly that he would 'marry her when she got older'. She had replied to him, innocently, that 'she couldn't do that, as he'd be dead'. Tragically he died that afternoon. In the Adult Attachment Interview (AAI) she abruptly adopted a little girl's voice and said that she 'had killed him with one sentence'.

When training child protection professionals we sometimes use a picture – the 'Bed Scene' (see Figure 5.1) from the Adult Attachment Projective (AAP; George and West 2001) – to illustrate how the three organized attachment 'styles' emerge when individuals are asked to make up a story about 'what they think might be happening in the picture and what might happen next' (see Shemmings 2004). The seven stimulus pictures contain no information about the internal state of mind or emotions being expressed by the cartoon-type figures in the pictures. The minimalist drawings and the prompts encourage participants to project their own experiences 'onto' the picture. There is no right answer; for example, in the *Bed Scene*, the 'mother' is drawn sitting at the end of the bed at 90 degrees to it, so that she is neither learning forward nor away from the 'child'. Whether the child is experienced as 'whining' and unlikely to receive comfort, or whether he or she is perceived as 'deserving of a cuddle', will depend largely on the attachment biography of the person doing the AAP.

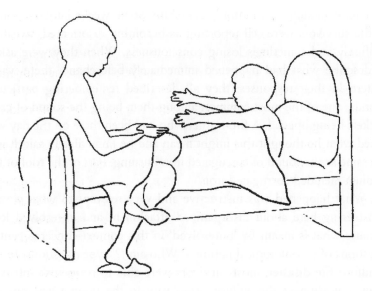

Figure 5.1 The Bed Scene from the Adult Attachment Projective (AAP) (George and West 2001)

On one occasion, one of us (David) noticed a participant becoming quite agitated and anxious while looking at this picture on screen. Others noticed too, so as it was near the coffee break, he suggested they stop. He asked the participant what was wrong. She said in a voice which sounded slightly 'ghostly' and in a strange monotone: 'Why is that lady strangling the child?' She felt 'unpresent', although in the room. David covered up the left side of the picture, so that only the 'child' was visible and asked her what she saw. She replied, startled and still speaking in the 'odd' voice, 'Where did he come from? I haven't seen him until now.' David then covered up the right side of the picture, so that only the 'mother' was shown. She again said, but this time in a less startled way, 'I thought she was strangling the child, didn't I? I don't really know why, now that I can see the full picture.' (She was 'seeing' the woman's knee as a child's neck, as one might in an optical illusion.) Such a response *might* indicate unresolved loss because it included an extreme reaction, with the possibility of a repressed or re-enacted memory along with a strong suggestion of dissociative behaviour.

In the context of attachment theory, the idea of a trauma remaining 'unresolved' doesn't simply mean 'not dealt with', or 'hanging in the air'. *Unresolved* loss and trauma is akin to PTSD. In the UK in the 1980s, for example, a tragic fire killed a large number of spectators in the stand of a football stadium in Bradford, Yorkshire. Some weeks later, a number of the survivors were self-reporting as becoming disoriented, sweating profusely and sometimes losing consciousness. When they were asked to describe what had happened immediately beforehand, there was a pattern in their responses: they all described remembering particular sounds, one of the most common among them being the sound of crisp packets being opened. A fire-fighter who had been there on the day was asked what he thought this might mean and he immediately said it was the same as the sound of corrugated iron burning. Part of the roof of the stadium included corrugated iron.

What happened was instructive and very relevant to what we are considering here about disorganized attachment and unresolved loss, because what is meant by 'unresolved' in this context concerns central questions of an ontological nature – 'Who am I?' type questions. In the Bradford fire disaster, most survivors were able to cope with intrusive sounds as soon as the auditory similarity to the trauma was pointed out to them. But some didn't and they were often those who had been sitting in the *opposite* stand at the time of the tragedy. The significance of this emerged later. Some of these people, it turned out, had felt that they had not 'done enough' to help those who perished in the stand that collapsed. Thus, they not only had the trauma to contend with – which, with help, most recovered from quite quickly when they were encouraged to talk about it to a person who would listen patiently and uncritically – but they also had to battle with the more ontological questions around 'Why did I deserve to survive, and not others?'

From an attachment-perspective, one can hypothesize that these survivors would have come to terms with the *unresolved* part of the trauma or loss in different ways, depending on their early attachment experiences. Securely attached individuals would be able to rationalize that they couldn't have done more or, if they concluded that maybe they *could* have, they would not then punish themselves. They would simply accept that they did not have the courage on the day; but they wouldn't tend to conclude that they were a 'bad' person. Avoidantly attached survivors would try not to think about the experience, but it would periodically 'leak' into their everyday experiences, and especially their close relationships. Ambivalently attached survivors, on the other hand, would seek a lot of reassurance but, like their avoidant cousins, they would not be able to talk about it, only act it out in attention-seeking behaviours.

As one can imagine, because parenting involves giving emotionally to another human being – the more so, the younger the child – it becomes almost impossible for those for whom losses and trauma remain unresolved to turn their attention away from their own confusion and pain. They are constantly grappling with the cold core within them, which tells them too regularly: 'You are worthless; you don't matter to anyone; nobody cares.'

How are unresolved loss and trauma related to disorganized attachment and maltreatment?

A number of factors determine the long-term effects of childhood trauma including: the resilience of the individual; the chronicity and nature of the abuse or neglect; and the relationship between the abused child and his or her abuser. However, it is less likely that abused children will gain the emotional support to help them overcome adversity (Belsky and Fearon 2002; Toth and Cicchetti 1996). Consequently, their experiences are more likely to be left unresolved. It is the ability to 'process' trauma which is at the heart of the future emotional trajectory of the child's development; to be able to process (i.e. 'make sense of') their experience reduces the likelihood of them repeating it when parenting their own children.

Abuse and neglect represent traumas for children, but other behaviours can also be traumatizing for them. When a parent is emotionally unavailable, and rejects his or her child's emotional signals, the child 'learns' to be overly independent and not express his or her emotions. The child of an intrusive and unpredictable mother, on the other hand, will adapt by being clingy and more unpredictable.

Parental sensitivity may also be affected if there is an absence of grief expression. It may lead to difficulties in mental and physical health, which may re-emerge subsequently if losses are experienced or when the task of parenting exposes the parent's vulnerability. During the AAI, it is noticeable that those with anxious attachments show 'marked discrepancies between the quality of childhood experiences they described and their facial expressions, for example, expressions of sadness or anger were noticeable while they were speaking about neutral or positive childhood experiences' (Shaver and Fraley 2008, p.59). It is thought that these discrepancies reflect anxious individuals' confusion and emotional dysregulation when they talk about emotional experiences (Cassidy and Shaver 2008). Such dysregulation manifests itself as confusing communication for an infant if the unresolved loss or trauma in the parent has been triggered by the infant's signals for comfort (Main and Hesse 1992). Soothing is not forthcoming and the parent experiences feelings of either fear or anger (or both) which are always frightening to an infant.

A child's attachment signals may not be read accurately by the unresolved parent, and he or she is likely to be distressed or frightened in these caregiving attachment interactions. As a response to this trigger, parents can 'display care-giving that is incomprehensible and frightening to the child, or communicate to the child that he or she is a source of alarm, perhaps because they confuse the child with their attachment figures. They may avoid the child when attachment needs are heightened' (Oppenheim and Goldsmith 2007, p.112). As a result, children seem to work out that their own attachment behaviour and needs are actually the cause of their parents' fear, in turn leading to their parents' frightening behaviour and increasing the chances that a disorganized attachment between carer and child develops (van IJzendoorn et al. 1999).

It was probably Freud who first identified the pernicious nature of the effects of trauma on parenting and on children. Referring to his work, Busch and Lieberman (2007) remind us that he wrote that 'traumatic experiences shatter the "protective field" that parents provide for their children, threatening the core of the attachment relationship' (p.139), because frightening events can 'dysregulate the parent–child relationship by triggering posttraumatic stress reaction in both the child and the adult, hindering the child's ability to seek comfort from the parent and the parent's reciprocal ability to provide reassurance' (Busch and Lieberman 2007, p.139).

A particularly difficult form of maltreatment often associated with unresolved trauma and loss is 'abnormal illness behaviour by proxy' or 'factitious or induced illness by proxy'. It is notoriously difficult to expose and assess but both loss and traumatic experiences were found to be common among mothers with abnormal illness behaviour by proxy (see Adshead and Bluglass 2005), mirroring findings from a study undertaken at Great Ormond Street Hospital which found an association with sudden, unexpected or violent bereavement with this form of abuse (Gray and Bentovim 1996).

But how does unresolved loss and trauma disrupt parenting and become associated with disorganized attachment? Referring to his study of parents who received a diagnosis of cerebral palsy or epilepsy for a child, Robert Marvin defines resolution as 'the integration of the experience of the diagnosis into the parent's representations which allows for a re-orientation and refocus of attention and problem solving on present reality' (quoted in Oppenheim and Goldsmith 2007, pp.112–113). In the AAI, some parents were reclassified as 'unresolved-depressed' with others classified as 'disorganized-confused'. Connections were also found between an acceptance of the diagnosis with the mother's sensitive caregiving behaviour. In other words, it is the extent to which the parent could accept the diagnosis, adjust to the new circumstances and 'see the uniqueness of the child beyond the diagnosis' (pp.112–113) that determined his or her ability to be sensitively attuned to the specific needs of the child (Marvin and Pianta 1996).

Parents' own attachment style is likely to determine how the diagnosis is received and, as a consequence, how the child is perceived (as well as their reactions to the person giving the news of the diagnosis). If a lack of 'realignment' becomes a barrier for sensitive caregiving by, say, denying the child's difficulties, or interacting with the child as if he or she were the 'wished for, typically developing child', it seems possible that parents may not respond to the child's attachment needs with sensitive attunement (quoted in Oppenheim and Goldsmith 2007, pp.112–113). The lack of resolution is demonstrated in different ways; some are overwhelmed with grief, while others focus on the professionals' failures. Consequently, parents' experiences of unresolved trauma or loss, combined with certain types of disability, can create additional risks for maltreatment. Children with congenitally based disabilities and high levels of dependence along with communication difficulties often display complex attachment signals. If their parent also has unresolved states of mind, they may be at heightened risk of maltreatment (Howe 2006).

The effects of relationally based trauma on the development of children is also well documented (Koenen *et al.* 2003). If, for example, during episodes of domestic violence parental behaviours represent traumatizing events for children, this can lead to disorganized behaviour. This is compounded if the adults believe that the child is too young to have noticed or to understand what was happening and thus do not respond sensitively to the child's emotional experience of the event.

Maltreatment resulting from 'childhood physical and sexual abuse in attachment relationships induces a cascade of physiological effects, including changes in hormones and neurotransmitters that mediate development in vulnerable brain regions' (Diamond and Marrone 2003, p.79). Patricia Crittenden powerfully describes the unresolved and traumatic experience for the abused child: 'the wrenching intestinal cramps of the distressed child waking up every day…the sickening taste, foul smell, that no-one else can perceive but which goes everywhere with the child' (Crittenden 2008, p.99). This produces at times a 'fear of breakdown', of disintegration; but Donald Winnicott was perceptive when he remarked that the fear of breakdown 'is the fear of a breakdown that has already been experienced' (Hesse and Main 2000, p.1119, referring to Winnicott 1974).

Trauma and loss also over-sensitize individuals to stress, leaving them more vulnerable in situations that remind them consciously or unconsciously of the trigger events. These effects can appear early. In a study by Nancy Kaplan and Mary Main (1986) they found that disorganized six-year-olds 'were likely to include bizarre or frightening elements in their family drawings – for example, whole figures might be scratched out, body parts might float freely in the air, or dark clouds might descend towards the family (Hesse and Main 2000, p.1109).

What is dissociation?

As the polar opposite of 'association', *dissociation* occurs when individuals unintentionally find themselves shutting down and disconnecting from experiences and the world *against their will*. This is not the same as daydreaming, which is usually voluntary and often pleasant. Individuals who dissociate may find themselves blanking out, clamming up or having terrifying nightmares, the world of dreams being the only place they (involuntarily) re-experience earlier trauma. It is adaptive because, in its absence, the result would be a complete breakdown. For a child, there is the additional cost of acquiring a 'sensitized and compromised neurobiology… Thus a child who repeatedly enters dissociative states will more readily enter such states under conditions of mild stress' (Dozier *et al.* 2008, p.728).

Mary Dozier goes on to offer the following theoretical explanation of what happens when a child begins to dissociate (which is similar to dissociative states in adults):

Early experiences with a frightened or frightening caregiver cause a child to develop multiple, incompatible models of the self and the other. In interactions with the caregiver, the child experiences rapid shifts in which the caregiver is at first frightened, then no longer frightened, then caring for the child. With each shift, a different model of self (perpetrator of fright, rescuer, loved child) and of the caregiver (victim, rescued victim, competent caregiver) is operative. (Dozier *et al.* 2008, p.728)

'Unresolved' parents have been found to have high ratings for day-dreaming and self-hypnotic states of consciousness. This dissociated behaviour in itself may lead to fear in the child (Hesse and van IJzendoorn 1998; Liotti 2004). The timing of the traumatic event or loss is also significant in the transmission of dissociative behaviour. It has been found that, if the event occurs within two years before or after a birth, it is less likely that it will have been resolved during this time, and this presents an increased risk for the development of dissociative disorders (Pasquini *et al.* 2002).

What has also been found is that the loss of a loved one, especially a child or baby during pregnancy, is linked with dissociation. For example, research by Giovanni Liotti found that 62 per cent of adults diagnosed with dissociative disorders had mothers who had lost a close relative within two years of their children's birth (Liotti 2004).

How can we tell if someone experiences unresolved loss and trauma?

As we have seen from the AAI, a parent's mental states are associated with unresolved trauma and loss. Furthermore, a meta-analysis by Mary Main and colleagues found a significant association with unresolved loss or trauma and infant disorganization (Main *et al.* 1985). Whilst organized ambivalent and avoidant insecure attachments affect maternal affective attunement and mentalization, it is the disorganized classification which is far more strongly associated with unresolved loss and trauma.

Main and Hesse (1992) found that, during the AAI, interviewees experienced lapses in monitoring of speech or in thinking. In other words, when talking about the loss or trauma, individual's emotions were so 'on top' that they talked about it as though it was happening in the present, and the way they spoke in the AAI showed clearly that they were still affected by it (which they often deny or make light of). When parenting, if the unresolved loss relates to a bereavement, a caregiver may become 'bombarded with intrusive images, thoughts, feelings and memories about the deceased and this, in turn, makes them likely candidates for complicated or prolonged grief' (Shaver and Fraley 2008, p.59). Importantly, the self-esteem of those saddled with unresolved grief can reduce significantly their capacity to be mind-minded and sensitively attuned to their infant.

In the AAI, individuals are asked if they recall any traumatic events from their earliest memories and they are then invited to reflect upon them. People who have unresolved memories tend to betray momentary mistakes in the monitoring of reasoning (sometimes referred to as 'metacognitive monitoring') and/or slips in the monitoring of discourse. The latter refers specifically to what Karlen Lyons-Ruth and Deborah Jacobvitz (2008) call a 'lost awareness of the discourse content'. Examples include 'falling silent in mid-sentence but then completing the sentence 20 seconds or more later as if no time had passed, or failing to finish the sentence entirely' (p.672).

'Lapses in the monitoring of reasoning' is not the same as illogical or foolish thinking (which we all exhibit from time to time!). It is indicated by errors in logic which are not then corrected or commented upon (as in 'What did I just say?' or 'I don't think what I just said makes sense. Let me explain'). Main, Goldwyn and Hesse (2003) give the following short extract as an example: 'It's probably better that he's dead, because he can get on with being dead and I can get on with raising a family.' Here are two longer examples taken from the transcripts in the study one of us (David) undertook some years ago (see Shemmings 2004):

Example 1

(Remembering her father) Yes, when he is stomping, I call it 'thumping', the big steps, I call it the 'heavy steps'. I can actually, memories, you know, I can actually feel almost physically sick. It upsets me to that degree. This authoritarian... This thumping and bumping... And when he's coming in, I think 'Oh, gosh, we have all got to be tidy, we have all got to get sorted'.

(Taken from David's transcripts)

Example 2 *[we return to this extract again in the next chapter]*

Erm, I am saying 'scared' but, I know that, you know, I was *scared* of her, but I wasn't *afraid* of her...I was very sensitive to her moods. If she was in a good mood, I would be the happiest girl there ever was...

In what way have you changed?

Erm, God how long have you got?! In what way have I changed? From what to what? Erm, I think I was, what's the word?...*(long pause)...* How have I changed? I very much, I am me, I think, it was very difficult when I was a teenager to...*(long pause and then changes subject).*

(Taken from David's transcripts)

It goes without saying one can never code an individual's attachment organization from such a short excerpt; we are just using the extracts to provide illustrations of disorganized discourse. In Example 1, one is almost drawn back with the speaker into the terrifying world in which she lived at times with her father. The use of reported speech, but where she speaks for herself in his presence, is also suggestive of intrusive memories which remain resolved. The fact that she says 'And when he's coming in' rather than 'And when he came in' suggests that the memories are still very alive for her. As we said earlier, with some exceptions, perhaps of a particularly terrifying nature – such as seeing close relatives being tortured, or oneself being kidnapped – it isn't events themselves that cause problems later...it is the sense we make of them. Consider this example:

Do you remember any incidents of violence as a child?

Yes once, when we went out as a family in the car for a trip, I ended up getting lost. We got out of the car and my dad was left to park the car and I must have become separated from my mum – no doubt I was interested in something else (I was only about 7 or 8). I think I was lost for about 20 minutes and a lady made me stand with her by our car. My dad came back and he really shouted at me and then he smacked my legs really hard and made them sore. I'd never seen this side to him. Then he and mum hugged me and cried. He was really sorry and said so a lot on the way back. I can see why he reacted like this: they must have been beside themselves with worry – and now *I've* got my own children, I can appreciate how frightened they were, what with all those horror stories in the papers. But he shouldn't have lost his temper like that and it took me a while to learn to trust him again, as he'd always been such a 'gentle' man.

(Taken from David's transcripts)

The narrative and discourse in this extract is of a different nature to the previous two examples. Here the speaker has experienced something unpleasant, but she can 'make sense' of it. She describes temporally what took place but with no lapses in narrative and no 'lost' tenses. The key to knowing that she has 'resolved' what happened is contained in the phrase 'they must have been beside themselves with worry'. This is also strong evidence of reflective function (RF), the significance of which is that it 'protects' individuals from assuming that, as young children, bad things happened to them as a result of *their* failings. In the above example, the individual remembers being hit by her father, and she clearly didn't like it – especially because she saw a dark, frightening side to her 'gentle' father – but she understands why it happened and she doesn't assume, unlike the girl whose arm was broken by her father (see pp.35–36), that it was as a result of *her* being unlovable. The speaker knows she did something wrong (or at least that her father thought it was wrong, but she could see why her parents would be worried); in the 'broken arm' example, the girl believes – indeed, 'knows' – that there is something wrong with *her*. She is highly likely to take this belief into all her subsequent relationships, behaving in ways that lasso others into seeing her as unlovable in order to maintain the integrity of her 'internal working model' of how she thinks other people must inevitably see her.

In Example 2 above the speaker doesn't see any need to explain or correct the contradictory statement 'I was *scared* of her, but I wasn't *afraid* of her'. Notice too how, in the final paragraph, the speaker doesn't finish any of her ideas, and sees nothing amiss by not doing so (as indicated by her *not* saying something like 'Forgive me, I can't seem to explain this' or 'I'm not being very clear here, am I? Can I come back to this later perhaps to give me a chance to work this out a bit more?').

We stress again that 'unresolved loss' is not the same as memories that are conflicted or painful, and 'on top' for much of the time. To illustrate this crucial difference we focus on two longer examples which point more to a preoccupied but organized attachment style. The reason they are not indicative of unresolved loss is that they don't contain protracted or recurring examples of lapses in the monitoring of reasoning or discourse. The first excerpt demonstrates many of the speaker's unfathomable and lingering feelings but it does not necessarily include unresolved loss. She is clearly engrossed and preoccupied, but nowhere in the complete narrative was there any strong evidence of unresolved loss. During the extract she is recalling, as an adult, a row with her mother:

> I think it was in my early thirties, something like that, and I thought, erm, I went round there one day and I said, erm – Oh, she wanted me to go to a party, she always had to have her own way – so she wanted me to go to a party and I said 'Sorry mum', I said, 'but I can't…' I said 'Mum, I can't do that', I said, 'because I've got, I've got to go somewhere else on that day' and she went into one, she went into a sulk, you got the 'silent' treatment, we had this all through when I was young: you get the 'silent' treatment. And…er…she started the silent treatment and I was sitting there and I was getting angry and I'm thinking, 'This is not acceptable, I can't have this'. Erm, so something in me, I said, I said to her, 'Why are you being like that, why are you being silent now, why are you doing that to me?' You know, 'Why can't you accept what I'm saying?' You know, I challenged her on it. It's the first time in my life I challenged her. Well she went into one, she went into such a rage – not physical rage but the verbal abuse that come out…she called me all the names you can imagine. So I said 'Do you realise', I said, 'Do you realise you have never once said you're sorry in all your life, not once. You must have been wrong once, it's always me saying I'm sorry to you', I said, 'but you never say you're sorry to me – or to anyone for that matter – you're never wrong'.
>
> *(Taken from David's transcripts)*

She had earlier recalled an incident as a child when prompted by the 'five adjectives' question:

> I asked for her help with something, I didn't expect her to react in the way that she did but I should have seen the signs, 'cos she started lighting up a cigarette and that's a sign that, you know, she's, she's struggling to cope with something there. I was just asking for her help in something I was doing and, erm, she was, erm, very short with me and I said, 'Well, I'm only asking you for help with this', and then she said, erm – I don't want to bore you with it, but she just started snapping at me – and I…and then she said, 'Well go on then, tell me what it's about', you know, and she's…but it was the way she said it, and with this smoking, and she's, 'Well go on then, what's it all about, I'm listening, I'm listening, go on, GO ON'.

Did you then tell her?

Well, I got frightened actually, I felt quite frightened of her at that point, I don't know why this is…I felt like that child again and I said, erm, 'Well actually I don't need your help really', I said 'Forget it'. 'No, no, no', she said, 'You tell me, you TELL me'. I said, 'No, I don't need you to, I'd rather not'. I said, 'Let's leave it, shall we?' You know, I said, erm, 'I don't need your help, so let's leave it at that'.

(Taken from David's transcripts)

Again we see evidence of preoccupation but not unresolved loss. As we have stated, disorganization doesn't mean 'all over the place': it refers to a specific set of behaviours which occur (or not) when a person's attachment system is activated. In the AAI this happens when the unconscious is surprised by, seemingly, innocuous questions about the past. The next speaker is recounting an incident when she was aged 'five or six':

I wanted a bathing suit and I think me and my mother were standing outside…I can't believe I can remember these things! *(She is very surprised by this 'awakening', slightly perplexed but also interested in 'telling her story'.)* I was standing outside and we were, I don't know what we did, I think we hung washing on the washing line and I think, as a little girl, I would normally have said 'Mother, I think I need a new bathing suit', and stuff like that, but I must have said it in a different way. I said to her 'I want a new bathing suit, I want it now and I want it to be, you know, "green", for example…' I don't know why I said it because – you know how the brains of little girls are when they want something – and at that moment I know my mother got so upset by the way I talked to her and she…I think she was so upset that I could be so rude to her. It seems like at that moment she was heartbroken but I can just remember that my mother went into the house and I went afterwards and I said 'I am sorry, I am sorry, I wouldn't say that again, I am sorry. I wouldn't…' you know, 'I am sorry that I spoke to you that way'.

(Taken from David's transcripts)

She had earlier recalled the following childhood memory, which also indicates the extent of her (and her father's) genuine fear of her mother's reaction and the degree to which she wanted to please (or is it 'appease'?):

I was wearing a hat to church and I was wearing this particular hat and this hat was my church hat so it was a very important hat. I couldn't wear it...you know, I wouldn't wear it in other places...and one Sunday I went with my father and I came out of church and I left my hat on the seat in front and we went to have...we went to the pool, we had a swim. I came back and I stepped into the corner and I sat on my hat and my hat went flat...and me and my father...I can recall my father was just as worried that my mother is going to smack, is going to be very, very angry. So we make a plan. We came back home and I hide my hat, I put my hat underneath my clothes and I think...in that whole week, the horror I lived through, knowing that Sunday is coming, and I have to wear my hat and I haven't told my mother, and on Sunday I did get a hiding, because I didn't tell her about my hat, and she found out...*that* is the scary feeling: when I couldn't tell my mother, because I knew that she would be so angry about this hat.

(Taken from David's transcripts)

Again, the reason for including these examples is that they do not indicate 'unresolved loss', in the precise sense in which it is used in connection with disorganized attachment. The speakers are, nevertheless, still very preoccupied by this incident (and possibly other incidents). Consider, for example, her use of tenses in the extract '...that my mother is going to smack, is going to be very, very angry'. Interestingly, she never revealed what her mother actually *did*. So she is preoccupied, but there were no unequivocal indications in the transcript that she displayed 'lapses of monitoring' or other indicators of *unresolved* loss or trauma.

Remember that this happened years ago. But she is not simply recalling it using the present tense; she re-tells the story in the future tense, from a temporal position just *prior* to her mother finding out about the hat. This indicates that the speaker is not only reliving the experience, she is reliving that part of it connected with her dread and fear of what her mother was likely to do. But her recollections are more a 're-experiencing' of the memory rather than the 're-enactment' of it. It is clearly painful, but she can both talk about and reflect upon it. These are important differences and we return to this distinction in the next chapter.

As we have seen, even some appallingly brutal parenting (e.g. the girl with the broken arm) or much more subtle, nuanced and perniciously adverse parenting does not necessarily lead to DA. The same is true of actual losses. It is not the *severity* of the actual loss itself but the *meaning behind it* that matters. So, for example, in a study by Ainsworth and Eichberg (1991), *unresolved* loss was a more powerful predictor of infant

DA than was the loss itself. This single result was confirmed by another meta-analysis by van IJzendoorn, Juffer and Duyvesteyn in 1995. They found a high effect size (d = 0.65) across nine studies (N = 548; van IJzendoorn *et al.* 1995). As Karlen Lyons-Ruth and Deborah Jacobvitz (2008) add, the same findings appear to hold true over time and across cultures – they cite studies in North America, Western Europe, the Middle East, Africa and Mexico – and 'this association occurs even when an adult's attachment status is assessed prior to the child's birth' (p.673). Even, it appears, the most dreadful and catastrophic events do not always lead to *unresolved* loss nor, as a consequence, to disorganized attachment in infants. Referring to the same study again, Erik Hesse and Mary Main comment that, 'intriguingly, about equal percentages of marked losses in the monitoring of reasoning or discourse during the discussion of loss or abuse within the AAI have also been reported in low-risk populations' (Hesse and Main 2000, p.1102).

One of the limitations of research looking at unresolved loss using the AAI is that codings can only be made when there has actually *been* a recalled loss or abusive experience. If the respondent cannot bring one to mind – either because nothing happened or its absence in the interview is the result of suppression/repression – then little or nothing can be classified from the transcript. Eric Hesse proposed a way to overcome this psychometric challenge by developing criteria to code an AAI excerpt as 'Cannot Classify' (or CC). From the perspective of attachment theory, individuals who do not (or cannot) recall specific loss or traumatic events tend to show significant signs of mixed attachment organization at other points in the transcript, in particular evidence of both preoccupied *and* dismissing strategies.

An alternative method of overcoming the problem has also been proposed by Karlen Lyons-Ruth and her colleagues (Lyons-Ruth *et al.* 2005). They argue for the transcripts to be coded from the point of view of 'Hostile-Helpless' (HH) states of mind, the key feature of which 'is the extent to which an individual has positively identified with the psychological stance of the infant caregiver whom he or she globally devalues elsewhere in the interview'. An example they give is 'We were friends…we were enemies. We're just alike, but we fought all the time' (Lyons-Ruth and Jacobvitz 2008, p.674). It is, of course, perfectly possible to hold such contradictory views, but they would need to be explained and commented upon (i.e. 'metacognitively monitored'). If they are, such a transcript might well be coded as 'Autonomous' (i.e. secure).

In the 'helpless' version of the HH classification individuals suppress or repress their anger and instead 'take the side' of an abusing or neglectful carer, often by recalling instances when, as the child, they 'take care' of their parent. Lyons-Ruth and Jacobvitz (2008) refer to three studies in high-risk samples which have looked at associations between adults classified as HH in the AAI and the subsequent effect on DA in their child/ren, which all revealed significant associations. The first focused on 45 mothers with high levels of childhood trauma (Lyons-Ruth *et al.* 2005), the second involved 62 mothers taking part in a methadone-dependence programme (Melnick *et al.* 2008), while the third studied a smaller number of patients diagnosed with borderline personality disorder (Lyons-Ruth and Jacobvitz 2008).

What can be done about it?

The problem is that individuals 'with a history of attachment trauma are liable to have profound difficulty developing and making use of what they most need to heal: secure attachments' (Allen, Fonagy and Bateman 2008, p.212). Not only that, they are more likely to be drawn to people who remind them of the initial trauma – so-called 'traumatic bonding' – or, indeed, who are still *part* of the trauma, in situations such as domestic violence, where a woman may stay with a violent partner when, financially, she doesn't 'need to'. Peter Fonagy offers the following explanation, based upon attachment theory:

> threatening behaviour heightens fear, and fear heightens attachment needs... Isolation from other sources of support cements the tie to the abuser – in Walker's (1979) words, as if by 'miracle glue' – and the bond is solidified further by the periods of loving respite that typically follow the battering episode. (Allen *et al.* 2008, p.212)

Exploring trauma treatments is beyond the scope of this book but we outline some general principles underpinning such approaches. First, children will rarely *talk* about their fears and trauma spontaneously; they are also unlikely to be able themselves to make connections in their own minds between what has happened to them and what they do or feel. Instead, children tend to communicate traumatic experiences by repeating them through play and in their interactions with others. They often appear inflexible and resist new experiences, 'preferring' to seek out the familiar and predictable which, perversely, is sometimes experienced as safer, even if it is a source of fear or abuse (Streeck-Fischer and van der Kolk 2000).

Second, when children are placed in foster care, for example, their complex behaviour will often puzzle new carers who will usually struggle to understand how best to respond. One foster carer with whom we worked was at a loss to understand why her five-year-old foster child of a few months always disrupted shopping trips when she went to buy her new clothes. The child would arrive at the shop and run around wildly, pulling at the clothes on the rails, refusing to try on dresses. Finally she had to be taken home after embarrassing tantrums made it impossible to continue. The effects of the trauma, caused by the abuse she had experienced before she was placed with the carer, were such that the child did not feel worthy of the time and effort involved, and could not cope with the idea that the carer could possibly care enough about her to make the effort. Such behaviour needs to be understood as symptomatic of previous disorganization, experienced in the context of earlier caregiving environments where the child could not seek comfort. Similarly, a residential worker with whom we spoke had planned a trip to the countryside to go trekking with an, initially, enthusiastic teenager. After weeks of planning, when the day arrived it proved impossible to persuade him to get out of bed. He said he preferred to stay at the home to watch the television. The trip may have represented to him an opportunity for him to 'fail', and for the day to 'implode', as he said from his experience that 'everything he touched fell apart'. He 'preferred' the safety of the familiar, and it confirmed his internal working model of being the 'bad' child.

Third, if parents or teachers become concerned about a child's excessive oppositional or controlling behaviour, it is important that it is considered as a possible symptom of something he or she finds impossible to express in other ways. Such children may be more susceptible to later dissociative disorders or to PTSD. Conversely, it is questionable whether the recent trend in medicating children to prevent these disruptive behaviours is the answer (Streeck-Fischer and van der Kolk 2000). Social workers, foster carers and other professionals are ideal people to help children talk about traumatic experiences. There is potential to use more direct work with children through their relationship with them, using play techniques to help them explore their trauma and experiences of loss. The power of play in understanding the internal worlds of children is fascinating and rewarding; using techniques such as Story Stem Completion opens up opportunities to help children.

Fourth, according to Nicola Diamond and Mario Marrone (2003, p.39), adverse events can be rated low, moderate, severe or catastrophic based on the following factors: the age of the child; the quality of support within and outside the family; and the intensity, repetitiveness, amplitude and combination of stressors. Furthermore, 'dysfunctional reactions to a child's trauma can be: dismissive, accusatory, over-reactive or incoherent' (Diamond and Marrone 2003, p.39). These factors need to be taken into account when planning how to help children and adults.

Fifth, from an attachment perspective, the key to helping a child (or an adult) be able to resolve loss and trauma is to move towards a gradual 're-*experiencing*' of it, rather than a 're-enactment' of it; indeed, 'recovering memories of past trauma will be futile if the patient is embroiled in ongoing re-enactments' (Allen *et al.* 2008, p.229), although 'mentalising emotions entails thinking about feelings *while remaining in the emotional state*' (p.232). The clear implication is that an excess of emotionality as part of the helping and healing process is likely to make matters worse. What is required is a supportive approach offering the individual a highly containing and boundaried experience. Trauma survivors cannot think about their experience because, for them, this means reliving it, which automatically leads an inability to mentalize the experience.

Lastly, there is evidence of an interesting rapprochement between some proponents of cognitive-behavioural therapy (CBT) and promoters of attachment-based trauma intervention. At a recent conference at the Anna Freud Centre in London in November 2009 David Trickey, a clinical psychologist specializing in CBT-based approaches to trauma, spoke and drew upon the metaphor of unresolved memories acting like a 'live wire in the body' which needs to be 'insulated' to reduce the shock of the trauma when touched. The insulation process progressively takes the form of words to reduce the recurrence of re-enactments in the form of nightmares and flashbacks. Intervention aims to increase the experience for the child (or adult) of *normal autobiographical memories* rather than *traumatic memories*. Progressively coherent and organized stories gradually replace vivid sensory information; trauma 'insulation' aims to replace 'static and frozen images' with 'fluid and updatable' ones. Continuing with the electricity metaphor, we would add that, when the live wire has been insulated, it also needs to be 'earthed' through a caring, supportive, mentalizing adult: the approach cannot be applied by reading a manual.

Chapter 6

Mentalization and Reflective Function

Introduction

A mother is pushing her toddler in a buggy. It is a very cold day and the child's shoe and sock have come off. The mother laid them on the top of the buggy and continued pushing. She was accompanied by a friend, who said 'Shall we stop and put his sock on – his little foot must be getting really cold?' The mother replied 'No...no...he's fine; my feet are like toast'. This was a mild example of a parent not appreciating the difference between her experience and that of her son. But a far more serious and pronounced example of such misattribution can be seen in the following example by Arietta Slade (2008):

> There's something rather inhuman about him – there's an absence of warmth, human feeling. He has deformed the family life and marriage. On a bad day, he's violent, ungovernable, and underemployed... He is always without that current that passes between parents and children... Never a moment where there's a bond...he's attached in a way that doesn't strike us as normal... He's an animal, a psychopath. (p.216)

Even more chilling than the content is the fact that the child referred to by his parent here is only five years old. Whilst children can, at times, be extremely demanding, how does a parent end up thinking such things about one of his or her offspring?

In this chapter we explore in more detail two interrelated components in the Pathway Model: *mentalization* and *reflective function* (RF). We have seen that this component may constitute something of a missing jigsaw piece in our appreciation of how evidence-informed moderator and mediator variables help link more global risk factors, such as parental mental ill-health, substance abuse, having been abused as a child, etc., to disorganized attachment when there is accompanying child maltreatment.

The concept of mentalization has its root in philosophy, specifically Daniel Dennett's notion of the 'intentional mind' (1989) along with writings on intersubjectivity by phenomenologists such as Maurice Merleau-Ponty and Edmund Husserl. But it is Peter Fonagy at University College London and the Anna Freud Centre who has been the inspiration behind its psychosocial application.

The skill of RF depends upon the adult taking what is known as the 'intentional stance' (Dennett 1989). In this context, taking the intentional stance means that the adult assumes the child has intentional states of mind (he or she *intends* things) or, in other words, the adult is conscious of the representational level that is underlying the child's behaviour. This is more complicated than it first appears and, in Dennett's own words, here is how it works:

> first you decide to treat the object whose behaviour is to be predicted as a rational agent; then you figure out what beliefs that agent ought to have, given its place in the world and its purpose. Then you figure out what desires it ought to have, on the same considerations, and finally you predict that this rational agent will act to further its goals in the light of its beliefs. A little practical reasoning from the chosen set of beliefs and desires will in most instances yield a decision about what the agent ought to do; that is what you predict the agent will do. (Dennett 1989, p.17)

Needless to say, much of this process usually operates in the non-conscious part of the mind with only occasional forays into the conscious realm. In essence, mentalization means recognizing – and remaining curious – that what others may think and feel is likely to be different from what one thinks and feels oneself; that other people's experience is likely be different from one's own. One of us (David) invites new social work students when they attend their first full lecture as a group every October to consider that probably everyone in the room is experiencing the session, the lecturer, the university campus, etc., in different ways: some will be excited, some nervous and apprehensive; for some, the lecturer will remind them of a teacher, which for some will be positive (but, for others, not so good). And so on.

Two colleagues of Peter Fonagy – Howard Steele and Miriam Steele – developed these ideas further, adding the concept of RF, which means mentalization in the context of *attachment relationships*. Low RF is what the mother showed in the example above of the 'toddler in the buggy with the cold foot': because *her* feet are warm she assumes her son's experience is the same. This inability to shift positions has little to do with intelligence; but it does have a lot to do with particular areas of the brain not having developed sufficiently during early childhood. The good news is that, if another human being can offer regular mentalizing experiences with the mother, previous unconnected pathways in those areas will (re)connect. She will then be able to recognize that she needs to read her son's experience as different from hers. And then put his shoe and sock on. We offer a glimpse in Chapter 8 of how these ideas are being translated into very promising interventions with caregivers, pioneered by Marinus van IJzendoorn, Marian Bakermans-Kranenburg and Femmie Juffer at Leiden University in the Netherlands.

Simon Baron-Cohen's work on autism at Cambridge University has added considerably to our understanding of mentalization. He has used 'false belief tasks' with people on the autistic spectrum to explore the difficulties they have appreciating the perspective of others. (An excellent novel devoted to the problems experienced by someone with Asperger's Syndrome relating to others is Mark Haddon's *The Curious Incident of the Dog in the Night-time*, 2003.)

A classic false belief task is Wimmer and Perner's (1983) *Maxi and the Chocolate*. To illustrate this we draw upon the gist of how one of us (Yvonne) introduces it to groups of multi-agency child welfare practitioners when working on skill and knowledge development. She first seeks a volunteer who likes chocolate (usually a number of hands are raised at this point!). She finds a volunteer (let's call her Ola) and Yvonne then says:

> So Ola likes chocolate and I am going to put her favourite bar into the right pocket of my jacket for her to have after lunch [Yvonne then places it there]. During lunch Ola takes a walk around the grounds. I absentmindedly move the chocolate bar to my left pocket and then drape the jacket round the back of the chair. When Ola returns I tell her to help herself to the chocolate I promised her. Which pocket will she look in – the right one or the left one?

Most people state that she will look in the right pocket, because that's where it was when she left; although on one occasion there was a person with autism on the course who was visibly perplexed. After a few minutes of painful deliberation he eventually said 'I can't work this out; I think she would look in both pockets', but he carried on puzzling and was unable to come to a firm conclusion. (As we saw in Chapter 2, there is no direct connection between autism, disorganized attachment and maltreatment: autistic children will only tend to show DA behaviour under the same circumstances as non-autistic children.)

A development of the Maxi story is *Ellie the Elephant* which begins 'Ellie the Elephant only drinks coke. Mickey the Monkey is a bit naughty and, when Ellie's not looking, he empties her can and fills it with milk (which Ellie really hates). How will Ellie feel when she goes to pick up her drink?' This false belief task includes the additional dimension of feelings. Six-year-olds correctly say 'happy', but at four years they will most likely say 'disappointed (or sad)'. Children, and many adults, on the autistic spectrum are very likely to say 'disappointed (or sad)'.

The relevance of mentalization and RF to disorganized attachment is that maltreated children over four years old can also find difficulty when feelings, or more complexity, is introduced into the scenarios. We outline the reasons for this later in this chapter but first we need to be more precise about what we mean by 'mentalization' and 'reflective function'. Here is an excellent attempt at a straightforward explanation, written by a patient taking part in a mentalization-based treatment programme. He is speaking about mothers (but it could be caregivers of infants generally) who have trouble connecting well with their babies:

> One thing that the research shows is that when…babies are really upset, these mothers don't calm the babies in a way that helps the babies to understand or learn what's their own distress and what's the mother's. It's a bit like the baby's distress is magnified and bounded back at the little thing rather than being soothed and dissolved by the mother… These things lead to many of us being unable to soothe ourselves in ways that are conventional, or not destructive, again reinforcing our tendencies to self-harm. (Allen *et al.* 2008, p.206)

From an evolutionary perspective there would have been considerable advantages to working out the intentions of other humans because this facility – which, as far as we know, is not shared with any other species – permitted us to accomplish two things; they are both somewhat manipulative, but each conferred on humans certain competitive advantages. First, the ability to mentalize enabled us to *portray* ourselves in a particular light in order to deceive others about our intentions: we could *pretend* to be happy, sad, etc., even though we were not. Second, we learned to detect when others were trying to deceive *us*. In short, the ability to mentalize enabled us to outsmart other people; but it simultaneously left us vulnerable to being outsmarted by them.

Why did humans develop the facility to mentalize? We need to turn briefly to the disciplines of palaeoanthropology and evolutionary anthropology to find an answer, where we quickly learn that it appears to be as a direct consequence of our bipedalism (Bramble and Lieberman 2004). Walking on two legs instead of four required a major redesign of our bone structure and led to at least three seismic and revolutionary developmental consequences.

First, species that use four legs have to inflate their lungs when moving, otherwise the chest cavity would collapse under the strain as, on four legs, the thorax cannot absorb high impacts when the body is travelling. Moving on two legs meant our lungs could be left deflated, which enabled us to make sounds other than grunts and cries, etc. Eventually we learned to speak, which we could never have achieved had we stayed on all fours.

Second, walking on two legs also led to a major redesign of the human hand and fingers – eventually giving us opposable thumbs – but the upshot left the infant unable to cling to the mother (unlike a chimpanzee, for example). Human mothers now had to hold their babies, for considerable amounts of time. Consequently, we evolved into a species with the most dependent offspring, and for a considerable length of time: around a year, when the developing infant can only just get around and begin to develop some independence. Because human mothers had to devote so much time, energy and resources to nurturing their offspring physically this necessitated a change in the behaviour of human males, who began to spend some time caring for the mother (otherwise his – and her – genes would not have survived). Sarah Hrdy's pioneering work also shows us that other women – 'allo-parents', such as grandmothers, sisters, female cousins, etc. – also provided much needed support to a new mother. Indeed the need for older women to take part in the care of younger mothers is thought to be the main reason for the menopause: to free older women from childbearing so that they were available to provide support to their daughters as well as to the other group females.

But the third consequence of bipedalism shows us how we evolved into the only species – as far as we know – that is capable of mentalization. As we 'stood up', the shape of our pelvis needed to change radically to absorb body weight on two legs. Tim Weaver at the University of

California and Jean-Jacques Hublin, Director at the Max Planck Institute for Evolutionary Anthropology, have now created a virtual reconstruction of a female Neanderthal pelvis. It demonstrates that the pubic arch – the 'gap' in the middle of the pelvis – became much smaller, in order to accommodate new muscle structures now needed at the top of our hips for us to stand and move on two legs for long periods. But, of course, it is through the pubic arch that the baby's head needs to pass in order to be born. This means that all human babies are, in effect, born at a time when they are far from fully formed (Leutenegger 1987; Weaver and Hublin 2009). For example, the top of their skull – the fontanelle – isn't completely fused until some months later.

Compared with other species, for whom birth is rarely as painful, nor indeed as dangerous as it can be to a human mother *and* her infant, our restricted pelvic size results in us being uniquely vulnerable and dependent. It may be the price we pay for walking and running around on two legs. But it all comes with a fascinating upside: our early development outside the womb immediately after birth brings with it the *unconscious* ability for babies to be aware not just of the physical but also the emotional availability of the caregiver (usually the infant's mother, in the early days). This explains, as Allan Schore put it, that the 'core of the self is...nonverbal and unconscious, and it lies in patterns of affect regulation... The activities of the "self-correcting" orbitofrontal system are central to self-regulation, the ability to flexibly regulate emotional states through interactions with other humans' (Schore 2001, p.38).

There is now a burgeoning literature providing the neurological evidence to argue convincingly that babies are aware of the intentional state of their mother at a very early age. This is because most new-borns have 'synaesthesic' capabilities until about four months: they can 'hear' colour and 'see' sound, for example. This is often referred to as cross-modulation, because parts of the brain, which are normally separated from one another, begin to link up, for example 'sight' and 'sound'. In addition to his work on autism, Simon Baron-Cohen has studied syn-aesthesia in babies, as well as in adults. Different ideas exist to explain how and why babies may have acquired this facility (see Baron-Cohen 1996) but, whatever the reason it developed in human infants, it enables them to interpret *unconsciously* (i.e. pre-verbally) the mind and intentions of a caregiver. At a very early age babies can 'read minds' (but they don't 'know' they can until much later). This ability is the precursor to both mentalization and RF, which develop fully when language matures.

To complement our knowledge of neonatal synaesthesia, much of Allan Schore's work draws together findings from neuroscience and molecular genetics, as well as Antonio Damasio's ground-breaking discoveries about the brain and 'consciousness', to show how brain development in the early months takes place predominantly in the right hemisphere, the primary site of emotion and the unconscious (see Damasio 1994). It was Schore's work into 'affective neuroscience' and attachment that broadened our understanding of early affect regulation experiences and their connection with subsequent mentalization capacity, which begin in the crucible of close attachments.

Understanding mentalization in theory and in practice

Although we said babies can 'read minds', this is really only a form of shorthand for a more complex process. Mentalizing is different from 'mindreading' because it refers and relates equally to one's *own* thoughts and feelings as it does to those of others. (And it most certainly is nothing to do with clairvoyance.) The notion of 'mentalizing' – knowing what's in Maxi's mind about the chocolate – also leaves out emotion. Similarly, mentalizing is not the same as 'ruminating', which can have a somewhat directionless, even anxiety-ridden, quality to it; indeed one of the benefits of secure attachment is the break it gives from excessive hypervigilance about one's own and others' mental states.

There are many definitions of mentalizing but the one written by the patient mentioned above gets to the heart of it. As Peter Fonagy puts it, 'Mentalisation is simply about recognising what's going on in our own heads and what might be going on in other people's heads' (Allen *et al.* 2008, p.203). What we mentalize about is complex and layered. The canvas is almost endless and the colours and hues include hopes, fears, beliefs, plans – even day-dreams, sleep-dreams and nightmares; and often our mentalizing is so fast we are barely conscious of it.

Thinking and feeling about one's own and others' thoughts and feelings in a dynamic, bi-directional and reciprocal sense also draws upon and reflects an individual's myriad relationships over the years. Recognizing the continuities and discontinuities within attachment and close relational biographies is a spontaneous accomplishment for those who are good at mentalizing.

Like most psychosocial phenomena, mentalization has its shadow-side and it can be deployed, consciously or unconsciously, by the bully

– or, at the extreme, by the psychopath – to tease, manipulate and even torture. We may have had experience of the 'friend' who seduces us into relational intimacy and trust only to abuse us later by telling others all our confided secrets. Betrayal is a hard lesson to learn partly because, as often as not, one doesn't see it coming; but the other reason is because the other person duped us into letting our hair down. They read *us*…but we didn't read them. Good mentalizers can also be highly deceptive charmers; the paedophile who grooms his victims to gain their trust in order to sexually abuse them is a powerful example of the flip-side of mentalization.

Finally, as the patient referred to earlier put it, mentalization is 'not just thinking clearly but *feeling* clearly' (Allen *et al.* 2008, p.59, emphasis added). And as Peter Fonagy adds, 'we can misunderstand what we feel, thinking that we feel one thing while truly feeling something else' (Allen *et al.* 2008, p.23). We tend to think that when a person says 'I feel sad' or 'I am scared' that this automatically means that the affect *described* is congruent with what he or she is actually feeling. We are not talking about deception here. It is perfectly possible to *think* we are feeling sad/scared, etc., even to *feel* that we are, but that doesn't mean that these are our true feelings: we may be denying or suppressing them, for example. In the same way as the Rogerian counsellor aims to accurately reflect feelings – and what led to them – back to the helpee, so too the good mentalizer aims accurately to identify and experience his or her own feelings, preferably before attempting to help others identify theirs.

The development of mentalization in the young child

Soon after the birth of the infant, the caregiver – again, usually the child's mother – realizes that she doesn't know precisely what the baby is feeling: he or she cries but initially it may be unclear what it 'means'. Slowly the carer tries out different things – changes nappies, feeds, soothes, sings lullabies, etc. – until the right action does the trick and the baby stops. When things work according to plan, the carer talks to the child during such times, even though in conscious terms the infant doesn't 'understand' what is being said. But, as we saw earlier, the infant is aware of the intentional state of the carer, in many ways that are unconsciously more sophisticated than most adults.

Again, when all goes according to plan, the carer mirrors back to the baby his or her feelings: that is to say, the carer reflects back to the infant *what the infant is feeling*, not what the carer is feeling. This is usually accompanied by what Peter Fonagy refers to as 'marked mirroring'. He contrasts this with *'unmarked* mirroring', when the mother shows the infant *her* feelings (not those of her baby). Marked mirroring has a slightly exaggerated quality – the child is unhappy so the carer makes an unhappy face back, ratcheted up just a little and accompanied by a gentle 'Is your tummy hurting?' – whereas unmarked mirroring would indicate the carer's feelings *about* the infant's internal state of unhappiness (for example, panic).

Miriam and Howard Steele add this important point: 'When the infant looks at the mother's face he can see himself, how he feels reflected back in her expression. If she is preoccupied by something else, when he looks at her, he will only see how *she* feels' (Steele and Steele 2008, p.137). If the carer's feeling of panic is communicated facially to the infant, he or she ends up experiencing his or her own feelings as panic rather than unhappiness. The result is a baby who remains in a state of confusion, possibly even overwhelmed, and in a heightened and under-regulated affect state. To the infant it feels as though he or she has been *infected* by the carer's feelings, experienced as though they are contagious (Allen *et al.* 2008). Hobson explains the desired state of 'separateness' needed:

> In reading her mother's reaction to a toy, the infant learns something about the toy; but, at the same time, the toy tells her something about the mother. What it tells her is that the mother is different from herself, in a particular way. It tells her that her mother has an attitude to the toy that is separate from her own attitude to the same toy. (Hobson 2002, p.109)

Secure parents can let themselves feel the same feelings as their child – they convey to the child 'Darling, these are *your* feelings, not mine, and it's OK, we'll get through it' – whereas insecure parents feel the child's feelings as though they were their own: when their child is sad they become sad too. You can observe these differences regularly when parents are with infants in supermarkets or any other public place; sometimes you will see quite worrying parental attributions to their children, ascribing to them all sorts of thoughts, feelings and intentions that, given their age, they couldn't possibly have.

Family members who encourage, or who are at least comfortable with, talking about negative emotions bring up children who understand the landscape of emotions as they develop. And as Peter Fonagy points out, 'parents whose disciplinary strategies focus on mental states (e.g. a victim's feelings, or the non-intentional nature of transgressions) have children who succeed in [*false belief tasks*] earlier' (Allen *et al.* 2008, p.25). This reinforces further the idea that most humans – but especially human babies – are only really stitched on when they enjoy the world *relationally and emotionally connected*. One study, for example, considered the 'pointing' behaviour of one-year-olds. If an adult just followed the child's finger, even if he or she smiled at the child when doing so, the child wasn't anything like as chuffed as when the adult 'responded by looking back and forth from the object to the infant and commented positively – implying that this sharing of attention and interest was indeed their goal… Such declarative and informing motives are apparently "purely social" in their aims' (Allen *et al.* 2008, p.31).

Conversely, it is now known that there are unfortunate consequences to prolonged exposure to unmarked mirroring and low mentalized parenting, one of which is a tendency to display disorganized attachment (Allen *et al.* 2008). Such infants and toddlers have problems with 'affect regulation, effortful control of attention and social cognition' (Allen *et al.* 2008, p.281). In respect to shared social attention such problems are particularly marked in cocaine-exposed children 'not only with the caregiver but also with an experimenter (e.g. they initiated joint attention less often)' (Allen *et al.* 2008, p.25). Fonagy goes on to identify the following 'non-mentalising' parental behaviour: 'affective communication errors (laughing when infant is crying); role and boundary confusions (demanding a show of affection); fearful behaviour (as evident in a squeaky voice); intrusive behaviour (pulling the infant by the wrist); withdrawal (not acknowledging the infant after separation)' (Allen *et al.* 2008, p.103).

Mentalization, maltreatment and disorganized attachment

We return briefly to the young girl in Chapter 1, whose father broke her arm in the most cold and brutal way. For her to 'resolve' what has happened to her – psychologically, not just physically – she has to be able to enter the mind of her father, to understand his intentional state, in order to conclude that he 'unloved' *her* rather than be left with the catastrophic feeling that she is 'unlovable'. But, of course, the last place she wants to 'visit' is her father's mind because it contains malevolence, hate and cruel feelings towards her. To contemplate that one's own father thinks about and feels towards his own daughter in this way is personally shattering: 'How can he hate me so much? I only did badly in my maths test, and I tried my best.' Such feelings will soon permeate other areas of her self, and she is likely soon to develop a very negative view of her own worth, about almost anything: personal achievement potential, ability, competence, likeableness, self-confidence and appearance, etc.

The negative downstream consequence is that she is deprived of the buffering effect of what she cannot experience, namely the opportunity of accurately understanding emotional and interpersonal situations, because she unthinkingly brings to them a 'false' self, but one which she feels increasingly is her 'true' self. To compound matters, if others do not respond to her 'false' self as her 'true' self, she will unconsciously lasso them into doing so, by engaging in progressively more 'unlovable' portrayals of herself until they do. This partly explains why children who have been abused and traumatized can become very challenging to adults who try to 'reach' them; and especially challenging to those who manage to connect.

Maltreated children and those showing disorganized attachment eventually withdraw from the world of close and intimate relationships; similarly, they avoid opportunities to mentalize the thoughts and feelings of both themselves and others. The child who demonstrates disorganized attachment 'is forced to look not for the representation of his own mental states in the mind of the other, but the mental states of that other which threaten to undermine his agentic sense of self. These mental states can create an alien presence within his self-representation' (Allen *et al.* 2008, p.34).

Peter Fonagy goes on to list three main reasons why children with disorganized attachment and who have been maltreated cannot integrate emotional awareness of others into their self-organization (Allen *et al.* 2008). First, they may have to devote too much time and attentional effort to make sense of the abuser's behaviour. Second, because the caregiver isn't responding to the child on the basis of what the *child* has done – rather, the caregiver is responding on the basis of his or her own needs, wishes and intentions – the child is not able to see what it is that has led to the maltreating behaviour (the child just thinks he or she is generally and specifically unworthy of love, care and affection). Lastly, the abnormal levels of intense watchfulness needed to make sense of the caregiver's unpredictable moods and reactions – which will not necessarily have much to do with what the child has or has not actually done – mean that the child may become attuned to the caregiver's state of mind 'but (we suggest) poor readers of their own mental states' (Allen *et al.* 2008, p.34).

Children who show disorganized attachment regularly have to put up with carers who minimize what they think, say and feel; who tell them off when it doesn't seem to make any sense in terms of proportionality or logic and contingency; or who make light of important things to the child. If we find ourselves in a situation when we are punished – or, worse still, ignored – no matter what we do, we will eventually conclude that we might just as well behave in a random way. This is a poor set of circumstances in which to develop and sustain an interest in the mental worlds of close and intimate relationships.

When children and adults develop a chronic inability to mentalize they experience the world in one of three different kinds of non-representational, pre-mentalizing, experiences. The first are 'too real' (what Fonagy terms *psychic equivalence*) while the second are 'too unreal' (which he calls the *pretend mode*). When we operate with 'psychic equivalence' we take things very literally with no room for alternatives. He gives an example of a person who phoned a therapist's secretary who was not able to answer. The therapist reminded him that all calls are returned within two hours if they can't be answered at the time. He replied angrily, 'What does that have to do with anything? No answer equals no help! Don't you even understand that?' (Allen *et al.* 2008, p.186). In the 'pretend mode' an adult will perhaps take on a Walter Mitty-type existence or will embellish and amplify events excessively; it can also take the form of intellectualizing or an over-reliance on 'psychobabble' to explain what is happening in one's personal or close interpersonal life. With the third type of experience – called the *teleological mode* – thoughts and feelings are only valid when they are linked to direct actions. Affection *must* be accompanied by touching or hugging and 'emotional pain can be expressed fully, for example, only via the sight of blood from cuts on the arms' (Allen *et al.* 2008, p.278).

It is not always abuse in its more direct and obvious forms that leads to low mentalization: neglect – and especially emotional neglect – is particularly pernicious because it represents to the child a direct interaction failure. Prolonged emotional neglect affects a child's cognitive and social development because 'children cannot learn words for feelings and adults have more difficulty learning facial expressions' (Allen *et al.* 2008, p.36).

Whatever the primary cause of low mentalization, be it autism or maltreatment, the result is usually children who just seem flummoxed by what's going on in other people's minds. They may also show little interest or enthusiasm. After all, in their way of seeing things and from their experience, what is the point? They have learned that trying to predict and read other people is too time-consuming and ultimately fruitless because, in their world, there may be only one predictable pattern: 'I am unlovable'. As we shall see, however, it would be quite wrong to conclude that such children grow up to become shrinking violets, permanently walking around with their heads lowered; on the contrary, they may deal with their chronic low self-esteem by seeking to take control of what is happening by being aggressive to others or by being self-destructive.

Reflective function

RF is mentalization in the context of attachment and 'is anchored in careful study of how adults use, or fail to use, mental state language (beliefs and desires) when pressed to give an account of their developmental history' (Steele and Steele 2008, p.135). The difference between RF and mentalization becomes more obvious when we compare *Maxi and the Chocolate* (which is primarily a cognitive task only) with *Ellie the Elephant and Naughty Mickey* (which involves affect and emotions). Interestingly, some children (and some adults, if the false belief tasks are modified to suit their maturity) will get Maxi 'right', but not Ellie. This is because different parts of the brain are involved in each task (Schore 2001).

In order to develop and demonstrate RF we must first *identify* the basic dimensions involved within the feeling/s being experienced: I am feeling sad...or is it really desperation...or perhaps I am actually disappointed, etc. Then we need to be able to *modulate* (or regulate) the intensity of this, now clearer, emotion. In other words, if we burst into tears whenever we have any feelings of sadness, it is difficult for us and others to appreciate, understand and imagine the true mental state being experienced. Third, we should then try to *express* the emotion; that is, the one that is as fully congruent as possible with the originating events.

To illustrate this we offer the following personal example. We were at home in September 2004. It was a Saturday and we were just about to go for a drive and then a walk with the dog. David was just about to turn off the radio when a story broke of an unfolding tragedy involving a group of terrorists in Beslan, in the Russian republic of North Ossetia. (The government did not give in to the terrorists' demands and eventually 330 people were killed, over half of them children.) We delayed going out for about an hour while we watched the events on the television (something we don't normally do in the middle of a Saturday). We were both shell-shocked but decided we would still go for a drive. David was quiet but rather grumpy and 'picky', a state of mind he was not experiencing before watching the television. He has noticed over the years that he gets mildly irritable if he doesn't express more powerful emotions; but doesn't always see it coming! This is where Yvonne comes in. When they arrived at their destination she asked how he was feeling, saying that she 'didn't think he was right'. He rather snappily and slightly sarcastically replied 'You *know* I'm not right…*and* you know why' (not the way he usually speaks to her!). She turned to face him and gently took hold of both his hands, which were by his side, and said 'Yes I think I do, my love…but I think you should speak about it.' He then burst into tears.

In terms of the three steps for mentalizing, David had *identified* that he *had* an emotion (sometimes we deny or suppress even that) but had not explored the 'shades, levels, contours and intensity' (Fonagy 2008, p.64). But he was in the 'wrong' emotional landscape too: he 'thought' he was feeling 'angry and irritable' whereas a more accurate emotional picture was one of 'desolation and desperation' at the plight of the powerless parents who had just witnessed what had happened to their children. In terms of the other two steps – *modulation* and *expression* – he was nowhere near the first rungs.

This matters because, when we are with people who activate our attachment systems on a regular basis, it means that we are in the 'wrong' emotional state in their presence – or worse still denying that we are actually experiencing an emotion. This increases significantly the likelihood of us projecting onto a family member the unprocessed affect, as David did with Yvonne: he became cross with her because he hadn't recognized and then fully experienced the powerful emotion he was feeling.

Recognizing, experiencing and expressing powerful feelings are not the same thing as *showing them in every situation*. For those involved in child welfare, processing and regulating emotion needs to be undertaken as part of supervision, where we can explore the more complex meaning and intention *behind* those feelings.

The Adult Attachment Interview (AAI) is the primary means of exploring people's capacity for RF. The points in the narrative containing the most indicative attachment-related information are just before and immediately following dysfluence and other specified discourse markers. As Nicola Diamond and Mario Marrone point out, 'the critical issue is not the kind of story the person tells, but where, when, and how the story breaks down' (Diamond and Marrone 2003, p.145); or as Patricia Crittenden put it, 'What s/he can't say coherently suggests what s/he doesn't understand' (Crittenden 2008, p.140).

Various questions in the AAI are designed specifically to see whether interviewees can reflect upon their experiences as a child and integrate seemingly disparate experiences. According to Miriam and Howard Steele, however, the following two questions are the key to giving interviewees the opportunity to demonstrate RF:

1. When you think about your childhood experiences, do you think they have an influence on who you are today (as an adult)?

2. When you think about your parents' behaviour toward you when you were a child, why do you think they behaved the way they did? (Steele and Steele 2008, p.139)

When assessing caregivers' capacity for RF, transcripts are rated low if they refer to the carer or the child in 'monotones', without reference to richer, more coloured depictions. So, for example, after being asked 'Please tell me about your child', responses such as 'She's naughty/funny/ bad', etc., and where little more is offered when elaboration is requested, would be rated 'Low RF'. Similarly, if carers only refer to themselves with under-developed responses such as 'I'm short-tempered/passive/ stubborn', etc., then the relevant passage would also be rated 'Low RF'.

The next level of RF is recognized by statements such as 'He's *sad*; He *likes* bananas; She *knows* I'm gonna feed her' (see Slade 2008, p.217). Assuming they are accurate, such examples would be rated as 'Moderate RF'. The difference between 'He's *sad*' and 'He *likes* bananas' – again, assuming they are accurate – compared to 'She's naughty/funny/bad' is that the latter contain no indications of the internal world of the child.

Sometimes our attempts to understand the intentions of others produce some rather bizarre attributions. We began this chapter with a particularly worrying extract but there are sometimes more subtle examples. We noticed a recent headline in the *Sun* newspaper (8 July 2010) following the shooting of the alleged murderer Raoul Moat. It was accompanied by a photo of Moat as a two-month-old infant. In the photo his hands were held tight. The caption ran 'Cute baby…but both his fists are clenched', the presumed implication being that his deadly outbursts as an adult could have been predicted at two months of age (a spurious and arguably irresponsible contention).

Metacognitive monitoring

In parallel with RF, 'metacognitive monitoring' – the ability simultaneously to 'think about thinking' – facilitates the development of coherence of mind and is evident in various discourse markers in individuals' AAI transcripts. Recent developments in neuro-psychobiology (see Damasio 1994; Schore 1994) make it possible to understand more precisely the processes occurring in the brain when it operates 'coherently', that is, when integrating other memory systems. Securely attached individuals tend to appraise situations as less threatening than insecure individuals – but especially people with a disorganized attachment history – and are generally more optimistic (Belsky 2002). They also have 'ready access to painful memories [but which] are not contagiously spread…[and they also] deal with conflict by compromising and integrating their own and others' positions' (Belsky 2002, p.167).

Metacognitive monitoring and RF are indicative of an individual's capacity to achieve psychological integration of his or her recollections of any early, non-optimal caregiving environments. Individuals' successful attempts at narrative coherence differ from the 'optimistic platitudes or lack of interest to avoid integrative thinking' (Crittenden 1996, ch.3, p.10) typical of avoidant individuals; it can also be differentiated from those who use 'psychological jargon borrowed from the media or popular culture but fail to see that they have not answered questions' (Crittenden 1996, ch.3, p.11) often found in the transcripts of people with an ambivalent internal working model of close relationships. Individuals who have experienced a disorganized attachment history will have the greatest difficulty processing the past in a meaningfully integrated and coherent manner.

We now consider some examples of high and low RF and *en passant* include high and low metacognitive monitoring. The examples derive from research completed in 2004 (by David). The results are not considered here but they can be found in Shemmings (2006a and 2006b). The research focused on later life filial relationships, which largely remain undiscovered within attachment theory and research. Attachment theory in general implies that one of the primary reasons for the maintenance of this bond in later life concerns the protection of the attachment figure; but adult sons and daughters and their parents are aware, consciously or unconsciously, that this relationship is moving inexorably towards its end and, hence, relational stress may be experienced by both parties. Such stress may be compounded if middle-generation adults invite their parent to live with them, especially if personal and intimate care involving role reversal is provided.

The study considered filial attachment relationships from the perspective of the adult 'child'. The overarching research question was 'How do adult children mentally represent their past, present and future attachment relationships with a parent?' Participants were selected using the Attachment Style Questionnaire to include equal numbers of the three main attachment styles. First, *Q Methodology* (see Shemmings 2006b) was used to factor analyse a Q-sort of 44 attachment-specific statements concerning this relationship. Second, the AAI acted as a guided conversation, from which transcripts were examined to illuminate the results of the factor analysis.

Examples of high and low reflective function from the Adult Attachment Interview (all names have been anonymized)

Example 1 – low RF

As a result of a rather conflicted relationship with her mother, opportunities for metacognitive monitoring and RF tended either to be missed or ignored by Valerie, as the following extract illustrates:

Why do you think she is the way she is?

I think it's probably the way she was as a child herself, I think she loved her mum actually...it sounded very sad when her mum died.

She seemed to get on very well with her mum but her father was such a contrast and very strict and she obviously didn't get a lot of love from him...he was a bully, there's no two ways about it, grandfather was a bully...I think my mum was very naïve, very naïve...we found out that she was pregnant before she got married, so my grandfather was supposed to have stripped all the sheets off the bed saying she's filthy and everything, so it must have been very traumatic for her at the time to be treated like that – she was 21, I think – but I don't think that mattered much, she was very naïve in as much as it came to having children...

Valerie can only really respond superficially with platitudes and, before her responses have developed, she quickly forecloses RF by making a derogatory comment concerning her mother's 'naivety'.

Example 2 – low RF

The next extract illustrates how – and *where* – Felicity overlooks or ignores the possibility of integrating incongruent information about her early childhood:

How do you think your childhood experiences with your mother have affected your adult personality?

I think it made me...very erm...I've forgotten what the word is... 'unsure' of myself...I am totally confident and have most of my life been very confident talking to people – anybody; I mean from headmasters to...I don't think it would honestly faze me talking to the Queen, I just don't worry about that sort of thing...but it made me very...erm...*(response ends, forcing the interview on to the next question)*.

She overlooks discrepancies between feeling 'unsure of herself' and being 'totally confident'; yet, at this point in the interview and at other points too, she is not surprised by this incongruence; hence, she misses the opportunity to integrate her memories.

Example 3 – moderate/high RF

Secure attachment organization is not necessarily the result of successive positive early life events: the event itself is far less important than its meaning constructed in the mind of the individual recalling it. Although the next extract contains a memory of insecure parenting, the event is processed by Marilyn in a way which underscores her acceptance of her own feelings, as well as other people's. She is explaining why she used 'insecure' as the first word to describe her relationship to her mother.

> Insecure, yeah…erm…I can remember once being frightened that my mother would run away and I knew that she had a boyfriend who was a farm labourer or brick worker… No, I think he was a builder… and he used to do a lot of work for the local farmer and he used to come and visit my mother, but I hadn't realized at the time that they had a relationship…

She then added 'I may have sensed it…and I think I could tell that my mother was not happy with my father at the time'. By this addition, she demonstrates that she is interested in the mental world of her mother and that she can appreciate other people's feelings as a result of her desire to consider events from their perspective. She follows this immediately by noting:

> I've discovered in later years that it was because of the incident of my father losing his business and the pressure that put on my mother and the bailiffs coming along. It left quite a scar and I think my mother was quite sort of…you know, she was younger than my father and I think she blamed my father, probably too much, without really meaning to…but I guess the blame had to go somewhere…

In this example of RF, we see that Marilyn can appreciate causal relations between effects; similarly, she can take her mother's perspective, but without slipping into inappropriate or premature exoneration. She concluded her recollection by exploring this uncomfortable memory, rather than by side-stepping it:

> …and so it had an effect on the relationship, and although they carried on together as a couple all through their years, initially it was quite a strained relationship, so I was always picking up tensions and vibes from my mother.

Example 4 – moderate/high RF

Barbara has a rather strained relationship with her mother and she would prefer to be reconciled. Nevertheless, she doesn't hold out much hope of it happening; although she has an open mind about the possibility of things improving, she says she is realistic that it probably won't happen. What helps her not become preoccupied about the current relational state of affairs with her mother is her well-developed facility for RF and her ability to metacognitively monitor discrepant information, which are evident within numerous integrative statements she provides, each of which is consistent with balanced, coherent and integrative mental functioning. At the end of the next extract, she uses a certain dry humour to make sense of her 'untidiness', although she monitors quickly that her reflection revealed a certain flaw in her logic, as well as contradictions. The dysfluence (in her case a few 'erms', and some pauses which were slightly longer than usual) evident within particular extracts is not deployed to distance or excessively confuse either the participant or the interviewer: the delays are needed merely to gain time for clearer thought and integrative reflection. A prompting question asked her to amplify a point she had made about a change from being excessively fastidious to becoming more untidy:

> I think my upbringing made me...erm...slightly over-precise...erm... I try to keep within rules...erm...and yet I'm also dreadfully untidy. I mean five people share this office. I don't take the responsibility for all of it, but a lot of the mess is mine, you know... Oh but I can see that this doesn't fit together properly...let me try and explain it another way: when I got away from home, I would purposely not do the washing on Monday, because not doing it held a wonderful freedom for me. But it would also feel wrong that I didn't...erm... It left me with feelings that there were precise and very rigid ways of doing things. And then I kicked over the traces...it took me years, by the way. I think I must have been 50 when I finally realized that if you didn't cut the grass on Saturday it hadn't actually grown a great deal by Sunday.

She returns to this point about breaking free from her emotional shackles a few minutes later when, again with humour but without resentment, she reflects that her own children's preferences were not necessarily the same as hers:

> I can remember when my kids were small, I felt I had to bake all our bread. Looking back, I can see that they didn't actually like it. They preferred Mother's Pride – different colour wrapper every day – erm...but, I felt that I had to bake their bread. I also had to go to work and...er...I had to juggle lots of things and I wasn't actually happy unless I had an awful amount to do...

Part of Barbara's capacity for integrating and synthesizing past experiences coherently is that she can evaluate unsentimentally her own contribution to past events. She was particularly insightful when she was asked to think about the effect of her early upbringing later in her life. Rather than simply blame her partners, she separates her own contribution to the marriage from theirs, without either preoccupation or avoidance:

> I think my upbringing may have caused two quite disastrous marriages because I was unable to say to either of these unfortunate men…erm…I couldn't say 'Well, actually, I don't like that' or 'No, I don't agree with you', which meant they were perpetually in the position where they were supposed to guess that I was overworked or that I couldn't pay the electricity bill or whatever…I think they had to second guess all the time what was happening in my mind. I would never actually have said, 'Come on – let's have a straight talk about money. This isn't enough housekeeping to keep three kids.' I would have never done that, so…erm…I think it made me slightly manipulative in a way.

Example 5 – low RF

When Jenny tried to make sense of some of her early childhood memories, her lack of narrative coherence resulted in partial, undeveloped or inaccurate RF, as evidenced either by a general lack of specificity, or by the deployment of 'media-generated platitudes' (Crittenden 1996, ch.11, p.4). For example, in the following extract Jenny is attempting to reflect upon her experience that her own childhood led to 'an increase in her own personal insight and self-awareness':

> I did a degree in social sciences and the [qualification in social work] as well. It's been a great teacher for me, my early upbringing experiences, and trying to, I think, coming into social work and studying psychology and all the rest of it has been a way of me trying to understand myself, and I understand myself, I think very, very well, and I can let that go now, do you know what I mean? It's like, erm, it's been a great teacher for me.

Your childhood or your experiences in higher education?

Yeah, a great teacher, my childhood.

What one thing would you say it taught you more than anything else?

One thing? I know it took me, I'd have to think about that one, that's a tough question, yeah, I don't know, it's er, I dunno, it just taught me to find out who I was really, you know, and I learned, I 'discovered myself' *(said with Jenny placing the words within inverted commas 'in the air' with her fingers),* let's put it that way.

Jenny often lapsed into incoherent and incomprehensible attempts at reasoning during the AAI; yet, after the interview was complete, when she was discussing other topics related to current affairs or her professional work, she was noticeably much more articulate, with very little dysfluence. These observations suggest that Jenny's capacity for handling her relationship with her mother, especially those aspects likely to become emotionally charged, could be severely circumscribed. Contained within much of the interview is an unending and eager longing by Jenny, simply to want to be *understood* by her mother.

Example 6 – low RF

As with Jenny, at no point did Lisa comment or reflect upon the contradiction between certain phrases and expressions. This suggests that she has a limited facility for RF. For example, she appears not to recognize the semantic imprecision in the following response to the question asking her to provide an example of being 'scared' of her mother. She wants to change her mind about her choice of the word 'scared' but she ends up confused about the difference between being 'scared' and being 'afraid', at which point she simply changes the subject and talks about how she always felt the need to predict very precisely her mother's moods (a known feature of the origins of relational preoccupation experienced by ambivalent individuals):

> Erm, I am saying 'scared' but, I know that, you know, I was *scared* of her, but I wasn't, I wasn't *afraid* of her, if you know what I mean. I was very sensitive to her moods, very sensitive. If she was in a good mood, I would be the happiest girl there was.

Being sensitive to her mother's moods may indicate heightened watchfulness and vigilance but this may have led to very inaccurate readings of her mother's intentional state of mind. And she may have perceived – accurately – *that* her mother was in a good mood, but may have had little understanding of the reasons and circumstances leading to it; hence, her awareness may have held little predictive capacity.

She does, however, immediately recall a remarkably powerful memory of being 'scared' of her mother. The incident she chose is another example of how unsurprising and undistinguished events hold immense significance for insecurely attached people – especially those with a history of attachment disorganization – because, unlike securely attached individuals, they have limited access to integrative mental processes by which to make sense of painful or traumatic events.

Example 7 – low RF (with some indication of unresolved physical and relational trauma)

The final extract demonstrates many of Jenny's unfathomable yet lingering feelings. In this account, she recreates for the listener the power of the event by shifting verb tenses regularly to the present. The resultant temporal immediacy is aimed at *involving* the interviewer in the same emotional experience and at the same intensity. As in the previous example, Jenny cannot distance herself to begin to comprehend the mental states of her and her mother; there is some dissociation, but mostly unresolved anger. Also, speakers in the AAI can sometimes try to involve the interviewer, who can be 'subtly drawn in as an internal mental support for the speaker…[who]…nevertheless, wanders away from the focus of the questions to topics of preoccupying interest' (Crittenden 1996, ch.11, p.2). One of the words chosen by Jenny to describe her relationship with her mother was 'anger' and she deployed a form of 'involving discourse', especially when she was asked to provide a specific example of the 'angry' relationship. At this point in the AAI she *became* rather angry – evident more from her tone of voice than in the transcript alone – and confrontational with the interviewer. The extract is also full of 'tense-shifting', in order to bring a particularly violent event into the present, thereby creating the potential for 'shared closeness' with the interviewer:

> *Can you think of an example of your mother's anger, from as early as possible?*

> Her anger? Well…erm…well, she nearly killed me one day, I mean, really nearly killed me, she would've killed me, she would've killed me *(shouting)*.

> *Can you say what happened?*

She didn't just hit me *(indignant)*, she picked up a chair and smashed it over my head. Erm, in fact she did it several times. She hit me on the first occasion, but as I kind of...we lived on the third floor of a flat, and...erm...I was being a nuisance – admittedly – because she...the boys were only babies...she was trying to get some sleep, so I wanted to go into the flat with my friend. I was knocking on the door and she kept saying, 'Go away'. I said, 'I want to come in'. She said, 'Go away'. I was about nine or ten. So eventually she lost her temper and she said, 'That's it' or words to that effect. I said, 'It's alright, I'm going now' and, as I'd gone to run down the stairs, she said, 'Come back here' and something in her voice... I knew what she was gonna... it was like... I didn't know what she was going to do to me, I knew she was gonna hit me but I still felt compelled to go back. My friend run for her life, 'cos my mum has an awesome voice – very, very loud voice. 'Come back here' she said, in words of few syllables, and back I went and...erm...with that she smashed the door, it was one of those heavy doors, and she picked up this chair and she just, and she picked up this chair and she just smashed me over the head with it and I kept moving around and she missed me and I just... I mean, she basically lost control of herself; totally lost control. I managed... I had a white dress on which made it worse and my head was gashed and all this blood coming down the dress. I opened the door, I managed to get out of the door and as I got out of the door... I mean that saved my life really, I'm talking to you now casually about it *(but re-listening to the tape, it is evident that Jenny was not talking 'casually about it')* 'cos even though I have discussed it before, it still affects me. She smashed the door behind me and I just went screaming down the stairs, you know, with all this blood flowing down, and my neighbour came out and... erm...anyway, I won't...you want an example of anger, that's an example of anger. Well, that's an example of rage, uncontrolled rage.

This certainly was an example of uncontrolled rage but for Jenny, who is not able to mentalize the traumatic event, it remains an *intrusive* memory, capable of taking over her daily experience, unannounced and unresolved.

We have considered the concepts of mentalization and RF at some length because it may be one of the crucial missing links in the pathways connecting caregiver characteristics – often seen as 'risk factors', such as parental mental ill-health, substance abuse, having experienced abuse as a child – with disorganized attachment via child maltreatment. But, until fairly recently, the reason why *some* people who abuse drugs, for example, go on to harm children, while others clearly do not, has bedevilled and bemused child welfare practitioners. We return to this conundrum in the final chapter, to re-examine how and why the moderating and mediating caregiver variables – *unresolved loss, dissociation, extremely insensitive and disconnected parenting* and *low mentalization* and *reflective functioning* – lead to disorganized attachment behaviour in children.

Specific Caregiver Behaviour

Introduction

Within secure parenting relationships, when we are frightened we go to an attachment figure (either in person or 'in our mind') who will offer comfort. Within insecure parenting relationships, the avoidant caregiver encourages the child to fend for him or herself, whereas the ambivalent carer ends up confusing the child (perhaps by cuddling him or her, well after the moment has passed). But abusive and/or frightening carers do something qualitatively different: when their child is frightened they end up frightening the child even more. We use the term 'end up' because it is thought that children's fear stimulates fear in carers, possibly reminding them of similar experiences that happened to them when they were children; 'end up' is thus used to suggest a lack of conscious deliberation on the part of disorganized carers.

Talk of 'insensitive parenting' soon conjures up its opposite but those parents among us can feel cheered by reflecting upon the finding that 'the ordinary mother has moderate levels of infant-state attunement with equal amounts spent in misattunement and repair' (Newton 2008, p.33). Furthermore, Hopkins (1996) stops us becoming too self-critical by pointing out that if a carer tried always to be there at the right time, in the right way, this would likely restrict a child's development. As Nicola Diamond and Mario Marrone put it, 'the importance of optimal frustration should not be underestimated' (Diamond and Marrone 2003, p.35). We need – indeed 'should' – only be 'good enough' (Winnicott 1958). Of course, if we are open and attuned enough to read the child's signals, it is the child who teaches us how to parent him or her when inevitably we get it wrong from time to time.

In their edited book *Promoting Positive Parenting: An Attachment-based Intervention* Marian Bakermans-Kranenburg, Marinus van IJzendoorn and Femmie Juffer describe sensitive caregiving as consistently offering warm, responsive and, more importantly, synchronous responses to their children by reading their signals accurately and then reacting promptly. They add that, 'with toddlers, other features of sensitivity include:

(i) attentiveness to the child, (ii) contingency response to non-distress vocalizations, (iii) mutual gaze and reciprocity and positive attentiveness and (iv) encouraging freedom to explore' (Juffer *et al.* 2008a, p.143). But it is also the child's *responsiveness* to the parent's initiations that is key to understanding the parent's sensitivity. The flip-side of parental sensitivity has led to a considerable amount of work to precisely define caregiver *in*sensitivity. As we saw in Chapter 3, Dorothee Out and her colleagues have recently divided the term parental insensitivity into *extremely insensitive parenting* and *disconnected parenting* – possibly the more damaging form of insensitivity due to its 'spaced out' quality, the parent seriously frightening the child because of his or her 'unpresence'.

According to a report for the World Health Organization in 2004 'sensitive and responsive caregiving is a requirement for the healthy neuro-physiological, physical and psychological development of a child. Sensitivity and responsiveness have been identified as key features of caregiving behaviour related to later positive health and development outcomes in young children' (Richter 2004, p.1). This conclusion is substantiated by various studies showing that, when considering the three organized patterns of attachment – secure, avoidant and ambivalent – the notion of caregiver sensitivity is significantly (if only modestly) associated with infant attachment security. It has also been established that interventions focusing on improving caregiver sensitivity are more effective than all other types of intervention measured in improving attachment security in the child and that interventions that were most effective in improving caregiver sensitivity were also most effective in enhancing attachment security in infants (Bakermans-Kranenburg, van IJzendoorn and Juffer 2003). Therefore, although there still remains some debate about the intergenerational transmission of organized attachment patterns – some continue to argue that a 'transmission gap' still exists in terms of our knowledge of this process – it is clear that caregiver sensitivity has an important role in this process along with the concept of mentalization and reflective function (RF).

However, when considering disorganized attachment patterns, caregiver sensitivity appears to be somewhat less relevant, or rather it is relevant but only at the extreme end of the spectrum and in combination with other problematic caregiving factors, such as disconnected caregiving and low RF. As we have seen, evidence has been accruing over recent years to indicate that the links between disorganized attachment patterns and caregiving approaches are much more complex than for the organized patterns. This evidence also suggests that the link between disorganized attachment and caregiving as originally conceived by Hesse and Main when they first developed their model of disorganized attachment was too simplistic (Madigan *et al.* 2006).

Organized patterns of attachment can show a remarkable degree of continuity across the lifespan, not just in child–carer relationships, with, as we have seen, studies indicating some continuity of attachment over the first 20 years of life. With disorganized attachments the picture is somewhat more complex and nuanced. By age three, most children with disorganized attachment patterns in infancy are found to have 'resolved' those patterns into more controlling forms of attachment (Hennighausen and Lyons-Ruth 2010). Children with these controlling patterns are more at risk of developing increased levels of dissociative symptoms and psychopathology in their teenage years. How individuals with – for want of a better term – resolved disorganized patterns relate to their partners, ageing parents and others is a new and rapidly developing field of research.

In attachment theory, the attachment system of infants and children is conceptualized as being in a reciprocal relationship to the caregiving system of parents or carers (George and Solomon 1996). This insight highlights the view that whilst the attachment system is a significant behavioural system for a wide range of animals, especially primates (Hansen 1966) and humans, it is not the only or even primary behavioural system that may be in operation at any one time. Depending on the context and the environment, other behavioural systems – such as the mating system – are just as (or more) important (Fisher *et al.* 2002). When considering how any one individual's behavioural system might be operating and what the underlying representational model might be for the behaviour, consideration must be given to how the individual's internal working model is interacting with reciprocal or opposition systems in other people.

Therefore, when thinking about the attachment of children to their caregivers, it is important to consider *at the same time* the responsive behavioural system of the caregiver to the child, namely the caregiving system. When thinking about the attachments of adults to other adults (partner to partner, adult child to ageing parent), the picture is further complicated by the fact that one or both of the individuals may be attached to the other, whilst at the same time playing the role of the caregiver (i.e. an adult child may view his or her ageing parent as an attachment figure whilst at the same time providing some form of care for the parent).

Caregiving and attachment

How are the two systems of attachment and caregiving thought to interact and how do they differ from each other? In any relationship, the attachment system and the caregiving system are conceptualized as organized systems in their own right – that is, they contribute a set of behaviours guided by a representation of the particular relationship. Although it is clear how they differ in terms of the different behaviours associated with them, what fundamentally distinguishes them at a representational level is their different aims (George and Solomon 2008).

Thinking first about the infant child to adult caregiver relationship, the child's attachment system has the aim of obtaining protection from and proximity to the attachment figure at times of heightened anxiety. In essence, the attachment system is about fear and the avoidance of harm. In order to achieve the goal of physical and/or emotional proximity to the attachment figure during times of perceived or actual danger, the child uses behaviours designed to make the achievement of this aim more likely. As the attachment system is goal-corrected – as is the caregiving system – these behaviours can change over time as the child learns which behaviours are more or less successful in obtaining the proximity the system desires. It seems likely that this system first developed because genes that had the effect of promoting behaviour which resulted in increased proximity to an interested and caring adult at times of increased risk or danger would have increased in frequency in the human gene pool at the expense of genes which did not.

Although the actual behaviours employed vary across the lifespan and are influenced by age, culture and situation, the goal of the attachment system always remains the same. This modification of behaviour to achieve the same end is the basis for the differentiation between the organized attachment patterns – insecurely attached children learn that they need either to minimize their affective behaviour (avoidance) or greatly exaggerate their affective behaviour (ambivalent) in order to achieve protection. Children with secure attachments learn that they can behave in a manner consistent with their affective states (i.e. they do not have to modify their behaviour to gain protection).

In a complementary fashion, the goal of the caregiving system is to provide protection and care to the child in response either to activation of the child's attachment system or to environmental cues that signal an increase in danger. Note that the adult's caregiving system may be activated at times when the child's attachment system is not activated and that there will also be times when the child's attachment system is activated (i.e. he or she feels the need for protection) and yet the adult's caregiving system is non-responsive. Incongruity between the attachment system of the child and the caregiving system of the adult is more likely in insecure relationships than in secure ones (although it would occur in both). However, when working in an ideal state, the attachment system and the caregiving system operate in a complementary fashion and, in the context of sensitive and secure relationships, the two systems often serve as bi-directional signals. The adult needs to be aware of and sensitive to things and events that the child considers fear-inducing and, at the same time, the child has the opportunity to learn about his or her wider environment in terms of relevant danger signals. One everyday example, familiar to most people, would be childhood fear of the dark, as almost all children are afraid of the dark during their toddler years. The combination of a developing imagination coupled with a fledgling sense of object permanency seems the most common explanation – that is, the toddler is not yet aware that objects remain the same, whether in the light or the dark (Miller 1979). Through the modelling of the attachment figure (i.e. the non-arousal of the caregiving system when the only differential input is the dark) in combination with normative psychological development (obtaining an understanding of object permanence), the toddler usually learns that night-time is not necessarily a more dangerous place than daytime.

Attunement between the two systems is thought to be a significant component in attachment theory's concept of sensitivity. Attempts to define 'caregiving sensitivity' have recognized that it is an umbrella term for a number of different factors, both explicit and implicit. Studies have now demonstrated that it is the *explicit* elements of the caregiving system that have the largest effect on attachment security. This includes elements such as responsiveness, response quality and mutuality, whereas implicit elements, including having a positive attitude, cooperation and physical contact, are less influential for attachment security (Dunst and Kassow 2008). This supports the notion that the two systems interact at a behavioural level. However, just as the attachment system of behaviour is derived from the child's internal working model of relationships, so the caregiving system of behaviour is also derived from a representational model.

A caregiver who combines a sensitive caregiving system with a high level of RF is able to play a vital role in the development of his or her infant's ability to comprehend interpersonal behaviour in terms of the underlying mental or psychological process. That is, the child is able to learn about behaviour and develop his or her own capacity for RF in response to the caregiver's ability to do the same. Although it is well known that caregiver security of attachment is a strong predictor of the likely attachment pattern of the infant (even when the carer is tested prior to the birth of the child), the degree of caregiver RF – the ability to understand behaviour in terms of states of mind and to be able to relate this to his or her own relationships – is an even stronger predictor of infant security and organization.

In thinking about the two systems in this way, attachment researchers have helped to define more tightly what is meant by the expression 'good-enough parenting/caregiving', an expression frequently heard (but perhaps less frequently well defined) within social work and other helping professions. Bearing in mind the outline above – that the goal of the caregiving system is protection of the infant – then a broad range of behavioural strategies can be considered as 'good enough', as long as they are organized around protection when the child is at an increased risk of harm. Viewed in this way, carers of infants with avoidant or ambivalent attachment patterns can be considered as 'good enough', despite the less than optimum insecure nature of their relationship, as long as under (non-extreme) situations of potential harm, the carer fulfils their protective role. This is in contrast to the carers of infants with disorganized attachments who, in situations of potential harm, often abandon or neglect their protective role by displaying disconnected and dissociative behaviour (being unaware of the risk or by omission of good-enough caregiving strategies) or by acting directly as the source of the threat (maltreating the child by commission of harmful acts or neglect).

Before considering the caregiving environments in which children are at higher risk of developing disorganized attachments, to offer a point of comparison it is helpful to outline what the caregiving environment is like for children more likely to develop a secure attachment pattern. Children with secure attachments come to understand through repeated experience that their caregivers will respond to their attachment behaviour in a sensitive manner – therefore, they do not need to adjust their behaviour to obscure or exaggerate their underlying affective states. Although there will always be times when their caregiver reacts insensitively, there is enough of a preponderance towards a sensitive reaction that the child's internal working model forms around this assumption.

The carer of a securely attached child is likely to have a caregiving system that is flexible, balanced and integrated (George and Solomon 2008, p.844). In addition, flexible, balanced and integrated female caregivers, on whom most of the research has been conducted, were found more likely to have other positive characteristics, such as 'commitment, trust, cooperation, knowledge of self and child as individuals, the ability and desire to communicate clearly about caregiving and attachment goals (especially when these goals are in conflict), and the joy associated with being a parent' (George and Solomon 2008, p.844).

Caregiving and disorganized attachment

As we saw earlier with organized attachment behaviours, findings on disorganized attachment also appear to transcend culture, as Erik Hesse and Mary Main (2000) describe:

> In Austin, Texas, the AAI was administered to 113 expectant mothers several months before the infant was born (Jacobvitz, Hazen and Riggs 1997). When the infants were eight months old, the mothers were videotaped in the home while feeding them, playing with them, and changing their clothing. In this study, unresolved…mothers were found far more likely to exhibit FR (frightening) behaviours than mothers who were not unresolved… Several other investigators have examined the relation between FR behaviour and infant disorganization. In a study of members of the Dogan ethnic group conducted in Mali, True and her colleagues found that a simplified assessment of FR behaviour, as recorded in the field or hut setting, was impressively associated with disorganized attachment in the strange situation (True, Pisani and Oumar 2001). (p.1116)

We now consider examples of both aspects of insensitive parenting.

Extremely insensitive and disconnected parental behaviour

Compared with children with organized attachments, caregivers of children with disorganized attachments have very different caregiving systems. They are either extremely insensitive in their caregiving, disconnected in their caregiving or they display very anomalous or disrupted caregiving behaviour. In an attachment context, *extremely insensitive parenting* is described as withdrawal, neglect, unresponsiveness (with regards to the child's need), lack of interaction or, conversely, over-intrusiveness and over-stimulation, aggression, rough handling, hitting, pushing and extremely hostile language. *Disconnected parenting* is taken to mean sudden and unpredictable changes in behaviour, not preceded by any explanatory gestures or vocalizations, and unaccompanied by signs of affection or playfulness. An aspect of dissociated parenting, anomalous or disrupted caregiving, is taken to mean frightened or frightening behaviour combined with disruptive affective communication.

Combined with dissociation or with maternal insecurity of attachment (paternal insecurity of attachment has yet to be examined in the same context), these types of caregiving, often triggered by the memory or a new incidence of unresolved loss or trauma, are mediated through the caregiver's low capacity for RF. The caregiver is unable to envisage or understand how the child will experience this caregiving and the child has only a very limited model from which to learn how to mentalize, leaving him or her unable to comprehend the behaviour of the attachment figure. Often, the consequence is that the child will develop a disorganized attachment to his or her caregiver, with or without the presence of actual maltreatment, but, in any event, children with disorganized attachments are often maltreated and children subject to maltreatment are often found to have a disorganized attachment to their abuser (Carlson *et al.* 1989).

Disrupted parental behaviours were then added by Karlen Lyons-Ruth and her colleagues (Bronfman *et al.* 2004) when she developed the Atypical Maternal Behaviour Instrument for Assessment and Classification (AMBIANCE).

The need to differentiate Ainsworth's sensitivity scale more accurately was identified in the first (1999) edition of the *Handbook of Attachment* by Karlen Lyons-Ruth and Deborah Jacobvitz and this has arguably now been achieved in the pioneering work by Dorothee Out and colleagues. (Because the Disconnected and extremely Insensitive

Parenting Measure is so comprehensive and clearly defined it is reproduced in full at the end of this chapter.) They found only a tenuous
connection between disconnected and extremely insensitive caregiving,
which tells us that the two factors are actually different: 'disconnected'
parenting predicted infant DA, whereas 'extreme insensitivity' was only
loosely associated with it. As the primary purpose of research is to explain behaviour, not just report it, here are the illuminating thoughts
of the authors about the pernicious effect of 'disconnected' parenting
behaviours, which are thought to be

> directly frightening, especially because their appearance is sudden,
> unpredictable and out of context... Even the infant may trigger
> disconnected parental behaviours when his or her behaviour reminds
> the parent of the traumatic experience... Consequently, at high levels
> of intensity or in stressful situations, disconnected behaviours are
> hypothesized to be extremely frightening for the infant. The infant
> is not free to approach the parent for comfort and repair and is left
> in a disorganizing state of fright without solution... From the child's
> point of view, disconnected behaviours appear suddenly and out of
> context, interfering with the parent's normal (and possibly warm and
> sensitive) way of interacting with the child. (Out *et al.* 2009, p.235)

Examples of disconnected parenting

What has become increasingly clear, therefore, is that extremely insensitive and intrusive parenting is only part of the story; equally damaging
– and sometimes more so, depending on the temperament and genetic
makeup of the child – are parents who are disconnected when parenting
a child. This is more akin to neglectful behaviour and, consequently, is
less amenable to illustration than the more active and intrusive forms of
'extremely insensitive' parenting. Hesse and Main's (2000) article about
parental frightening behaviour towards their children makes for sombre
reading and we draw on it in this section because, as will become apparent, it is impossible to paraphrase the examples they give. As we have
seen in other studies, going back to Main and Solomon's (1990) initial
findings from the Strange Situation Procedure, they picked out 'inexplicable, odd, disorganized, disoriented, or overtly conflicted behaviours
in the parent's presence' (Hesse and Main 2000, p.1102), which they
coded as 'unclassifiable'. Karlen Lyons-Ruth points to the following
example: 'early on, [Janie] shared one particularly vivid incident in her

relationship with her father when she was six or seven years old. They were having fun playing in a pool when he suddenly held her underwater for a frighteningly long period; when he finally let her go, he was laughing' (Lyons-Ruth and Spielman 2004, p.328).

Some people may retort by wondering whether this is taking things too far and is redolent of an intrusive nanny state – 'Can't we have a joke with our children any more without some child protection official saying that we are abusing them?' But, in this example, the father wasn't *playing* with his daughter: he was terrifying her, whether or not that was his intention. It is the way the child perceives the 'play' that is so important. If the father had looked closely at his daughter, who would have shown clear signs of being upset, he could have corrected any misunderstanding.

What must have bemused researchers who discovered disconnected parenting – especially when they witnessed it at 'soberingly' high levels in low-risk samples – was that when invited to reflect on the session soon afterwards many of the parents observed had little or no recollection of what they had been doing with their child. Returning to an earlier study by Ainsworth and Eichberg in 1991, Erik Hesse and Mary Main (2000) refer to 'a particularly dramatic example of a lapse in reasoning in a high-functioning individual':

> Immediately upon being asked about loss, one woman responded 'Yes, there was a little man'…and then began to cry. The person 'lost' was an elderly workman who had been employed briefly by her parents when she was eight years old. Jokingly, he had asked her to marry him when she grew up, and she replied 'No…you'd be dead'. (p.1112)

Two features were noted, which recur in more recent studies: she seemed unable to rationalize and correct – 'metacognitively monitor' – what she had said; indeed she seemed *unaware* of what she had just said, and she spoke in a noticeably different voice – in fact, as a child might have said it. The attendant 'dissociation', unresolved loss and oscillating but unmonitored change of 'voice' is a recurring theme in parents who exhibit 'extremely insensitive' parenting (Out *et al.* 2009). Not surprisingly perhaps, this mother's own child was coded as 'Disorganized'.

Sometimes this kind of parenting will be observed in 'naturally occurring' situations and we now give two examples. The central feature is the 'unpresence', as distinct from the 'absence', of the parent. We both felt unnerved by what we saw, which made us powerfully aware of what it must have felt like for the children concerned.

Case study 7.1 Disorganized attachment in a naturally occurring situation 1

One of us (David) was travelling up a long escalator on the London Underground. About a quarter of the way down the other escalator was a mother with her young son who was, at a guess, around five or six years old. She was talking to her friend, and suddenly her son broke free and proceeded to run down the remaining stairs. She shouted to him – but in a very deep, croaky, monotone voice, rather like a Dalek and, obviously, quite unlike her normal speaking voice – a series of injunctions and commands, but which didn't actually make any sense as they were muffled by her extremely bizarre tones, which sounded terrifying and certainly not at all funny. Her behaviour frightened everyone on the escalator (including her friend). Her son just froze, stared ahead and then just proceeded, motionless, on the escalator, as it descended. Fortunately another traveller picked him up as he got to the end (otherwise his tiny feet could have got caught under the grille). He continued to stare ahead; he didn't cry or respond to the helpful traveller; he didn't greet his mother when she arrived at the bottom. She just grabbed his hand and carried on talking to her friend, whose jaw was by now near the floor.

Case study 7.2 Disorganized attachment in a naturally occurring situation 2

We were travelling on a bus when a mother got on with her toddler in a buggy. As we were sitting in the areas marked for parents and young children, we offered her the seat. She declined, replying she could 'manage OK'. She was perfectly pleasant, and was reading a book. Her little boy began to whimper and then cry a little more strongly, at which point she stared at her child for about a minute (but what seemed like an eternity), rather like one of those 'human statues' that remain unnervingly motionless whatever the crowd around them does to bait, goad or generally communicate with them. The child's cries became more insistent, so the mother then almost imperceptibly turned up her top lip. Her eyes then widened a little, which had the effect of removing an appearance of disgust only to replace it with a face that created an impression of overwhelming ghostly terror. The child stopped crying and appeared to be in a trance. Immediate passengers noticed this and were visibly shocked. We were just about to say something when a man, unrelated to her, but standing close by, smiled at her. She smiled back and then smiled at her son…who carried on looking terrified (we don't know for how long, as we needed to get off at the next stop). From the research, if we had filmed the scenario (which we didn't!) and then played it back to her, the chances are that she would not have recalled doing it. We had probably witnessed an example of unresolved loss or trauma, played out in a dissociated form with her son as 'disconnected parenting'.

But why is extreme insensitivity different? Erik Hesse and Mary Main suggested that when parents are insensitive, but not *directly* frightening, 'the infant can develop "conditional strategies" for coping with the limitations or restrictions imposed by parental behaviour' (Hesse and Main 2000, p.1117). It needed Dorothee Out and colleagues' empirical study to tease out more precisely the linkages between variables.

Karlen Lyons-Ruth outlines two additional hypotheses about the precise nature of parental behaviours that lead to infant disorganized attachment: first, unresolved states of mind – not simply frightening/ frightened reactions – on the part of a parent may go some way to explain what is actually happening; and, second, the way a parent fails to help a child regulate his or her own fearful experiences may also be a factor. In this way, 'parental withdrawing behaviours or role-confusing behaviours that leave the infant without adequate parental regulation of fearful affect would also be potentially disorganizing, *whether or not the parent's own behaviour was directly frightened or frightening to the infant*' (Lyons-Ruth 2003, p.889, emphasis added). As we have seen, an additional dimension to these findings is that frightening behaviour may be a mediating or moderating explanatory mechanism for *insecure* carers only (van IJzendoorn *et al.* 1999): research with low-risk samples 'may indicate that secure attachment operates as a protective factor in high-risk environments' (Deklyen and Greenberg 2008, p.647).

Working with disorganized attachment

The implications for professionals working with disorganized attachment are numerous. Although people with disorganized attachment histories are generally thought to have mostly non-integrated representations of the self and others, whatever fragile level of integration is present can suddenly collapse under situations of stress or trauma, especially when related to separation or loss. This can activate confused, unstable working models of attachment and attachment behaviour (Fonagy and Target 1997). Therefore, child protection social workers, whose very involvement with a family implies a significantly increased risk of separation through the possibility of children being removed from carers, or counsellors attempting to help an individual understand his or her own behaviour, may stir up intense feelings of shame, hate or anger, essentially deriving from a fear of abandonment in childhood. This will be worsened if the individual concerned experiences the fear without a sense of possible resolution. Indeed, by playing the part of 'being the source of the fear', the social worker or other helping professional will only be confirming the internal working model of such individuals, who will already be expecting those purporting to be able to help and protect to also and at the same time be the source of the danger.

Simply being aware of these potential issues is not enough. The professional needs to appreciate that a carer with a history of disorganized attachments cannot be helped simply by the application of what would otherwise be 'good enough' relationship standards – that is, being sensitive, respectful, keeping one's word, etc. Essentially, such individuals have a persistent sense of insecurity and mistrust and are likely to be unable to enter into a committed and mature relationship, whether with their children, their ageing carers, a partner or a helping professional. They may initially behave in an engaged and open way, but then withdraw suddenly or actively denigrate the work. The information provided by them may be contradictory, especially when referring to relationships – for example, describing their family as 'the nicest people in the world', before recounting how their mother or father was mean and lived a sad life (Gubman 2004). This contradiction will often go unnoticed by individuals and they may react defensively if challenged. Indeed, they may well question their need for professional help at all, since they had 'such a happy childhood' and a 'fulfilling adult experience of relationships'. They may blame others for being insensitive or demanding of them whilst simultaneously blaming themselves for being unworthy of sensitive or undemanding relationships.

When working with such adults, professionals are not simply working with people as they present now but also with all of their difficult experiences of attachment relationships and representations. Models of the transmission of attachment have attempted to capture some of the levels of influence on current attachment representations and many people with histories of disorganized attachments will have had challenging experiences at every level of the model (Bakermans-Kranenburg and van IJzendoorn 1997).

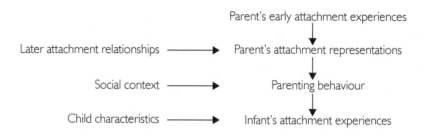

Figure 7.1 A model of attachment transmission

Looking at the top half of the model in Figure 7.1, adults with histories of disorganized attachments are likely to have had significantly difficult if not actually abusive early attachment experiences. In addition they are likely subsequently to have had difficult attachment relationships, leading to very conflicted and hostile attachment representations. The social context in which they are living may well be very challenging in terms of lower levels of educational achievement and a higher likelihood of lower socio-economic status (especially if they have come to the notice of child welfare services). It is within this web of complexity that the helping professional is hoping to intervene.

Working with people with a history of disorganized attachment is always going to prove challenging and difficult, not least because the individuals in need of help will oscillate between being apparently desperate for help, to blaming everyone else – especially the professional – for their difficulties, to indicating they have only themselves to blame for what has gone wrong for them. People with histories of disorganized attachments are also likely to be resistant to conventional methods of intervention. As we will see in the next chapter, recent evidence indicates that working with individual carers with these types of histories is more successful when a mentalizing professional discusses filmed recordings of them actually parenting their own child; such targeted, highly skilled interventions appear to lead to marked changes surprisingly quickly.

The Disconnected and extremely Insensitive Parenting Measure: dimensions and categories (Out et al. 2009)

Dimension 1. Disconnected behaviour (adapted from Main and Hesse 1998)

Frightening/threatening parental behaviours

- Pursuit movements, assumption of attack postures, attacking or threatening to attack.

Frightened parental behaviours

- Parent suddenly retreats from the child or startles in response to the child's behaviour.

- Parent appears frightened by the child, indicated by a frightened facial expression, comments to or about the child and/or by posture and movements.

Dissociative parental behaviours

- Stilling or freezing in trance-like posture with trance-like expression.

- Voice alterations.

- Handling as though the child is an inanimate object, and other handling indicating lack of sense of child's animate status.

- Sudden inexplicable and unpredictable change or shifts in mood.

- The parent shows inexplicable fear regarding aspects of environment which have no intrinsically frightening aspects.

Deferential and romantic/sexualized behaviours

- Handling the child or interacting with the child in a timid, submissive and/or deferential manner.

- The parent is overly responsive, deferential and submissive in response to the child's anger, rejection or displeasure.

- The parent fails to stop the child from parent-directed aggression.

- Spousal/romantic and sexualized behaviours.

Disorganized/disoriented parental behaviours

- Simultaneous and sequential contradictions in behaviour and/ or vocalizations.

- Anomalous movements and postures.

- Disoriented parental behaviours.

Dimension 2. Extreme insensitivity (adapted from Bronfman et al. 2004)

Parental withdrawal and neglect

- Failure to initiate responsive behaviour to the child

  o When the child is in distress, the parent does not respond or the parent's response is too minimal.

  o The parent does not intervene when the child engages in potentially dangerous or harmful behaviour.

  o The parent does not respond to the child's repeated vocalizations and cues.

- Actively creating physical distance from the child

  o When the child is in distress, the parent actively creates physical distance from the child.

  o When the child seeks contact or approaches the parent, the parent responds in such a way as to create distance from the child.

- Lack of interaction between parent and child

Intrusive, negative, aggressive or otherwise harsh parental behaviours

- Intrusiveness

  o The parent displays physically intrusive behaviours towards the child.

- Rough, negative, aggressive or otherwise harsh parental behaviours

    o The parent handles the child in a rough and insensitive way.

    o The parent displays aggressive behaviours towards the child.

    o The parent makes negative, rejecting or hostile comments concerning the child or to the child.

Part 3

THEORY AND RESEARCH INTO PRACTICE

Chapter 8 (with David Phillips)

What Produces Successful Interventions?

Introduction

There are two major and significant reviews into the relationship between interventions and organized and disorganized attachment security. They have both been undertaken by Marian Bakermans-Kranenburg, Marinus van IJzendoorn and Femmie Juffer at Leiden University and they are both meta-analyses of previous studies. The first is called 'Less is more: Meta-analyses of sensitivity and attachment interventions in early childhood' (2003) and involved analysing 70 published studies which included 88 intervention effects on sensitivity (N = 7636) and attachment (N = 1503). This meta-analysis did not focus specifically on disorganized attachment but, because one of the types of intervention – video feedback with the carer – led to positive changes in disorganized attachment, a second meta-analysis was undertaken entitled 'Disorganized infant attachment and preventive interventions: A review and meta-analysis' (2005).

We now consider each of these meta-analyses in turn and conclude with an example of one of the most promising interventions: the *Video-feedback Intervention to promote Positive Parenting* (VIPP), designed and pioneered at Leiden University.

First meta-analysis (2003): 'Less is more'

The combined sample was coded with respect to design, sample and intervention characteristics. *Design characteristics* comprised: sample size, randomization, whether a control group was established, and attrition rate. *Sample characteristics* consisted of: economic status, whether the carer was referred by a professional, and whether the carer was considered to be a 'high risk' (poverty, social isolation, single parenthood). *Intervention characteristics* were: number of sessions, the child's age, whether the facilitator was a trained professional, whether the intervention took place at the carer's home, and whether video feedback was used (as this was thought to be a likely intervening variable). Lastly the intervention was coded as: aimed at increasing carer sensitivity, aimed at changing the carer's mental representation, providing social support, and, finally, any combination of these three approaches.

First, *sensitivity-based* interventions operate from Mary Ainsworth's formulation that 'sensitivity' involves two features: (i) perceiving and interpreting the child's signals correctly and (ii) reacting to them quickly and well (enough). Different sensitivity-based approaches tend to concentrate more on one of these two components.

Second, *representationally based* interventions are altogether different because they attempt to get the carer to explore and, it is hoped, change his or her working models of attachment relationships. They are in one sense insight-based and founded on psychodynamic principles and beliefs that lasting change – in this case in terms of changing caregiver skills, capacity and competence – will only occur if the individual processes more effectively his or her past and present attachment relationships. Representationally based approaches rely on child–parent or parent-focused psychotherapy whereas sensitivity-based interventions use methods such as 'speaking for the baby' or 'minding the baby' (to which we return later in this chapter).

Third, programmes based on *social support* offer practical help and advice, and are relationship-based, in the main using Rogerian principles to engage family members by building trust. Later on, when trust has developed sufficiently, project workers will model positive caregiver behaviour with children. In some senses the popular TV series *Supernanny* epitomizes the latter component of approaches aimed at developing and sustaining social support.

The results showed that 'interventions can enhance maternal sensitivity and infant attachment security, but infant attachment security to a lesser extent than maternal sensitivity. In particular, interventions that only focussed on sensitive maternal behaviour were successful in improving insensitive parenting as well as infant attachment security' (Bakermans-Kranenburg and van IJzendoorn 2007, p.73). Furthermore, very specific and clear interventions were far more effective than 'broadband interventions'; hence, the main title of the resulting paper: 'Less is more'. Family characteristics counted for little in determining outcomes, although interventions aimed at infants less than six months of age were much less effective (it is suggested because to do so disrupts a process which is often assumed by the mother to be 'natural' – but the authors admit this is only a speculative explanation).

Interventions aimed at increasing carer sensitivity were more effective than any others in reducing levels of attachment disorganization, but attachment insecurity in general appears to be more difficult to change than carer sensitivity. The authors point out, however, that this may be due to an insufficient time-lag between measurements: increased carer sensitivity may take a while to translate into lower levels of attachment disorganization in the infant. Interventions aimed at modifying carers' representations of themselves and their infants were less effective than perhaps some practitioners would have expected; interestingly, interventions that combined both approaches fared no better.

Second meta-analysis (2005): preventing disorganized attachment

In the second meta-analysis, 10 studies with 15 interventions were analysed but this time the aim was to review specifically whether the interventions studied could be related directly to disorganized attachment. Although no studies at the time of their review had been focused specifically on 'preventing disorganized attachment', the 15 selected all included DA behaviour as outcome measures.

The types of interventions in both meta-analyses were varied but always had as their 'golden thread' that of being 'attachment-based' (rather than, say, 'parenting education' approaches). In the second study it was again convenient to sub-divide the approaches into those that were 'sensitivity-based' and those that were 'representationally based'.

Even though this second review includes more narrative detail about the approaches analysed, the results are remarkably similar to those found on the first meta-analytic study: the most effective interventions were those that did not start until the infant was six months of age and when a *sensitivity-based* approach was deployed. The only additional finding that emerged was that more risk-intense infant characteristics (such as being adopted) were associated with a greater reduction in disorganized attachment behaviour than characteristics associated with the parent.

Sensitivity-based approaches were routinely more effective than others at reducing attachment disorganization because 'interventions that teach parents to follow their children's lead or to observe their children by means of video-feedback focus parents' attention on the children's behaviour, *thereby diminishing dissociative processes in the presence of the children*' (Bakermans-Kranenburg and van IJzendoorn 2007, p.198, emphasis added). They were also thought to be have been successful because they directed parents' attentional focus onto the immediate situation in which the child found itself.

Other reasons for the marked differences were that, compared with representationally based approaches, the more precisely and behaviourally focused nature of sensitivity-based intervention may hold the key. Also, facilitators often found sensitivity-based approaches easier to follow and implement.

It will be of little comfort – but probably come as no surprise – to social workers and others trying to help dysfunctional families that it 'might be easier to prevent or change disorganised attachment when the parent is relatively well-functioning and free of psychopathology' (Bakermans-Kranenburg *et al.* 2005, p.208) because the parent is more likely to see the problems, want to address them and also work collaboratively with the professional.

Both meta-analyses point to the importance of interrupting parental non-involved or intrusive behaviour and frightened, frightening or dissociative caregiver behaviour and this is likely to feature in intervention programmes aimed at preventing disorganized attachment behaviour in children in the future. As infant disorganized attachment is a powerful predictor of a range of subsequent mental illnesses, the design and evaluation of more proven effective interventions would seem to be justified at both the individual and policy level.

Some sensitivity-based approaches are similar to mentalization-based interventions and we now consider these in more detail.

Mentalization-based approaches with caregivers

Before we conclude this chapter with an example of an attachment-based intervention – the VIPP – we provide a brief review of mentalization-based approaches because there are, in our view, some similarities. As we have seen already in Chapter 6, adults who find mentalization difficult are likely to respond with minimalist attempts at answering Adult Attachment Interview (AAI) type questions aimed at giving them an opportunity to reflect. Here is an example:

Q: *Why do you think your parents behaved as you did?*

A: I've no idea...you're the social worker.

Of course, this could have been said in a belligerent, irritated way, and not be indicative of low mentalization at all, but the professional would be in a good position to assess this. But it's also worth remembering, however, that hostility towards the AAI interviewer – but we accept that a social worker, for example, may not be perceived to be in the same role – can be an indicator of attachment insecurity and low reflective function. Consider another example (modified from Fonagy 2008, p.50):

Q: *Do you think your childhood experiences have influenced you in any way?*

A: Nothing really springs to mind at the moment...no, nothing in particular...no, nothing I can think of at the moment.

Again, assuming this was not simply a reflection of the caregiver's irritation with the professional's power, the response indicates a lack of curiosity, rather than simply a memory lapse, which is one of a number of markers of low mentalization. Peter Fonagy lists a number of 'elements of the mentalizing stance', the opposite of which, therefore, imply low mentalization: 'i) inquisitiveness, curiosity and open-mindedness; ii) uncertainty, not-knowing and an interest in understanding better; iii) consistent focus on the mind of the person; iv) adaptation of interaction to the person's mentalizing capacity; v) orientation toward generating alternative perspectives; vi) authenticity' (Fonagy 2008, p.183).

An individual's restricted capacity for mentalization can be expressed non-verbally, as a powerful visual example by Alicia Lieberman (2004) attests. She described a three-year-old boy who came for an assessment with his mother; he was dressed as a 'punk', with a spiky hairstyle, a black leather jacket and a skull-and-crossbones sign painted on the back. Lieberman describes him as looking like a 'diminutive gang member' (p.108). Social workers will sometimes retort by saying that we shouldn't criticize people's lifestyles, but the point here is that the toddler isn't expressing his lifestyle preference: his mother is expressing *hers, through him.* To reinforce the point that this is such an extreme projection of her state of mind, Alicia Lieberman tells us that the mother's son resulted from her being raped at gunpoint. She remembered an occasion when her son sought comfort from her. She said to the worker,

'See? What did I tell you? He just pretends to need me, but he is really mean' (Lieberman 2004, p.108).

When working to increase a caregiver's mentalizing capacity there are two key conditions which have to be met: first, the professional aims to focus the person's mind on to *someone else's* mind – often the *professional's*; second, to develop mentalizing capacity, an individual needs to receive regularly mentalized experiences *from the professional*. In one sense, the experience is rather like a bi-directional empathic interplay, with both partners trying to understand each other's state of mind.

The idea of the caregiver being invited to consider what it is in the *professional's* mind may be an unfamiliar one to many, especially those trained within the Rogerian paradigm, where regular empathic responses from the practitioner are considered *de rigueur*. So, for example, someone who becomes angry with the professional would most likely receive a response along the lines of 'When I did/said (X), this makes you angry because...' A mentalized response would look more like this: 'I'm finding it really difficult to hear what you are saying at the moment – and I very much want to. Can I ask that you stop shouting as I can't concentrate and I know I'm likely to become a bit defensive.' Then, assuming the person *does* stop...or at least calms down sufficiently... 'If I've done something to upset you I'd really like to know what it is, because I may be able to explain myself better or stop doing what's upsetting you.'

An example will illustrate this approach more directly. A social worker visited a mother (we'll call her Jean) who quickly became angry with her, but not, so it seemed, about anything specific. Jean admits that she 'can often fly off the handle at nothing'. All of a sudden, apparently out of the blue, Jean railed against the worker, along these lines: 'Who do you think you are? You get on my nerves, coming here in your brand new green car. You have no idea what it's like for me living on this estate. It's a dump.' The mother had, in fact, become very close to the worker and had already said that she could talk to her about aspects of her life that she'd never discussed before. The worker asked the mother (gently but firmly, and without any hint of annoyance) if she could try and stop shouting, and offered to make a cup of tea for her and find her favourite chocolate biscuits. When a sufficient amount of calm had ensued, the worker said: 'I'm really sorry if I've said or done something to upset you, Jean. I'd like you to try and tell me what it was but could you explain one thing first please: am I correct in thinking that you believe that I am kind of rubbing your nose in it when I pull up in my new car?' If Jean apologizes, they can then both reflect on what happened and how it might relate to any patterns around anger expression. If, on the other hand, Jean holds her ground and continues with the point about the car, then the worker will need to explore this non-defensively – 'How and when did this develop?', etc. – but the key question that the worker and Jean need to discuss is 'What does Jean think is in the *worker's* mind, when she drives up in her new car?' Provided the worker can explore this openly – as it is possible that she *is* unwittingly giving this impression – it is likely to reveal problems with mentalization. The point of this approach is to encourage Jean to mentalize with the worker, not for the worker *solely* to empathize with Jean.

It is important that the worker is able sensitively to challenge Jean… but if she becomes hectoring or confrontational, she will miss opportunities to model the desired approach; the worker will also need to mentalize with Jean's thoughts and emotions in a gentle, confident and 'boundaried' way. The aim here is to help Jean see that 'the same behaviour may be experienced differently and thought about differently by different minds' (Fonagy 2008, p.189). Furthermore, the aim is not that of raising insight about why they hold a particular view of the worker 'but rather to engender curiosity as to why, given the ambiguity of interpersonal situations, they choose and stick to a particular version. In wondering why they might be doing this, we help them give up the rigid, schematic…mode of interpreting their subjectivity and others' behaviour' (Fonagy 2008, p.189).

Such novel, possibly even skewed, thinking starts a process of reviewing inflexible forms of logic – and especially *psycho*logic – which permits the worker to introduce ideas to free people from the shackles of non-mentalized thinking. The aim is almost to *surprise* people with new insights and fresh ways of seeing things, through the different lens that a mentalization-based approach offers. The individual progressively moves out of his or her mind into another's by being gently nudged into considering questions such as 'What do you think might have been in his/her mind for him/her to do that?' and 'What indications did you see to make you think s/he was thinking this way?'

Remembering that this is very difficult for some people, the worker needs to be tentative and move slowly. Peter Fonagy urges us to avoid non-mentalizing words and phrases such as 'clearly', 'obviously', 'what you mean is' and 'it seems to me that what you are saying is' but 'this is not quite the same as merely encouraging tentativeness – which is a worthwhile trait for a professional to develop anyway' (Fonagy 2008, p.194). He advises instead phrases such as 'I'm getting the impression that...', 'I'm wondering if...', 'It occurs to me that...' and 'Here is what I'm thinking...', 'When you brought that up, I started feeling...', 'Have you considered the possibility that...' (Fonagy 2008, pp.186–187).

Arietta Slade brings a mentalization-based approach into her *Minding the Baby* intervention (the double-meaning is intended). It has attracted interest because of the way it incorporates theoretical principles directly into practice. She starts off by inviting the caregiver to describe the kinds of feelings a baby might have, and why. Here is an example in which a caregiver needs help to make sense of her baby's behaviour.

Case study 8.1 Low RF in a naturally occurring situation

One of us (David) is behind a very young mother in a supermarket check-out queue. Her baby is only a few days old and is beginning to cry uncontrollably. The mother gets progressively flustered and within seconds raises her voice (but to no-one in particular) and says 'He f...g does this on purpose to get at me, the little b...d'. David offered to help her with the packing and loading and both he and the checkout worker tried to divert her attention (asking the baby's name, finding out how old it was, etc.). But if he had been professionally involved it would have been important to establish whether she could identify other reasons why a new-born infant might cry, without relying on attributions about its state of mind that it couldn't possibly hold at such a young age. It would have been interesting to see whether she would have said that her baby wasn't hungry simply because the *mother* had eaten recently (i.e. can she separate her own intentional states from another's?).

Lois Sadler and colleagues, based at Yale University and working on the *Minding the Baby* Project, come to the rather sobering conclusion that 'understanding that the baby *has* feelings and desires is an achievement for most of our mothers' (Sadler, Slade and Mayes 2006, p.280). They continue:

One mother, for example, began to tease her child when he cried after catching his finger in the door. 'You're a faker' she exclaimed, mocking him. The home visitor gently spoke for the baby: 'Ooh, that hurt. You're kinda scared and want Mommy to make it feel better.'

Thus, she was first trying to help mother to *accurately* perceive the child's intention. (Sadler *et al.* 2006, p.282, original emphasis)

We conclude this chapter with a more detailed outline of the *Video-feedback Intervention to promote Positive Parenting and Sensitive Discipline* (VIPP-SD) in practice. It is written by David Phillips, a key member of the ADAM Project.

Case study 8.2 Using video feedback to promote sensitive discipline

Introduction – speaking for the child
Our Family Centre Service has used ideas from attachment theory to provide a useful map to help us make sense of parent–child relationships and assess significant harm to young minds. Along with techniques such as Story Stem profiling and Child Attachment Interviews, we have been using camcorders and feedback discussions to help assess parenting capacity. An episode of parent–child interaction is filmed in the family home (or for children subject to care proceedings during supervised contact at the Centre) and later parents are encouraged to 'speak for the child', by providing subtitles for the behaviour of their child on screen.

This attunement exercise has proved useful in exploring parents' understanding of their child's developmental needs (for example, whether or not they place negative attributions on age-appropriate behaviour) and clarifying their capacity to be reflective and 'mind-minded' about their child's inner world of thoughts and feelings.

Many parents report that seeing a mirror of themselves and their child on screen is a powerful and revealing experience. For those watching positive interactions this can be delightful and affirming; for others watching negative images it can have the opposite effect. Coincidentally, the one element of the Webster-Stratton 'Incredible Years' (Webster-Stratton et al. 2001) parenting programme that we run jointly with the Child and Adolescent Mental Health Service (CAMHS) that some parents report difficulty connecting with was watching video clips of *other* people and *their* children. Until recently we've used this video feedback technique for assessment purposes only and not as part of a structured intervention that might promote parental sensitivity.

However, at the Centre for Child and Family Studies at Leiden University, Femmie Juffer, Marian Bakermans-Kranenburg and Marinus van IJzendoorn have developed a programme based on video feedback whose effectiveness has been demonstrated in randomized control trials and pre- and post-tests (Juffer, Bakermans-Kranenburg and van IJzendoorn 2008b). The latest version of their programme – *Video-feedback Intervention to promote Positive Parenting and Sensitive Discipline* (VIPP-SD)

– is aimed at increasing the sensitivity and discipline strategies of parents to prevent or reduce behavioural problems with children aged one to four years. Prospective facilitators receive intensive training and practice exercises in VIPP-SD, and learn how to use a detailed manual on the VIPP-SD. There is also a VIPP-SD website: www.leidenattachment researchprogram.eu/vipp/en.

The VIPP-SD programme is carried out in the family's home and consists of seven home visits of approximately 60 to 90 minutes each. After the preliminary assessment session, the remaining six visits follow the same structure, starting with a recording session, after which the recordings of the previous visit are viewed and discussed. The two themes of *sensitivity* and *discipline* run throughout the programme. Even though the intervention follows a standard protocol, it becomes specifically aimed at the particular parent–child relationship when giving feedback to the parent regarding the recordings.

In the Family Centre Service we're starting to pilot the programme with families considered hard to reach, help and change and where young children are subject to protection plans due to physical and emotional abuse as well as neglect. Many of these parents have very low RF and difficult relationships, not just with their children but also with partners and helping agencies.

Theoretical framework of VIPP-SD

The VIPP-SD programme is rooted in attachment theory and ideas from Bowlby and Ainsworth; in particular the relation between parental sensitivity and attachment security. The central theme is that, for an infant to learn to recognize and regulate his or her own feelings, the parent needs to show contingent marked mirroring. For normal development the child also needs to experience a mind that has his or her mind in mind. The parent needs to be able to react to the child's intentions and behaviours accurately and to not overwhelm the child.

The programme also incorporates Patterson's 'coercive cycle' (Patterson 1982). This model describes how a child escapes a parental request through escalating negative behaviour and the parent escapes his or her child's tantrum by escalating yelling or physical aggression and, crucially, finally gives in to the child's demands. Behaviour is better improved by positive rather than negative consequences yet parents usually provide less attention to positive behaviour. The model explains how negative or aggressive child behaviour is inadvertently rewarded and reinforced by parents.

Overview of the working method

A cornerstone of the VIPP-SD programme is the use of film as a revealing and reinforcing mirror. The process of seeing themselves and their child in the mirror provides the opportunity for parents to reflect on and make sense of their own and their child's behaviour (for example, 'What do you think your child is feeling here?' 'Do you think s/he understands what you want him/her to do?'). To use Peter Fonagy's term, this process helps the parent to mentalize.

The method used also has an empowering effect by emphasizing and building on the parent's strengths. By pausing and replaying the film the parent's attention is focused on specific moments of positive inter-action (for example, 'What a lovely moment, look how s/he enjoys play-ing with you. A toy doesn't smile back but you do!').[1] Repeating positive moments, perhaps with only fleeting eye contact at first, is rewarding for parents struggling with their role. The technique enables parents, per-haps for the first time, to see themselves as being competent. ('Here you are sharing a moment together, looking at each other. This is important as it helps him/her feel understood. You are very important to him/her.')

The technique also enables a parent, again perhaps for the first time, to learn to read his or her child's signals more accurately and have more realistic expectations (for example, 'Looking at it again, do you think s/he had finished playing with that? Adults know just by looking at a toy what it does. A child needs to learn and discover everything for the first time, which can be time-consuming').

It is difficult to overstate the impact this technique can have. In my own thus far limited but swiftly developing practice experience, this has appeared to trigger in several parents a fledgling sense of self-belief that they can make changes after all. In this way, by positively reinforc-ing sensitive behaviour shown on the film, parents become their own models of intervention. In addition, increased parental sensitivity to their child's signals is rewarded by a more responsive child. By reinforcing his or her parent's sensitive behaviour in a positive feedback loop the child becomes a 'co-facilitator' in the programme.

As with any other parenting programme, the effectiveness of the intervention is at least partly dependent on how it is delivered. The VIPP-SD guidelines stress the importance of preparation, and building and maintaining a confident, relaxed, professional relationship with the parent. Programme facilitators are trained not to adopt an expert model of parenting, but rather parents are considered to possess pockets of expertise about their own children and encouraged to discover and then solve their own problems. However, facilitators do bring in their own professional knowledge of child development and parenting.

Facilitators are advised against promoting too much interaction with the child, as the aim of the intervention is to help build the parent's rela-tionship with the child, not the worker's. At the start of the programme negative interactions are deliberately not addressed so as to keep a

---

1   All citations are from/based on the VIPP-SD manual.

clear focus on the child's perspective and on the positive moments. In later sessions negative interactions are addressed by suggesting alternative positive solutions, preferably from the parent's own behaviour repertoire. There is a further expectation that the facilitator maintains a neutral position, listening to the parent but not being drawn into long conversations about subjects not part of the intervention. However, sharing heightened and joyful moments with the parent during the video feedback helps the facilitator build a close alliance. One advantage of the short-term nature of the intervention, only seven home visits in total, is that both parent and facilitator remain motivated to work hard together.

Delivering the programme requires formal training, and additional preparation and practice. Initially there is a lot to juggle with: working the DVD player, stopping the film in the right place, using the time code, keeping to the manual, making the points you want to make while still maintaining an interactive approach with parents and remaining alert to their responses. For example, anxious to skip over negative material and focus on the next positive interaction, I had not been prepared for a parent to suddenly request that I pause the film instead. However, she had noticed that her child appeared tired and this led her to reflect that perhaps the child had not been deliberately disobedient as she had first thought.

Structure and content of the intervention
The VIPP-SD programme is divided into three phases, each containing two sessions. Phase One (home visits 1 and 2) focuses entirely on the child's behaviour. The facilitator starts with the first part of Ainsworth's definition of sensitivity: accurately perceiving the child's behavioural signals. Exercises are undertaken together with the parent to help him or her to observe, 'tune in' and empathize with the child's perspective. At the same time distraction and induction strategies are discussed that help to offer the child an alternative to disobedient behaviour.

Parents are also encouraged to praise their children and give them compliments when they behave in a positive way. When viewing the previous week's recordings positive interaction is highlighted, encouraged and reinforced.

In Phase Two (home visits 3 and 4) the behaviour of the parent when dealing with the child is also addressed directly. Here the facilitator continues with the second part of Ainsworth's sensitivity definition: prompt and adequate responding to the child's behavioural signals. The parent is shown how and when positive parenting behaviour is effective through the use of 'sensitivity chains' and the facilitator discusses how this positive behaviour can be used in different situations. Sensitive time-out is introduced as a way of dealing with a temper tantrum (we are encouraged to use an alternative phrase such as 'particularly difficult behaviour').

Phase Three consists of two booster sessions (home visits 5 and 6) in which all the themes are addressed again. The first four home visits have their own themes regarding sensitivity and discipline and each theme of the previous session is integrated into the following home visit.

Using the camcorder
Using a camcorder effectively takes a little practice. The five-day facilitator training does not include any filming, but advice is given and you quickly learn from mistakes. Camcorder tripods are too formal and intrusive; instead facilitators need to learn to hold the camera in a quiet and steady way. Sitting down and supporting the camera by resting your elbows on your knees works well. Getting down to child level is helpful too as it's important to film facial expressions and hand gestures of the child and parent, if possible.

Using a camcorder with a zoom lens is recommended as this enables you to sit far enough away not to interfere with the interaction but you still need to be close enough to capture the sound. Filming outside is not recommended; it's generally too noisy. Likewise it's sometimes necessary to ask for the TV or radio to be turned off as background noise interferes with the recording. Before starting you explain that you will not speak when filming. This can be difficult if the child tries to communicate with you but focusing on the camera or partially hiding your face behind it can help. Finally you are encouraged to end the recording at a quiet moment and if possible on a positive note, filming for a little longer if necessary. The importance of this becomes clear when you're watching the film back with the parent on the next visit.

Preliminary assessment visit
The manual provides clear and detailed instructions, including a suggested script for the facilitator to follow on each home visit. On the preliminary visit an explanation of the video feedback is given, something like, 'Each visit I will make a recording of your child and you together and also your child playing alone. In the beginning it can be quite difficult to play with your child or perform a task in front of the camera. Most people find this difficult, but try and act as you would normally do. I'll fit in with you. Next time I visit we will watch the film together.'

You are encouraged to bring your own selection of toys and story books for the recordings of all home visits as children usually get bored quicker and are less motivated to play together with their parent when using already familiar toys. New toys are more engaging and I have found that the recommended small selection – a few 'cause and effect' toys plus wooden building blocks, play pots and pans or a tea set, a furry animal and puzzle – works well.

During the preliminary visit it's further explained that all parents have to say 'no' to their children from time to time as not everything is allowed and that during the home visits we will look at those kinds of situation and give advice about how the parent might deal with difficult behaviour.

Three 'base-line' recordings are made at this preliminary visit; initially the child plays alone with an age-appropriate toy (3 minutes) and then the parent joins the child and they play together, following the introduction of a selection of toys (5 minutes). After these toys have been quickly cleared away, and without involving the child in the process, a third recording is made of the child not being allowed to touch a new selection of attractive toys (2 minutes). Once the filming has stopped the child is allowed to play with these toys for a short while.

At this initial recording parents are given the opportunity to choose where they play with their child and this is often illuminating. My experience so far has been that parents who do not sit to enable eye contact report not being used to playing with their child.

Using sensitivity scales to create a parent profile
The goal of the intervention is a 'sensitive' parent, as described by the Ainsworth scale (Ainsworth, Bell and Stayton 1974), that is, a parent who accurately observes, interprets the signals of his or her child correctly and reacts to them promptly and appropriately. More generally, a sensitive parent is one who: reacts responsively to the seeking of physical contact; who doesn't interfere when his or her child is exploring; who is responsive or affectionate when playing with the child and when the child needs comfort or support; and who is sensitive or empathetic when disciplining his or her child.

Using 14 sensitivity scale questions, an initial profile of the parent–child interaction is developed based on the ten minutes of recordings made during the preliminary visit. This is watched back with a time code, freeze-framing at significant moments. Positive and negative symbols are used as shorthand to highlight observations, and help identify what will be most important to focus on in the first intervention home visit.

These themes include the following: 'Noticing of signals, learning to observe', 'Reacting appropriately to positive signals', 'Thinking of alternative ways to react to negative symbols; not sticking to the same ineffective way of reacting', 'Giving explanations to the child in a sensitive way about why something is not allowed' and 'Reducing interfering or disturbing behaviour from the parent when the child is exploring or playing'.

I was initially sceptical that such short sequences would be useful; previous practice in the Family Centres had been to film interaction for 30–60 minutes. However, the training programme teaches you how to look at and analyse the micro-detail of parent–child interaction and short pictures become a rich source of material (perhaps another example of the VIPP-SD principle that 'Less is more').

Observing parent–child interaction is not a purely neutral, technical activity, however. We interpret the behaviour of others through our own lenses, influenced by our underlying beliefs, values and expectations. To accurately code these interactions using the sensitivity scales it is therefore necessary to develop increased self-awareness about your feelings towards the parent–child relationship you are observing and to consult with colleagues to get their views too. It is therefore advised to regularly meet with colleague VIPP-SD facilitators and discuss each other's families (*inter*vision, rather than supervision).

First intervention home visit – using the feedback script
The first intervention home visit focuses on continuing to build a trusting relationship with the parent while the facilitator uses the technique of 'speaking for the child' to promote the parent's accurate perception of his or her child's signals. This involves providing specific and detailed subtitles to the child's signals, feelings and behaviour on screen and encouraging the parent to do the same. The first and second intervention visits don't directly address the parent's behaviour at all but focus entirely on the child's perspective and behaviour.

The initial part of the first visit involves filming several activities including the child playing alone with toys (3 minutes), playing together with toys (4 minutes) and clearing up toys (2 minutes). The second part involves the video feedback based on the recordings that you made during the introductory session.

The VIPP-SD manual is very detailed and identifies the key themes to include in each video feedback script. For example, for the five-minute sequence of 'Playing together with toys' from the preliminary visit the feedback focus is on highlighting the difference between the child's *exploring signals* and *contact-seeking* or *attachment signals*.

Messages about exploring behaviour are given when the child is focused on or playing with the toys and might include comments like 'Look how curious s/he is about how this toy works', 'Play is like work for him/her, here s/he's really busy concentrating' or 'At this moment it looks like s/he wants to do this on his/her own.'

When speaking for the child you try to find the right words to describe the child's mood and expressions while you try to involve the parent in the process: 'Here s/he looks happy (or surprised/frustrated/angry/sad). Do you agree?' Sometimes it may not be entirely clear whether a child's expression or gesture is meaningful or not. On these occasions you pause the film and involve the parent: 'What do you think s/he is feeling/meaning/thinking here?'

Feedback messages to the parent to highlight contact-seeking behaviour are given through the child's perspective. For example, 'Look how s/he likes you sitting near him/her' rather than 'It's good how you sat next to him/her.' Other contact-seeking comments might include, 'S/he's showing you the toy, you're very important to him/her' or 'What a lovely moment. A toy doesn't smile back – you do!'

Any examples of the parent supporting the child when he or she is learning something, or comforting the child when he or she is distressed, or helping when the child can't manage something, are all commented on but, again, this is done from the child's perspective by using the 'speaking for the child' technique. For example, 'Look how s/he is listening to you. It really feels good when you support him/her', 'At this moment s/he loves getting a hug', or 'This is a difficult task at his/her age. S/he's looking for your help and getting it. This makes him/her feel understood.'

When giving important messages the film is always stopped and replayed to reinforce the message. The film is also always stopped at a positive image like a close-up, especially when there is clear eye contact.

The parent profile guides what specific themes relating to sensitivity or discipline you want to work on but the manual includes a range of helpful messages, some about child development. For example, 'Children need a lot of time to play. Adults know just by looking at a situation what needs to be done, while a child needs to learn and discover everything for the first time.' Explaining that children are really interested in the world around them is also a helpful message; for example, 'By asking you all sorts of things, children get to know the world around them. That's how they learn to understand things.'

Having watched the 'playing together' section with the feedback script, the facilitator summarizes the key messages. These are that the parent is really important to the child and that playing together even for a few minutes each day reduces difficult behaviour and helps the child handle difficult moments more easily. The parent is encouraged to try and play with his or her child for a few minutes over the next few days.

Whereas the 'playing together' sequence introduces the sensitivity themes of exploration and attachment, the 'don't touch' video sequence is used to explore the issue of *discipline* and in particular the techniques of *distraction* and *induction* (or explanation).

Prior to watching the sequence the facilitator explains that all parents need to say 'no' to their child on a daily basis or tell him or her not to touch something. Parents are then asked to give their own example and also asked how they deal with the situation. The facilitator then explains that it can be difficult for young children to just hear what not to do as on these occasions it's as if it keeps playing through their head, or they can't think of anything else to do. The manual suggests something like 'Saying no can be done in different ways. For a young child it can really help to distract the child by offering an alternative. You replace the forbidden thing with something that is fun, which makes it easier to forget the other thing.'

The two-minute 'don't touch' sequence is then watched back. Using the technique of 'speaking for the child' the facilitator specifically explains how difficult the task is for a child of this age. The point is made that young children don't touch things out of disobedience or to deliberately irritate the parent but instead from a healthy urge to explore the world around them. By touching and exploring everything, they begin to know and understand the world around them.

The facilitator highlights any examples of distraction the parent uses in the sequence and, still 'speaking for the child', describes how the child feels (for example, 'S/he finds it very difficult not to touch, especially with all those bright colours!'). For distraction to be an effective technique the alternative has to be made attractive to the child and the importance of using an enthusiastic voice is encouraged.

The technique of induction is also explained; the manual suggests something like 'You can also try to make it a habit to explain why your child is not allowed to do or touch something. Slowly, but surely, you teach your child why certain things are allowed and others, that seem similar at first, are not. Stay calm so your child can get back to being calm too.' If there are any examples of the parent already doing this, then these are also highlighted in the video feedback. So far it has been my experience that parents are not using induction at this first intervention visit but can be encouraged to do so over the programme.

The first intervention visit ends with parents being asked about how they experienced seeing themselves with their child on the film and a clear ending statement like, 'Well, that was it for today.'

Parents are told that you would like to record them having a meal or snack next time and the timing of the visit is arranged to coincide with this. Finally they're reminded that the order of the next visit will be the same as today, starting with recording the new situation during meal time and then looking at the material filmed today. After this and every other visit the facilitator immediately completes the logbook. This contains 12 questions to help reflect on the parent–child interaction, the parent's response to the intervention so far and the specific focus of future work.

Second intervention visit – praise, empathy and distracting
The second intervention visit follows the same structure as the first; an informal discussion including the parent's experience of using the tips, recording the next parent–child activity and then reviewing the recordings of the previous visit.

During the video feedback the 'speaking for the child' method is used again, to help the parent be more sensitive to both the child's exploration and attachment signals. The parent is encouraged to use this method by asking questions about the child's behaviour and expressions. The discipline techniques of distraction and induction are repeated with *praise, empathy* and *postponing* also being introduced after watching a sequence of the parent and child 'tidying up toys'. The manual provides detailed guidance. For example: 'Lots of research has been done into ways of getting children to do as they're told. It turns out that it's much better to praise your child and give compliments when s/he is doing things well than to punish him/her when things go wrong. Sometimes it's even better to ignore difficult behaviour because that way your child is not receiving any attention as a result of the behaviour. If you do pay attention your child may repeat the difficult behaviour because s/he is rewarded with your attention and then can't think of another way to get it.'

Third intervention visit – sensitivity chains and corrective messages
The third intervention visit marks the start of phase two of the programme, when the behaviour of the parent dealing with the child is addressed more directly. Watching the film of the meal time recorded at the last visit, the facilitator works on the behaviour to be improved by giving (a) *corrective message(s)*. The guidance is careful about how corrective messages are given; the facilitator must always show empathy to the parent, and a corrective message should only be given after compliments have already been delivered and never made at the start or end of the video feedback.

Non-responsive behaviour can be approached as 'Here, you could also have done...' followed by an example of where the parent does show the desired behaviour, or something approaching it, to reinforce the message that he or she can do it – 'Look, here you are doing it really well!'

In addition to 'speaking for the child' and encouraging the parent to join in during the video feedback, the facilitator introduces the parent to a 'sensitivity chain'. This has three elements: what the child is trying to tell the parent with his or her behaviour, how the parent responds to the child's signal and how the child reacts to that. These are used to illustrate how the parent is responding sensitively to the signals of the child and to explain the importance to the child of feeling understood.

The facilitator starts by selecting a positive interaction and, while pausing after replaying the film, puts this chain into words. The *child's signal* can be any behaviour specifically directed at the parent (for example, crying, making noises, talking, reaching, pointing, smiling, combined with looking at parent). Even though exploring behaviour is not directed at the parent, it can also be understood as a signal ('I'm playing').

The parent's *sensitive reaction* is all behaviour that is an appropriate and a prompt reaction to a signal from the child. An appropriate reaction is one that connects with what the child is trying to tell his or her parent – for example, an answer to the question posed by the signal. Examples might include: answering the child's babbling, naming something the child is pointing at, picking the child up when he or she reaches up, or comforting the child when he or she is crying. For young children the reaction of the parent has to be prompt (within a few seconds) to enable the child to link it to his or her own behaviour, and thus feel understood.

The *child's reaction* is all behaviour that follows and confirms the sensitive reaction of the parent (smiling, laughing, vocalizing, combined with looking at the parent, or stopping whining or crying).

In any fragment of parent–child interaction there are likely to be at least several sensitivity chains. In preparing the feedback script you are looking to highlight a particular chain that illustrates that the parent is competent to respond sensitively and that this sensitivity is acknowledged and rewarded by the child.

After watching a positive sensitivity chain together the facilitator delivers a key message: 'If you react to your child you give him/her the feeling s/he is being listened to and understood. This is important because that makes his confidence in you and him/her grow. That in turn will make him/her feel secure and at ease and s/he will feel supported in undertaking new things.'

The facilitator reassures the parent that reacting sensitively does not mean always having to let the child have his or her own way, but that it is important to let the child know that the parent at least understands what the child wants or means. Parents cannot be the instruments of their child's will and for children aged over one year of age the parent should not reinforce imperious, demanding behaviour and instead warmly encourage and reward behaviours that are inviting or requesting.

The video feedback also repeats any *discipline* messages from the last visits including the importance of giving praise, ignoring negative behaviour, announcing changes in advance ('in two minutes…'), giving the child an active role in the change of activity ('Would you like to help me? You're really good at clearing up') and letting the child know you understand it's difficult for him or her.

General messages about *child development* are also given as appropriate (for example, 'Children like to be praised. It helps them stay on track'; 'Young children often don't know how they feel. As adults we sometimes forget how young they are. It's a trap we fall into').

After watching the mealtime film and completing the feedback the discipline technique of 'sensitive time-out' is introduced and clear instructions given, including: 'If s/he gets angry like that it may help to tell him/her that you want him/her to calm down and that you'll talk with him/her when s/he has calmed down. Research shows this works best if you carry on talking calmly, don't start shouting, explain that you want to talk but this isn't possible as long as s/he's shouting, and also you are briefly out of sight. This method only works if there is enough positive attention to balance it out, which means giving compliments when s/he's doing things right.'

Fourth intervention visit – sharing feelings, empathy and induction
The fourth intervention follows the same order as previous visits: an informal discussion, explanation of the session, a recording sequence with

the camcorder and then watching the recordings made at the last home visit. The same techniques are repeated: speaking for the child, reinforcing positive behaviour of the parent, highlighting specific sensitivity chains, the importance of being understood, and giving corrective messages.

While watching a film of 'playing a song game together' the final sensitivity theme of *sharing feelings* is introduced. The facilitator explains the importance of having fun together as well as sharing distress and 'tuning in' to each other's feelings as this enables the child to learn to share his or her positive and negative feelings and build relationships, not just with the parent but also gradually with other people. It's further explained that, for a child, sharing feelings starts with close body contact with his or her carer so parents are encouraged to have their child sitting on their lap, hugging and playing games together, as this way they learn to understand each other.

The facilitator repeats a message from the third intervention (with a subtle addition): 'If you react to your child's reactions and emotions you give him/her the feeling that s/he's being listened to, that s/he's being understood. That's important because it makes his/her confidence in you and him/herself grow. That in turn will make him/her feel secure and at ease, and s/he will feel supported in undertaking new things.'

During the video feedback any actual examples of, or potential for, using discipline techniques are highlighted. These might include giving compliments and praising good behaviour, announcing when a change of activity is coming up ('in two minutes…'), giving the child an active role, giving an alternative ('You can't have *this* but you can have *that* instead'), postponing something ('Not now, but later') or ignoring negative behaviour in combination with praising good behaviour.

After the video feedback discussion the facilitator reinforces the discipline themes of *empathy* and *induction* using the manual guidance: 'Research shows that it is really important for a child to feel that s/he is being understood. It's therefore important to show your child that you understand how difficult s/he finds it to stop doing something.'

A few specific examples of how the parent might say this are then rehearsed, something like, 'It's really difficult to stop playing with this, isn't it?' The facilitator continues, 'Children also have to learn how to put themselves in someone else's shoes, but they need help with that. Giving explanations helps your child learn to take your feelings and other people's feelings into account. Research shows this is true even for children aged just one year.' Parents are encouraged in the coming weeks to put themselves in their children's shoes when telling them what to do or not do and to try to explain why they have to do what they are being told.

As before when rounding off the visit, the parent is told 'That's it for today' and then asked what he or she thought of the video and how it compared with last time. An appointment is made for next time, but in about two months' time, rather than in two weeks. This longer interval is to give the parent the opportunity to put the suggestions into practice in daily life.

At this point the parent is also asked whether he or she would like his or her partner to be present, but it is explained that this is not compulsory. Previous research has suggested that completely joint parent interventions may reduce or inhibit the beneficial effects on some mothers' interactions (although more research is needed).

Fifth and sixth intervention visits
The fifth and sixth sessions make up the third and final phase of the intervention. These are booster sessions designed to integrate all the previous sensitivity and discipline themes and principles. If partners (usually the father) are present they are given an explanation of the visit: that there will be filming of the parent and child (for session five only) and then film material from the previous session will be shown, stopping from time to time to talk about something on the film. Unless the parent insists on the partner being included, filming with him or her only takes place on the sixth and final intervention visit. This is as a memento and all the recordings from the intervention are given to the parent at the end.

An example of a video feedback script
Below is an example of a video feedback script from a fifth intervention visit with a 20-year-old mother and her two-year-old daughter. The mother has a complex history that included a period as a *looked-after child*. Previous concerns included: her apparent lack of emotional availability and warmth to her child, a lack of adequate stimulation and further concerns that she was not coping with her daughter's behaviour.

The parenting profile, completed with the base-line observations made during the initial assessment visit, identified that the mother was not sensitive to many of her daughter's cues and had difficulties managing challenging behaviour.

The aim of previous feedback scripts had been to help the mother learn to notice her daughter's signals and increase her understanding of what moves her child, and to help her to react more appropriately both to positive signals (e.g. eye contact, smiling) and negative signals (e.g. defiance, protesting, crying). In the initial sessions, the mother's tone of voice often appeared flat so feedback scripts were also aimed at improving warmth in her voice and facial expression when interacting with her child.

Despite initial ambivalence about the intervention the mother has made progress. For example, having previously described considerable difficulty playing with her daughter she has begun to do so and, significantly, has noticed positive changes in her daughter's behaviour as a result. She has shown some signs of being more sensitive to her daughter's cues and also managed to apply some non-coercive discipline strategies at times. However, she has also reported not always staying calm and has resorted to shouting and smacking her daughter.

The aim of this feedback script, which features mother and daughter playing together with toys, is to try and reinforce mother's sensitivity behaviour and improve playful interaction and the sharing of feelings. I also want to encourage her repertoire of discipline techniques, such as giving praise, distraction and 'time out', so that she is better equipped to manage disobedient behaviour.

Example feedback script
'On my last visit we talked about the importance of your child feeling understood and how this happens when you react to B's signals. Do you remember this? Let's look at the film of you and B playing together with the toys.'

Time code (when film is paused)	Comment
00.06.21	So, look how eager B is. She's really enjoying sitting with you.
00.19.03	Look how curious she is about these coloured pots and how they can fit together. Play is like work to her and she's really concentrating hard.
00.35.00	This is really good. You're giving B time to explore all the pots herself. At this moment it seems like she wants to do this on her own. She's concentrating so hard.
00.58.07	How clever she is. She loves those pots. Now she's put the blue one back inside the red one. Adults get bored with this play but children like repeating it. She's learning a lot. By repeating things children learn about the world around them.
01.13.06	This is a great moment. Look how she likes to share with you. She's holding the green pot up in her left hand for you to see. You're very important to her.
01.34.49	Now, what do you see here?... Has she lost interest in the pots or has she something else on her mind?
01.39.20	Ah, she likes the look of your bag. What do you think she is thinking right now? Children like to explore. She's curious to look inside the bag.

01.58.18	Okay, here you move the bag on to the table. At this moment do you think she understands that you don't want her to play with it?
02.14.25	Here she's still trying to reach the bag. Look at her expression, she looks very determined. Try to imagine how hard this must be for her. She really wants to explore.
02.26.45	Okay, here you've said 'Leave it' a second time. Look how frustrated B looks. It's a difficult moment for both of you. You really sound annoyed. Does this often happen? It's important to set rules but it takes time for young children to learn them. You have to tell rules over and over again.
(Induction message)	Your message to 'Leave it' was very clear. Here you could have also said why she's not allowed in your bag or why it's bad for you. It's good for her to know why she can or can't do something. For all of us it's easier to follow rules if we understand why. As adults we don't like having to follow rules we don't understand.
02.50.08	You've done really well here. You've stayed calm and ignored her throwing the beaker. What would have happened if you hadn't ignored that? If things got more difficult do you think you would have used time-out? We can talk about this again after looking at the film.
03.17.05	Again here your tone of voice is very encouraging. She's listening to you and paying attention to how you're putting the bricks on top of each other.
03.26.12	What do you think she's thinking right now? That tower looks interesting Mum! Here you've done a really great job distracting her from thinking about the bag. It's difficult for children just to hear what they can't do; it really helps if you give them an alternative by telling them what they can do instead.
03.39.43	Now here I want to show you the importance of reacting to what your daughter is doing. She's joined you on the floor and picked up a yellow brick. She's asking to make a tower.
03.41.24	It's nice how you understand her. You point to the red brick she can put her brick on top of. What happens next?

03.47.15	Look, B quickly reacts to your invitation and puts the yellow brick on the red one. This is a lovely moment; she's so excited by her achievement.
Rewind to 03.39.43 and play through to 03.47.15	Let's watch that again. By reacting to B, you give her the message that she's being listened to and is understood. That makes her confidence in you grow and makes her feel safe and supported to undertake new tasks. Do you recognize this?
04.02.21	Look how well she listens, how clever that she can follow your instructions about putting the bricks on top of each other.
04.11.05	She looks relaxed and happy here. Is that right? She's having a great time playing with you.
04.19.20	Now this is a very short but lovely moment I want to show you. Look, here you follow her giggle with your own laugh. It's important to B because it shows her that her feelings are understood. If she feels that she is being understood she can start to understand others too.
04.56.47	Wow, she's very clever! With your encouragement B has made a tower of four bricks. This is a really difficult task at her age. You've made it interesting for her with your tone of voice.
04.59.19	And just here there's a shared moment of eye contact. What do you think she's thinking right now?
05.12.15	Here B is so excited to knock the bricks down. How nice to get praise from Mum. It's good for children to know they're doing well. It gives them confidence to try new things. You can't spoil your child with compliments. How do you feel when you get compliments?
05.27.10	Look at her smiling here. Playing with Mum is great! A toy doesn't smile back – you do.
05.35.40	Again, this is a lovely moment for B and you too. Look how you're both sitting. You are a mirror of each other. It's like the two of you have a secret understanding together!
05.49.20	The film is about to fade out here but look how well she is still listening to you. She really likes playing with you.

Summary
Within our Family Centre Service we are still in the early stages of piloting the VIPP-SD programme with families where young children are subject to protection plans due to physical and emotional abuse and neglect. In collaboration with other interventions – for example, those aimed at addressing issues of domestic violence, substance misuse and adult mental health difficulties – we are hopeful that the VIPP-SD programme will contribute to improved outcomes for children and parent–child interactions and relationships. There are several reasons for this:

- Many parents, who might be characterized as 'hard to reach' or 'resistant to change', are unable or unwilling to engage with any group work parenting programmes. The VIPP-SD intervention takes place in the family home and parents report finding the technique engaging and rewarding.

- Although short-term, the intervention enables the worker to empathize and establish a close alliance with the parent while still maintaining a clear sense of purpose and focus on the child's experience.

- Because the intervention is aimed at making observable changes to parental sensitivity and the quality of the parent–child relationship, the intervention guards against the 'rule of optimism', where superficial changes (redecorating a bedroom, for example) are seized on as evidence of significant change to the child's caregiving environment.

The Assessment of Disorganized Attachment and Maltreatment (ADAM) Project

Introduction

Conclusive evidence, much of it summarized in reports from Harvard University's National Scientific Center for the Developing Child, now confirms unequivocally that early abusive caregiving environments lead to extremely poor outcomes for children. One of these is the appearance of disorganized attachment which is, as we have seen, a strong predictor of subsequent problems in adolescence and adulthood, particularly dissociative and personality disorders, both of which are difficult to change. The shoots of frightened or frightening behaviour, unresolved loss and low mentalizing take root in the maltreated child and are likely to be passed on to his or her own children intergenerationally in a vicious cycle. Remember that, although most children who are abused do not go on to abuse others, children who have experienced disconnected and extremely insensitive parenting, and show clear signs of disorganized attachment behaviour, *are* likely to develop serious and unremitting mental health problems in adolescence, and *are* likely to repeat this kind of parenting if they go on to have children of their own.

One of us (David) was part of a team commissioned through the UK government department to undertake a review of 'resistant families' in child protection work. In the final report, he wrote that

> recent discoveries in the neurological, biochemical and genetic dimensions of child development now expose that disorganised attachment – fear, abuse, and neglect – produces abnormal hormone levels, which in turn lead to excessive and unremitting stress. In the absence of the cushioning shield of supportive relationships, these hormones stay out of balance which, in turn, damages neurological brain architecture and circuits in young children (National Scientific Council on the Developing Child 2005, 2007, 2008). Environmental

factors, such as deep and persistent poverty, as well as threatening neighbourhoods, can further destabilise the foundations for optimal development. When these two factors combine with very poor child care – specifically, harsh, inconsistent, neglectful, frightening, hostile, frightened, helpless, but particularly *psychologically harmful* caregiving – the mixture becomes more toxic. (Fauth *et al*. 2010, p.10)

Furthermore, according to Marian Brandon and her colleagues, one of the 'major predictors of poor-quality parenting from Sroufe *et al*.'s (2005) Minnesota study was a lack of parental understanding of the "psychological complexity" of the infant'. Equally, 'parents who fail to recognise or understand their children as complex emotional and psychological beings are less sensitive and available at times of need. The feeling of abandonment that this engenders in young children only adds to their arousal and distress, putting the parent under further stress' (Brandon *et al*. 2008, p.64).

When undertaking the research for this book a number of high-profile cases of child deaths and maltreatment hit the headlines of virtually all UK press and media. The reporting of the death of Peter Connelly ('Baby P') and the case of Karen Matthews, who managed to hoodwink most of the country, along with its media, when she claimed her daughter Shannon had been kidnapped, severely criticized child protection professionals – especially social workers – and demonized many parents who come to the attention of Children's Services.

In this final chapter we outline an innovative project we developed in London in 2009. We conclude with examples to demonstrate how we are trying to put into practice the research discussed in this book. We begin by summarizing the main challenges, as we see them, facing professionals charged with the role of helping families protect children.

Challenges and problems with child protection practice

To contextualize the discussion, during the year ending 31 March 2009 there were 547,000 referrals to children's social services departments in England (total population 11.7 million children aged 0–18) with 23 per cent being repeat referrals. Some 37,900 children became subject to a Child Protection Plan. When children are physically harmed by their caregivers or neglected by them, they are likely to have suffered trauma, and for some this will constitute 'significant harm'.

At present, professionals tend to rely on three approaches, either individually or in combination, when investigating abuse and neglect. First, they rely almost exclusively on interviews with the adult family members (Brandon *et al.* 2008; Holland 2000). They hope that abusing carers will admit that they are placing children in danger or are failing to protect them. But many parents cannot or will not accept such responsibility; indeed, recent high-profile tragic cases also have introduced a shocked public to the phenomenon of the highly manipulative parent (in the case of Karen Matthews) or 'disguised compliance' (in the case of Peter Connelly's mother). Disguised or feigned compliance refers to parents who try to dominate a visit by, for example, talking about their own problems and worries rather than those of the child. This kind of behaviour can hoodwink an unsuspecting social worker or health visitor because it seems to be 'giving them what they expect', that is, self-disclosure, even insight. Other families will consciously or unconsciously use dogs or other animals as diversions, especially if the animal is violent. Similarly, having other people in the house at the time of the worker's visit can divert attention away from professionals' observations and assessments.

Second, child welfare practitioners often use the relationship the parent has with them as a proxy indicator of the relationship the parent has with his or her child. But it cannot be correctly assumed that if carers are hostile to the worker that they behave in the same way with their child; equally, it cannot be assumed that if parents are co-operative that they are similarly responsive to their child. An almost exclusive focus on the adult carer carries with it another problem: numerous enquiries find that children are often not seen; and when they are, they tend to be asked a number of unfocused questions, aimed at establishing their wishes and feelings by practitioners who freely admit to us that they lack the skills and the time required to undertake creative, direct work needed with children. Sometimes they seek to develop a trusting relationship with children so that they will eventually feel safe enough to disclose. The problem, of course, is that it can take too long, or it may never occur.

The third way practitioners investigate allegations of abuse and neglect is by the interpretation and risk assessment of 'caregiver characteristics'. But relying on the caregiver characteristics used to assess abuse is imprecise because so-called 'risk factors' are notoriously unreliable as predictors of future behaviour. Although witnessing domestic violence and serious drug or alcohol abuse are never optimal for children, if we were to remove every child where this happened it would result in a huge demand for residential or foster care. And most children would be deeply unhappy to have been taken away from their parents.

At a conference in 2009 Marian Brandon presented the findings of two studies into over 350 Serious Case Reviews in the UK. She included the following bullet point: 'Most cases were too complex for serious injury and death to be predictable'. She explained later that this meant that if workers had known at the beginning all the information they eventually knew by the end they still would not have been able to predict what happened at the end. This is a very important message for social workers and other child welfare practitioners, because it is mostly within the 'prediction gap', between risk factors and maltreatment, that mistakes are made.

Eileen Munro (2002) explains why caregiver characteristics can only rarely be used confidently to predict future harm or neglect to a child. Because there is little evidence available to help child protection professionals beyond simple correlational research, all they actually know about are *associations* between maltreatment occurrence and recurrence and 'carer' or 'family characteristics', such as a family member's history of abuse, parental substance misuse, mental health problems, domestic violence, etc. The problem is that although maltreated children *do* tend to come from families with these problems – singly or in combination – whilst never being optimal for a child's development, as often as not, they don't lead to *maltreatment*. For example, current estimates are that about one third of child abuse survivors go on to abuse their own children (Crittenden 2008; Fonagy 2008; Lösel and Bender 2005) – and, therefore, two thirds do not. This level is only just above the proportion who turn to crime later (about 26 per cent; see Widom 1989). As Patricia Crittenden puts it, 'what can be understood retrospectively cannot be predicted prospectively' (Crittenden 2008, p.9). She explains further: 'if you maltreat your child, you almost certainly were maltreated. But if you were maltreated, it is more likely that you do not maltreat your own children' (p.117). An example of this 'prediction gap' is that, in respect of sexual abuse, girls are more likely to be abus*ed* than boys...but men are far more likely than women to be abus*ers* of children. To further complicate matters, it is known that most men who abuse their own children have not themselves been sexually abused (but probably have been physically and emotionally; see Crittenden 2008, pp.158–160) whereas most women who sexually abuse their own children have themselves been sexually abused, either from within their immediate family or by a close relative, such as an uncle (see Crittenden 2008, p.165).

Such overreliance on incorrect causal assumptions about maltreatment leads to children being overlooked when risk thresholds are set too high or it leads to the problem of 'false positives', when families are brought into the system by mistake. Referring to Browne and Saqi (1988), Eileen Munro came up with an interesting epidemiological estimate: if we tried to screen 10,000 families in the general population, seven high risk cases would be missed, 33 would be identified correctly, but a further 1195 families would be falsely identified as being high risk (Munro 1999, p.24). No wonder child protection professionals are damned almost whatever they do.

Finally, professionals are encouraged to bring out strengths in families but in our experience they sometimes are muddled about what this means in practice. To illustrate the confusion, a few years ago one of us (David) saw in a social work file a well-argued and evidenced assessment of a father's sexual abuse of his five-year-old daughter. It was an excellent analysis, but the next paragraph began 'However...' David wondered what he would read next and was astonished to find that the worker continued '...whenever I visited he has always been civil; for example, he always offers me a cup of tea and is always polite'. When David asked her if she could say why she had written this, she said she hadn't wanted to but her supervisor said she should always 'balance weaknesses or difficulties with a search for strengths'. But this is to miss the key point: in child protection work, 'strengths' should only be identified if they can be recruited into the plan to offset difficulties and weaknesses. In this example, the social worker would have needed to argue precisely how the father's 'civility' could be used to stop the sexual abuse. An impossible task, surely? Balancing families' strengths and weaknesses is more than an accounting process where 'pluses' and 'minuses' are first tallied and then cancelled out. This problem also contributes to the well-known phenomenon of 'false optimism', whereby the worker is so desperate to find positives that he or she then ignores danger signals.

Towards a new mindset and approach in child protection practice

As a consequence of these challenges and problems we argue that child welfare practitioners need a change of focus. First they need progressively to reduce their reliance on interviewing parents about their parenting skills when trying to assess parenting capacity. Instead, more attention should be paid to assessing, through the use of skilled observation, caregivers actually parenting (see Juffer *et al.* 2008a). After asking a carer simply to be with his or her child, doing ordinary things, such as playing, bathing or nappy-changing – whatever needs to be done at the time – a series of progressively more challenging tasks are introduced. For example, the carer might be asked to tell the child not to touch a particular toy, or to clear up the paints. The advantage of observing parents actually parenting is that simulating sensitive parenting is very difficult to sustain for long (for one thing, the child's behaviour soon indicates that something different is happening). To accomplish such a shift in emphasis, specific observational techniques such as understanding and recognizing disorganized attachment behaviour will need to be acquired by practitioners. This is a markedly different approach to that of asking the parent to comment or reflect upon his or her parenting which, for someone feigning compliance, offers a wonderfully simple opportunity to deceive the worker. The use of standardized questionnaires and assessments can help here too.

What else should practitioners be doing to feel more confident detecting abuse and neglect, given the criticisms they have experienced recently in the media? We argue strongly that they need to start by taking, to use David Jones' neat phrase, a 'child's eye view' (Jones 1997). As we have seen throughout this book, the key is in understanding how the child's *mind* operates. We have seen that, when children are abused by those who are meant to love and delight in them, their brain 'protects' them by creating a series of internal messages basically saying 'this must be happening because I am unworthy and unlovable'. It is rare that a young child being abused – especially in cases of sexual and emotional abuse – would actually hold the *adult* responsible. And here lies the true horror of child maltreatment: not only do children suffer the abuse, they are very likely to believe it was their fault. But it is precisely such pernicious and powerful internal messages that, if the social worker is trained to understand and recognize them, can provide much of the evidence needed to protect the child.

A good deal has rightly been made about the need to speak to the child alone, but to do this effectively social workers need to be confident about conducting such a meeting. Experienced practitioners know that asking children if they have been abused is unlikely to produce a reliable response, partly because children may have been threatened with violence if they talk to anyone. And professionals know only too well that many children are not *able* to speak about their unimaginable fear and sorrow. It goes without saying that for a child to feel safe enough to disclose maltreatment a high level of trust with a practitioner is required but, according to a number of reports, this is unlikely to be forthcoming if social workers are spending too much time at their computers. But even if they did have the time, if a child is being abused, it is important that we don't wait until he or she feels confident enough to tell an adult: we need to act more quickly than that. Practitioners at all levels regularly tell us that, when they say they have 'seen' a child, it may be literally that: they *saw* him or her in the garden; but they didn't necessarily *speak* to him or her. They tell us that they don't have the time to do so, because they must return to the office to write up the report and to meet deadlines. More worrying is their often unsolicited admission that, other than asking the child how he or she is and 'how's school?', etc., they don't possess the skills and knowledge to develop the interview any further. This is one of the main reasons why we developed the Assessment of Disorganized Attachment and Maltreatment (ADAM) Project, because they are desperate to learn more and, in our experience of working with over 8000 qualifying and qualified professionals during the past 20 years, we would say that they want to put the best interests of children and families at the centre of their practice. As we have seen throughout this book, recent developments in attachment theory and research offer such a prospect because, if certain assessment techniques are used, they focus on the way the *mind* of an abused or neglected child quickly betrays what is happening to him or her.

There are ways of knowing that a child is being abused or neglected which do not rely on visible signs, such as bruising. We mustn't forget or overlook the more basic signs of maltreatment, such as avoiding intimacy in close relationships, being excessively vigilant and distrustful, or indicating low self-efficacy by passively accepting what the child is given. Similarly, where there are irrefutable physical signs, it is vital to act quickly. But in many cases of abuse and neglect there are few or no signs at all (sometimes because abusers are good at covering their tracks). For example, sexual abuse is rarely accompanied by tell-tale physical indicators that a social worker will see during a visit. Similarly, emotional abuse, involving persistent derogation or humiliation, rarely produces unambiguous accompanying outward signs. What emerged in the reporting of the case of Peter Connelly ('Baby P') is that adults can be extremely convincing when giving accounts of physical injuries.

In the ADAM Project we use a modified version of the Pathway Model outlined in Chapter 2 (see Figure 9.1) to introduce workers to the idea that investigating DA in the child's behaviour is a necessary – but not sufficient – condition of effective assessment. The next step is to concentrate on the mechanisms that will indicate whether a carer is struggling. They achieve this by observing directed parenting tasks to spot the presence of disconnected and extremely insensitive caregiving behaviour and through the use of specialized interviews to uncover with the parent unresolved loss and low reflective function.

Maltreatment Pathway Model

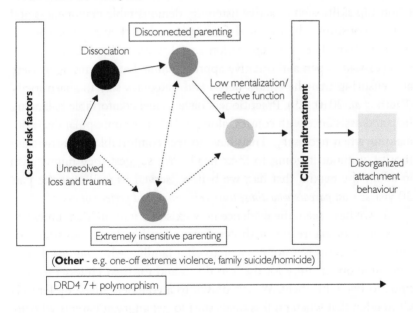

Figure 9.1 Maltreatment Pathway Model

Practitioners using the model routinely make the point that they find it most helpful in situations when they are in some doubt over whether the child is being maltreated (if they already have evidence of abuse, then they don't need to use the methods incorporated within the model). The modified model used in the ADAM Project differs in only one respect: we have included an additional circle to denote that the methods used are aimed primarily at detecting chronic maltreatment, abuse and neglect; it is not able to identify or uncover the predisposing factors likely to lead to a one-off catastrophic incident, such as a parent who kills him or herself and his or her children as a result, for example, of having been rejected by a partner or after an acute episode of mental ill-health.

An advantage of starting with an analysis of whether the child experiences DA is that it is 'relationship-specific'. This is of immense importance for child protection professionals when assessing allegations of abuse and neglect because it suggests strongly that infants, toddlers and young children are likely to exhibit DA patterns only in the presence of particular carers or adults.

The approach buttressing the ADAM Project requires child welfare practitioners to use well-developed communication skills. But what are they precisely? There is no doubt that empathy and other established relationship skills such as active listening, demonstrable genuineness and respect constitute the essential foundations; but they are not enough on their own. The child protection social worker also needs to bring an 'eyes-wide-open authoritative approach aimed at containing anxiety and ensuring that the child's needs and outcomes stay in sharp focus' (Fauth *et al.* 2010, p.9). Practitioners have to feel comfortable balancing help and assistance with control, along with firm or unpopular decision-making when necessary. They have to feel comfortable with their authority, without it going to their heads. We suggest they might wish to adopt the maxim that has, we believe, served us well over the past 30 years: *most parents who abuse their children would prefer not to.*

As we have seen, the evidence now exists to indicate that, unless an assessment of maltreatment shows an irretrievably dangerous situation, only in rare cases is it not possible to offer families who want to change a genuine opportunity for them to do so and for their children to continue to live with them. We are drawn to a comment made by Patricia Crittenden that when professionals start to get angry at parents who are significantly harming a child, 'as a colleague of mine said, as soon as he reads the AAIs of parents…he suddenly finds compassion for them' (Crittenden 2008, p.34).

But although empathy and compassion must always be present – on tap and on demand – this is not the same as being sentimental. Getting this balance right has always been difficult and an elegant and creative study by Donald Forrester shows that this is still the case. He presented 24 social workers with two child protection scenarios which incorporated different levels of concern. They were simulated by an actor using a loosely worded script (to encourage improvisation). Workers were asked to respond in the way they would normally behave. What prompted him to do this research was a parallel study in which social workers prior to a training course on motivational interviewing were asked to respond to scripted vignettes. Having found some evidence of 'low levels of empathy' and the 'use of a highly confrontational style' (Forrester *et al.* 2007, p.42), he decided to introduce a more realistic design to the scenario than is possible with scripted vignettes. He found similar results: even though they achieved clarity over the main points of concern, there was the same low level of empathy and, sometimes, worryingly hostile communication. He concluded that 'the fact that... social workers were not using good communication skills is a serious challenge to the profession' (p.49).

It is understandable that professionals will feel anger, frustration and anxiety when working with abused children in resistant families. They often find themselves in situations where they are convinced that the child is experiencing significant harm but without sufficient evidence to protect the child. This dynamic was first documented in the early 1950s by the pioneering work of the late Isabel Menzies. She demonstrated in powerfully poetic language how the organizations within which professionals work under extremely anxiety-provoking circumstances develop unconscious 'practices' to protect them from that anxiety. She found, for example, that nurses would wake patients in the middle of the night to give them their sleeping tablets – and when questioned about it, didn't see anything odd about doing so (Menzies-Lyth 1959). In our view, her work is still as fresh and relevant as it ever was. It underlines the need for workers to process their feelings, ideally through mentalized supervisory provision.

We already know that one of the attractions of the ADAM Project methods to social work practitioners is that they are child-friendly and reliable if used in conjunction with confident professional judgement and sound analytic skills. The approaches used in the ADAM Project require workers – to quote the father of attachment theory, John Bowlby – to be 'bigger, stronger, wiser...and *kind*'. Consequently they need to *demonstrate* open, accountable and ethical practice (Shemmings and

Shemmings 1996). But there is another, more pragmatic, reason for en-suring that the highest communication and professional standards are shown to family members right from the start. We argue that the worker who does the assessment should be the one to try and help the family later. We know from the research on intervention that critical, confron-tational or hostile communication – which is not the same as being sensitively open and honest – is likely to scupper any offers of help later on; at minimum, the consequences of poor communication can be very difficult to retrieve.

The Assessment of Disorganized Attachment and Maltreatment (ADAM) Project

We established the ADAM Project in 2009 to offer a complementary way for professionals to investigate allegations of abuse and neglect. We established a series of discussions with practitioners and supervisors as an action research project to apply attachment-based assessment methods in child welfare practice. At present the core member authorities comprise seven boroughs within London. These organizations have helped pilot the approach, with their own staff and with other agencies including the judicial courts. Consequently, we sought practitioners and their supervi-sors who were interested in discussing these ideas to build them into workable, transferable techniques, tools and protocols.

The ADAM Project offers a four-day intensive training event, evenly spread at monthly intervals to enable practitioners to try out new skills acquired. An online facility is also available for one year, so that partici-pants can receive immediate support and advice when putting the meth-ods into practice. The website also offers guided reading (with access to contemporary online articles, synchronous chatrooms and discussion boards). Invited 'guests' also host chatroom slots at pre-published times. The option to print the full 'chat' text is also available. For example, we recently received an email from a participant in which she wrote:

> I visited a child in a residential home yesterday and she wanted to show me her bedroom. I was astonished: it was like a bomb had exploded! Is this an example of disorganised attachment?

We replied that it was more likely to be an example of 'a teenager'! We then explained that the conditions – a mildly anxious situation into which a carer enters, or the child is asked to think about (or draw) his or her reaction to an attachment-saturated story – were not present. Another email said:

> A 13-year-old boy in care went for an interview with a male psychiatrist and, immediately upon entering the room, proceeded to take down his trousers and masturbate. Is this an example of DA?

Again, we stated that, while this was certainly very disturbing behaviour, the conditions were not there to determine the presence of disorganized attachment.

The project is particularly timely in the light of the UK's National Social Work Task Force, as well as the forthcoming review of social work in the UK by Professor Eileen Munro. It had already proved popular with social workers. For example, David was asked recently to speak about the Project for a whole day to the entire workforce of the Children and Families Service at the London borough of Tower Hamlets. The London Mosque in Whitechapel was hired for the event and over 300 people attended.

The methods outlined in the ADAM Project are used in situations when the practitioner is concerned that a child may be being maltreated but does not have sufficient evidence to proceed (we always stress to participants that, if they *do* have that evidence, they have no need to use these methods).

Stressing the limits of the Project

We always stress that the purpose of the Project is not to train practitioners in the use of these assessment devices in their strict clinical sense, where the aim is to arrive at a more precise classification of secure, ambivalent and avoidant attachment. Instead, professionals acquire a deeper understanding of the theoretical principles upon which disorganized attachment and the other constructs underpinning the methods are based in order to observe, understand and analyse children's behaviour *pragmatically and with a purpose*. But the results of such assessments still need to be incorporated with other emerging and accumulated evidence; it is unlikely, for example, that isolated observations of disorganized attachment would be accepted as evidence in a court.

With these caveats, however, we argue that social workers and health visitors are often in the best position to utilize the techniques already used by psychologists and therapists. It is also true that waiting lists are prohibitively long for children who need to see fully trained professionals skilled in the use of these methods of assessment and intervention. Because the training provided covers the theoretical and evidence base behind the concept of disorganized attachment, and as DA behaviours do tend to 'stand out', then we argue that the average child protection professional can be shown how to recognize it. The online facility we offer does, however, act as a fail-safe mechanism because we have a number of experts who are more formally trained in the use of the methods.

We are clear with participants that the four-day training does not enable them to claim they can identify the full range of attachment behaviours. They have access to the website and will respond to practice-related queries that need more detailed analysis and advice. Nevertheless, we stress to participants that they should try and attend expert programmes at, for example, the Anna Freud Centre in London and we recommend that organizations second some staff, as this widens the skills available within teams, as well as to the Project.

The ADAM Project programme

Interested practitioners are invited to an initial one-day seminar in the authority. By the end of the day participants:

- are familiar with new techniques to assess why some parents who are thought to be 'high-risk' go on to abuse a child, whereas others do not

- understand the meaning and significance of *disorganized attachment behaviour* and why it is a strong predictor of child maltreatment

- learn about the contribution of three key mediating factors to our understanding of child abuse:

  o *Unresolved Early Loss/Trauma* and accompanying *Parental Dissociation*

  o *Disconnected* and *extremely Insensitive Parenting*

  o *Low Parental Mentalization* and *Reflective Function*

- are introduced to a modified *Toolkit of Measures* to assess these key mediating factors

- gain an awareness of neurobiological and genetic explanations (kept simple!)

- consider the evidence about which *Interventions* work best.

By the end of the four-day course participants are able to use a number of measures, which have been adapted for use pragmatically by busy child welfare practitioners who tell us that they feel confident as a result when presenting assessments in court and at child protection meetings.

The ADAM Project organizations have become increasingly interested in moving beyond the use of the methods solely for the investigation and assessment of allegations of child abuse and neglect to include interventions to help families. To that end we are working with Leiden University to train small groups of Project members in the use of *Video-feedback Intervention to promote Positive Parenting and Sensitive Discipline* (VIPP-SD), which we outlined and gave examples of in the previous chapter.

Evaluation and research

A high level of interest in the Project has already developed, hence we plan to evaluate the project because questions will be asked about its effectiveness. However it is phrased, the press and the media, as well as the research community, will ask: 'Does it *work* and, if so, how do you know?' We have already attracted four PhD students to undertake evaluative research, one of whom was funded by the University of Kent, UK. (We are attempting to be very precise about what 'Does it work?' might usefully and realistically mean, and this question features early on in an action research project.) Additional research areas being explored include:

- What are the characteristics of those children selected by professionals?

- What do we need to understand better about the processes involved?

  o At what stage in an investigation should these methods be introduced? (We do not advocate their use as part of general 'needs assessment'.)

○ What happens if a parent refuses to allow a child to be interviewed?

○ How can family members be fully involved in a transparent, open and sensitive way (thereby modelling what they may not be able to offer to their children)?

○ How does attachment-based assessment of allegations fit in with and complement other aspects of safeguarding practice (such as working with families to promote safer and more sensitive parenting)?

• What is the predictive validity of the techniques – are the children who exhibit DA/AD *actually* being abused?

• Are the measures being used correctly?

We are using a variety of research methods including: action research, case studies and multiple and logistic regression. In the area of child protection research random allocation is likely to be resisted by practitioners as unethical and, hence, RCT-based proposals are unlikely to pass through relevant ethics committees. Consequently we are using path analysis and structural equation modelling to assist in our understanding of how intervening variables interact.

We also hope to attract interest in the use of neuro-imaging techniques as well as research methods capable of exploring the biochemistry and genetics of disorganized attachment. Eamon McCrory and his colleagues at University College London offer the following exciting prospect:

> the possibility that neuropsychological screening informed by biomarker research…approaches may one day help us better predict differential treatment outcome. Similarly, genotype markers may also help predict differential treatment responsiveness. For example, it has been demonstrated that response to a parenting intervention for externalising problems in infants depends on which form of the dopamine receptor (D4) gene the child is carrying. (McCrory *et al.* 2010)

Finally, because the overall aim of the project is to share findings in accessible ways with practitioners and families, we are encouraging ADAM Project participants to publish their experience using the methods; indeed, three of them have each contributed to chapters in this book. We conclude this chapter with an example of how the ADAM Project operates in practice, written by Tania Young, another of the key ADAM Project members.

Case study 9.1 An example of the ADAM Project in action (all names and details have been anonymized or changed)

Hannah (9), Ben (6) and Danielle (4) came to the attention of the Local Authority following a referral from the primary school in June 2009. Ben disclosed to a staff member that his mother had slapped him on the face and his father had hit him on the back of the head. He was very tired and explained that he had not slept the night before. He said he had been woken and beaten by his mother. He reported that his parents kept beating him and he didn't know why. Ben also reported that his sisters were sometimes hit on the legs with a belt. He talked about his parents banging a belt on the wall to frighten him and his siblings. The school reported both Ben and Hannah as being very emotional at school, especially Hannah. Both children were reported as being clean, attended well, but found it difficult to settle at times. There had been some concerns about the children not having enough food and that Hannah had suffered from extended periods of cystitis (urinary tract infections) which left her in a lot of pain and her parents needed reminding to take her to the GP for treatment. The children lived with both parents.

Following these disclosures, all three children underwent a child protection medical examination, which revealed a number of marks and bruises on Ben and Hannah, some of which were in protected areas. The parents were unable to provide explanations as to how these marks were caused. The paediatrician who carried out the examinations reported that some of the marks were consistent with being hit with a belt. Both parents admitted that occasionally they had smacked their children but said they had never hit them with a belt or any other implement. The father admitted to using a belt to threaten them but suggested that Ben knew this was meant as a 'joke'. Both parents were arrested but not charged because the children were considered unreliable witnesses.

An initial child protection case conference was held in 2009 and all three children were made subject to child protection plans under the category of physical abuse. In addition to the allegations of physical abuse, the conference discussed concerns about the children, including extensive tooth decay of all three children that required immediate attention. Hannah was described as an emotionally demanding and needy child who often cried at school. She was reported as 'standing out' in comparison to other children. The school was also concerned about

Hannah complaining of being in pain and having difficulty sitting down. The mother explained that this was because of constipation.

Further assessment was carried out, despite considerable resistance from the parents, especially the father. There were particular concerns about Hannah, who had developed certain fears and would quite often refuse to go upstairs by herself, saying that 'walls have ears'. Concerns were raised about the children's routines and their sleeping arrangements. Hannah was said to have refused to sleep in her own room and therefore shared with Ben and Danielle in one room. Both parents regularly reported that the father had a closer bond with Hannah than the mother but Hannah was frequently observed to be seeking her mother's affection. Overall Hannah was perceived by the mother as being difficult and controlling and this was the cause of much of the mother's stress. The concerns were shared with the parents but they were unable to engage with professionals because they found all intervention intrusive into their family life. The parents refused all parenting and therapeutic intervention. They presented as aggressive and defensive and their responses to being challenged were, however minor, extreme. They seemed unable to develop any insight into the emotional needs of their children, which heightened concerns.

Over the course of the assessment it became apparent that the children had been coached by their parents not to talk to professionals. Both Danielle and Ben, the younger of the sibling group, made cautious remarks such as 'we are not allowed to say anything rude about our daddy'. This made it even more difficult for the social worker to develop a trusting relationship with the children where they felt safe enough to disclose what was really happening in their home. Our concerns were increasing and, because we believed that the children were being coached about what they could and could not say to social workers, we had to find alternative methods to investigate and gather evidence. This was the stage that we were introduced to a variety of methods to identify disorganized attachment but for this case in particular we used Story Stem profiles.

As a group of social workers we spent five days in total being trained to use the various methods – including Story Stem work and Adult Attachment Interviews – in order to detect signs of disorganized attachment behaviour as well as unresolved loss and trauma and low RF. Following the initial training, the social worker asked the parents whether she could see the children at school on their own. The mother gave consent for the children to be filmed.

The social worker met with Ben at school. She carried out 10 of the 13 stories. The process itself was non-intrusive, and Ben was asked to show and tell what would happen next in response to the different Story Stems. He was not asked specific questions about himself or his family that might ordinarily cause him anxiety. He appeared relaxed and happy to play out the stories with the social worker (something that was in marked contrast to his demeanour during home visits).

At the beginning of the session Ben appeared comfortable. He was smiling and asking questions about when the social worker was going to see his sister. His initial interactions were very much those you would expect to see in a typical six-year-old boy. As the stories were played out, however, Ben's behaviour began to indicate a completely different picture. Two of the most striking stems were the 'spilled juice' and the 'burnt hand' stories, although in all of them we saw signs of disorganized attachment.

The 'spilled juice' story

For this story the family is thirsty and they are all going to have some juice. They are all sitting around the table drinking their juice when Child 1 gets up and reaches across the table: 'Uh oh, he spilled the juice all over the floor. Now can you show and tell me what happens next?'

Ben's immediate response to this scenario was 'now I go to the hospital and report it at the hospital'. The social worker prompted Ben, asking 'Who cleans up the spilled juice?' He said 'me' and then added 'quickly...before mum...', then he swished the little boy around the room cleaning up the mess and said 'Oh I wish mum and dad would wake me up'.

His story began with a very dramatic reaction to what is a minor mistake (spilling the juice). He has to go to the hospital to report that he spilt some juice. This suggests that, when mistakes are made, the response is extreme; interestingly this is exactly how the parents behave in any interactions with professionals: when simple questions are asked, their responses are almost always extreme. For example, they were once asked whether they might think about changing the front door lock as it was a potential fire hazard. Their response was to write a letter of complaint calling the social worker evil for suggesting that they would burn their children.

Throughout Ben's story he at no point sought help or reassurance by either of the 'parent dolls'. The outcomes were fairly catastrophic, given the trivial nature of the event. Even when asked who would clean it up, *he* quickly cleans up before mum...(what, we wonder...?). He stops there and it seems to make him feel uncomfortable. This is when he seems to change the subject saying 'I wish mum and dad would wake me up'. This diversion and lack of coherence appears to be a way of coping with these unpleasant feelings.

The 'burnt hand' story

For this story, the family are in the kitchen. 'Now, Mummy and (Child 1) are at the stove [interviewer points at them]. Mummy is making dinner for everyone. Daddy and (Child 2) are sitting at the table [interviewer points at them]. Mummy says: "We're going to have a really good supper but it's not quite ready yet. Don't get too close to the stove." (Child 1) says: "Mmmmmmmm…that looks good. I don't want to wait, I want some now" [interviewer shows child leaning over and knocking the pan off the stove onto the floor]. (Child 1) says: "Owww!! I've burnt my hand! It hurts!" Now can you show me and tell me what happens next?'

Ben's first response was 'I need grandma' but this seemed only because he had seen a 'grandma' figure elsewhere on the table. The social worker prompted him saying 'What about the burnt hand?' He said 'Put water, put water', but splashes himself. The social worker prompts again saying 'What about his burnt hand, does anyone do anything about his hand?' He bluntly says 'No…because it's his own…dead'. The social worker asks 'What about the spilled food?' He said 'Um, um, um, um, um… Oh, I have to clean up'. The social worker asked 'Does anything else happen?' He said 'No'. The social worker finished with 'So the little boy is dead?' and he said 'Yes'.

In this story, Ben's reaction was again catastrophic. You can't get much more catastrophic than dying. He presented as anxious to clean up the spilled food, no-one looked after him when he burnt his hand and even at the beginning he splashes himself with water. No-one offered him comfort. It was if he was the only person in the story, even though the entire family are depicted in the scenario. When he was specifically asked about the spilled food, the little boy cleans this up himself, despite having a burnt hand.

Ben's play was overall very worrying, characterized by catastrophic events, 'dead' play and unresolved finality. He could neither enact any help-seeking, comfort-seeking, resolution of conflict, nor could he deal with unpleasant feelings. The only time he did involve his parents was either to be violent to someone else (e.g. 'Mervyn' in the 'headache' story) or he was violent to them (he 'boofed' his entire family off the sofa in the 'crying outside' story). At times his responses were bizarre and seemed disconnected – as if it were too difficult for him to manage the feelings associated with the story. He actually runs away in a lot of the stories, seemingly scared of the consequences of ordinary behaviours or mishaps in childhood. He at times looked sad and vacant as his internal working model of attachment began to unfold in front of our eyes. Ben's stories reflected a history of caregiving that was neglectful and unavailable at the very least. The parents in his stories were either not present or not interested. He was left to resolve all of the problems on his own without any adult assistance.

Most striking was how Ben changed from looking like your average six-year-old chatty boy to a very sad, confused, lonely little boy as his attachment system was activated and his mind began to unfold. The stories proved to be a powerful tool in gaining a greater insight into how he was parented in ways that were not possible to discover through standard social work methods, particularly in light of the fact that these particular children had been told very clearly not to talk to social workers.

One of the aims of the Family Support and Intervention Service has always been to ensure that its most vulnerable children have their individual needs identified and addressed in such a way that improves their future outcomes. The problem, however, is that, with the best intentions, the needs of vulnerable and mistreated children are at times either overlooked by the various professionals or are such that the child protection training and subsequent practice is inadequate thoroughly to assess and tackle such complex needs.

The case of Peter Connelly (Baby 'P') has been a tragic example of how, in spite of the best intentions and achieving performance indicators, the system at times still fails us. The reliance on children to develop a trusting relationship with a social worker in order to disclose is an approach that is still heavily relied upon in assessing children at risk. But it is time-consuming and arduous, especially when some parents work so hard to prevent it. The introduction of Story Stem work is one of the methods that we have used that has helped overcome some of the difficulties we regularly face when working with children where we suspect maltreatment. In this particular case example, the use of Story Stem profiles did, by default, lead to the development of a trusting relationship between the social worker and the child. However, it also enabled us to explore Ben's perceptions of family roles, attachments and his relationships without the need to ask him any questions at all. These children in particular were especially anxious during social work visits and were very wary of being asked anything about their family life.

One of the benefits of using Story Stem profiles is that the child tells us so much about their family life without specifically having to mention their family. This reduces significantly feelings of anxiety and apprehension that we observe frequently during interviews with children. In this case, it was clear that, because the usual anxiety that exists when social workers ask questions was not present, Ben appeared relaxed and unaffected by the process. The safe atmosphere, of itself, both builds upon the child's relationship with the social worker and also provides the child with the opportunity and space to disclose. One might say that this is an example of standard social work practice and this may be true. In my view, however, it is the mere use of playing that leads to additional opportunities for disclosures.

Second, and more importantly, this technique allows for the identification of disorganized attachment. Once identified, and combined with the evidence gathered using standard social work methods of investigation, such as observation, interviews, police checks and history gathering, it strengthens and adds weight to the overall assessment of risk. It often tells us something that we would have no way of finding out through the standard methods of assessment.

On the other hand, it can provide an alternative tool to reassure us that maltreatment is less likely when there is no evidence of disorganized attachment. There have been examples since we have been using these techniques where we initially had significant concerns that were somewhat alleviated by the use of these methods. What we got in contrast was a more reassuring picture that home life was more settled than we had imagined. These techniques help social workers gather a deeper understanding of life at home for children and to act in ways either to facilitate the process of change by providing them with therapeutic support or, alternatively, they can be used as evidence-gathering at the commencement of care proceedings.

In this particular case it achieved just that. What transpired after the interview with Ben was an interview with Ben's younger sibling Danielle. She also displayed several signs of disorganization (although not quite as marked as with Ben). However, rather strikingly after the stories had concluded, Danielle disclosed to the social worker that her father beat her regularly. She added that her father beat her siblings as well.

Following Danielle's disclosure, the social worker went back to see Ben with the police. He too immediately opened up explaining that his dad beat him all the time, often with a belt. He again appeared very tired and withdrawn and stated on several occasions that his dad was 'horrible'. He said he was frightened and did not want to go home in case something else happened to him.

It is difficult categorically to say that this disclosure would not have come about at some point without using Story Stem profiles; however, it may have taken a lot longer for it to happen. We already suspected from the family history reports that these children were subjected to excessive physical chastisement at the very least. What we were not aware of, in as much detail, was the harmful effect their home life was having on the children's emotional wellbeing and that the predominant message being depicted was emotionally abusive and neglectful, over and above the physical harm that we already had concerns about.

The difficulty, however, once disorganized attachment has been identified, is knowing what to do about it, in the sense of how best to use this valuable information to guide an intervention (as distinct from the investigation and assessment process). The unfortunate reality of modern social work, however, is that some other agencies – and, it feels, particularly the courts – seem not to value the expertise of social workers and this perception may be difficult to change in the near future (given depictions in some of the media). However, as a beginning, the identification of disorganized attachment in care proceedings cases will at least act as a platform for other experts, whom the Court deems more qualified to conduct such assessments, to make their own enquiries and form their own conclusions. If this process helps to keep children safe and allows us all to make better decisions for them, it will, of itself, have proved invaluable.

Concluding Comments

We have concentrated in this book on the connection between disorganized attachment and maltreatment but we want to conclude with some observations about parenting generally. We confess we are worried by what we see, when we are just out and about where parents are with their young children: at shopping centres, parks, swimming pools, etc. And we are not alone: recent publications by Sarah Hrdy, in her formidable anthropological treatise in 2009 on the evolutionary roots of caregiving, *Mothers and Others*, and Bruce Perry in his 2010 book *Born to Love: Why Empathy is Essential – and Endangered* (Perry and Szalavitz 2010), also reflect our unease.

What are we nervous about? That we may be losing touch with our children. Unlike in the rest of this book, where we have been scrupulously evidence-informed, we accept completely that our anxiety is based on little more than our day-to-day observations. Here are two case studies which, compared with what we have discussed in the book, are certainly not examples of 'maltreatment', in the sense of the state needing to intervene, but we believe they are troubling:

Case study 1 What do I mean to you?

At lunchtime in a London department store's self-service restaurant a mother and father brought the toddler's buggy to a table and discussed who would go and get the food. Eventually, the mother sat the small girl (of about two) at a table; she sat next to her, facing us, while the father set off to join a long queue for food, well out of sight of the child. Having glanced at the child, the mother took out her mobile phone and made a call, during which time the child periodically looked at her. She would only very occasionally glance down at her, but without talking to or even smiling at her. After making the call, she continued to use the keypad for some ten minutes, playing a game, but again without any reference to the child, who impassively stared around her. She periodically glanced up at her mother; but she got no response. When the father returned with the food, neither of them spoke to her, but conversed briefly to each other about the long queue. Nothing was said directly to the child for 20 minutes; neither was she smiled at or even looked at.

Case study 2 The 'unpresent' parent

Two small boys aged about seven and five were left playing with small packaged toys, newly purchased, while their father bought them cake and juice in a coffee shop. Sitting at an adjacent table we could hear them chatting while they unwrapped their toys. The father returned to the table and, having given them their food and drink, he began texting, which he continued for a protracted time. They were excited about constructing their new figures and car and spoke to their father about what they were doing. He did not look up or acknowledge what they were saying in any way and, on leaving, we offered our newspaper to him. He had been so engrossed in his activity he looked startled, as waking up from a dream, and could hardly articulate an answer. He seemed completely unaware of his surroundings or that his children had been talking to him.

We wonder, therefore, whether our momentous technological advances are having the unintended consequence of cutting us off from our surroundings; including, at times, our children. Obviously we need a break from children – they can be exhausting – and parents have always 'switched off', *but not normally for prolonged periods when they are in their immediate vicinity.* What we are seeing is different from dad going off on his own to play football or mum having an evening out with her friends. It feels as though we are witnessing the isolation of children *while they are surrounded by people.* In these two case studies, whilst the parents were physically present, they are likely to have been perceived by their children as significantly emotionally unavailable. If this behaviour is chronic and regular, it is likely to lead to some of the outcomes identified in this book.

But we need to progress beyond merely bemoaning what we are noticing. In their recent review on the 'neurobiology and genetics of maltreatment' Eamon McCrory and colleagues consider disorganized attachment and maltreatment through anthropological and evolutionary lenses:

> If the infant is to respond optimally to the challenges posed by their surroundings then early stress-induced changes in neurobiological

systems can be seen as 'programming' or calibrating the stress system to match the demands of a hostile environment; this will in turn maximise an individual's ability to compete for resources and survive to sexual maturity… Two core assumptions make such atypical adaptation of clinical relevance. The first is that chronic exposure to early stress establishes a neurobiological response associated with a higher biological cost and increased risk of mental and physical health problems. (McCrory *et al.* 2010)

Jay Belsky adopts a similar evolutionary 'take' when he convincingly suggests that the organized ambivalent style was as an adaptive response to a more complex and threatening evolutionary environment, one which would have been recognized by its *unpredictability*, unlike in both the secure and avoidant attachment organizations which are much more foreseeable. Our immediate surroundings may, at one time, have appeared safe and then become – or have been perceived as becoming – capriciously dangerous. He argues that the aim under these environmental conditions would have been unconsciously to induce levels of helpless dependency in offspring and to interfere with the growing infant's autonomy and exploratory instincts in order to promote dependency (Belsky 1999). There is a consequential reluctance to reward or encourage the child's initiative because, in order to ensure better survival of their genetic progeny, the instinctive aim of parents would have been to convey doubts about the child's ability to survive on its own. The parent's behaviour thus mirrors the evolutionary environment. Young children would have been encouraged to act as a caregiver of other kin because 'maternal caregiving is excessively taxed, possibly because surrogates are not reliably available' (Belsky 1999, p.156). What evolved were not merely attachment behaviours but the ability to organize them into a pattern to fit prevailing child rearing conditions and in so doing promote reproductive fitness, not just survival.

Evolutionary anthropologists invite us to consider questions such as 'Why, in terms of our reproductive fitness, did disorganized attachment ever develop; why didn't children who were frightened of or by their parents simply not survive?' The reason is that, in our more distant past, their behaviour would have been a signal to the immediate community that all was not well; neither for the child, nor for the parent. Thus, in the 21st century, disorganized attachment behaviour should sound alarm bells in us all. This is another reason why we wrote this book: to encourage child welfare practitioners and others to attract the attention of a wider audience to the danger signals of disorganized attachment, unresolved loss and trauma, and disconnected parenting.

So where do these insights leave us? We believe with some stark choices. James Leckman refers to the 15 per cent level of disorganized attachment in low-risk samples as 'sobering' (Leckman 2005). He continues: 'knowing that attachment strategies are, in many instances, passed on transgenerationally, it seems likely – even without factoring in further social chaos in the world – that the number of children in this category is going to increase' (p.336). For him this 'raises the question about whether our descendants – who presumably will still be bipedal and clever – will be "human" in the same way that we apply the term today' (p.337). His concerns echo the last paragraph of Sarah Hrdy's book. The title of her chapter is 'Are we losing the art of nurture?' and we quote the paragraph in full:

> I have no doubt that our descendants thousands of years from now (whether on this planet or some other) will be bipedal, symbol-generating apes. They will probably be technologically proficient in realms we do not even dream of yet, as well as every bit as competitive and Machiavellian as chimpanzees are now, and probably even more intelligent than people today. What is not certain is whether they will be human in ways we now think of as distinguishing our species – that is, empathic and curious about the emotions of others, shaped by our ancestors' heritage of communal care. (Hrdy 2009, pp.293–294)

These authors are hard-nosed academics, not given to sentiment or rhetoric; but they are worried and, as we said, so are we. So what is the choice? We think the following stanza written by the poet Mary Lamb (1765–1847), called 'A Child', expresses it perfectly:

Thou straggler into loving arms,

Young climber-up of trees,

When I forget thy thousand ways

Then life and all shall cease

Notes on Contributors

David Phillips qualified as a social worker from University College, Cardiff in 1992. He is currently Head of the London Borough of Enfield's Family Centre Service. This provides parenting assessments, supervised contact and outreach work for vulnerable children and families where children are subject to care proceedings and protection plans.

David Wilkins is a Senior Lecturer in Social Work at Anglia Ruskin University and the Deputy Team Manager for the London Borough of Enfield's Disabled Children's Team. This role involves overseeing child protection investigations and interventions as well as working with children in need and looked after children. David qualified as a social worker in 2005 and is currently studying for a PhD at the University of Kent.

Tania Young is a Team Manager in the London Borough of Lewisham's Family Support and Intervention Team. After gaining her degree in 1998 she went on to study social work at the University of Tasmania and qualified in 2000. She currently manages a team of social workers working in child protection. She also has two therapeutic social workers in the team who offer therapeutic interventions to the most hard-to-reach families.

References

Abrams, K.Y., Rifkin, A. and Hesse, E. (2006) 'Examining the role of parental frightened/frightening subtypes in predicting disorganized attachment within a brief observational procedure.' *Development and Psychopathology 18*, 345–361.

Ader, R. and Cohen, M. (1993) 'Psychoneuroimmunology: Conditioning and stress.' Annual Review of Psychology 44, 53–85.

Adshead, G. and Bluglass, K. (2005) 'Attachment representations in mothers with abnormal illness behaviour by proxy.' *British Journal of Psychiatry 187*, 328–333.

Ainsworth, M.D.S. and Eichberg, C.G. (1991) 'Effects on Infant–Mother Attachment of Mother's Unresolved Loss of an Attachment Figure, or Other Traumatic Experience.' In C.M. Parkes, J. Stevenson-Hinde and P. Marris (eds) *Attachment Across the Life Cycle.* New York: Tavistock/Routledge.

Ainsworth, M.D.S., Bell, S.M. and Stayton, D.J. (1974) 'Infant–Mother Attachment and Social Development: "Socialization" as a Product of Reciprocal Responsiveness to Signals.' In M.P.M. Richards (ed.) *The Integration of a Child into a Social World.* Cambridge: Cambridge University Press.

Ainsworth, M.D.S., Blehar, M., Waters, E. and Wall, S. (1978) *Patterns of Attachment: A Psychological Study of the Strange Situation.* Hillsdale, NJ: Lawrence Erlbaum Associates.

Allen, J.G., Fonagy, P. and Bateman, A.W. (2008) *Mentalising in Clinical Practice.* Arlington, VA: APP.

Armstrong, J., Putnam, F.W., Carlson, E.B., Libero, D. and Smith, S.R. (1997) 'Development and validation of a measure of adolescent dissociation: The Adolescent Dissociative Experiences Scale.' *Journal of Nervous and Mental Disease 185*, 1–7.

Bakermans-Kranenburg, M.J. and van IJzendoorn, M.H. (1997) 'Intergenerational Transmission of Attachment: A Move to the Contextual Level.' In L. Atkinson and K. Zucker (eds) *Attachment and Psychopathology.* New York: Guilford Press.

Bakermans-Kranenburg, M.J. and van IJzendoorn, M.H. (2004) 'No association of the dopamine D4 receptor (DRD4) and −521 C/T promoter polymorphisms with infant attachment disorganization.' *Attachment and Human Development 6*, 211–218.

Bakermans-Kranenburg, M.J. and van IJzendoorn, M.H. (2007) 'Genetic vulnerability or differential susceptibility in child development: The case of attachment.' *Journal of Child Psychology and Psychiatry and Allied Disciplines 48*, 1160–1173.

Bakermans-Kranenburg, M.J. and van IJzendoorn, M.H. (2008) 'Oxytocin receptor (OXTR) and serotonin transporter (5-HTT) genes associated with observed parenting.' *Social Cognition and Affective Neuroscience 3*, 128–134.

Bakermans-Kranenburg, M.J., van IJzendoorn, M.H. and Juffer, F. (2003) 'Less is more: Meta-analyses of sensitivity and attachment interventions in early childhood.' *Psychological Bulletin 129*, 195–215.

Bakermans-Kranenburg, M.J., van IJzendoorn, M.H. and Juffer, F. (2005) 'Disorganized infant attachment and preventive interventions: A review and meta-analysis.' *Infant Mental Health Journal 26*, 191–216.

Barnett, D., Ganiban, J. and Cicchetti, D. (1997) *Maltreatment, Emotional Reactivity, and the Development of Type D Attachments from 12- to 24-Months of Age*, unpublished manuscript.

Baron, R.M. and Kenny, D.A. (1986) 'The moderator–mediator variable distinction in social psychological research: Conceptual, strategic and statistical considerations.' *Journal of Personality and Social Psychology 51*, 1173–1182.

Baron-Cohen, S. (1996) 'Is there a normal phase of synaesthesia in development?' *Psyche 2*, 27.

Bartholomew, K. and Horowitz, L.M. (1991) 'Attachment styles among young adults: A test of a four-category model.' *Journal of Personality and Social Psychology 61*, 236–244.

Beeghly, M. and Cicchetti, D. (1994) 'Child maltreatment, attachment, and the self system: Emergence of an internal state lexicon in toddlers at high social risk.' *Development and Psychopathology 6*, 5–30.

Behrens, K.Y., Main, M. and Hesse, E. (2007) 'Mothers' attachment status as determined by the Adult Attachment Interview predicts their 6-year-olds' reunion responses: A study conducted in Japan.' *Developmental Psychology 43*, 1553–1567.

Belsky, J. (1999) 'Interactional and Contextual Determinants of Attachment Security.' In J. Cassidy and P.R. Shaver (eds) *Handbook of Attachment: Theory, Research and Clinical Applications*. New York: Guilford Press.

Belsky, J. (2002) 'Developmental origins of attachment styles.' *Attachment and Human Development 4*, 166–170.

Belsky, J. (2005) 'Differential Susceptibility to Rearing Influence: An Evolutionary Hypothesis and Some Evidence.' In B.J. Ellis and D.F. Bjorklund (eds) *Origins of the Social Mind: Evolutionary Psychology and Child Development*. New York: Guilford Press.

Belsky, J. and Fearon, R.M. (2002) 'Infant–mother attachment security, contextual risk, and early development: A moderational analysis.' *Development and Psychopathology 14*, 293–310.

Benamer, S. and White, K. (eds) (2008) *Trauma and Attachment*. London: Karnac Books.

Berlin, L.J. and Cassidy, J. (1999) 'Relations among Relationships: Contributions from Attachment Theory and Research.' In J. Cassidy and P.R. Shaver (eds) *Handbook of Attachment: Theory, Research and Clinical Applications*. New York: Guilford Press.

Bernstein, E.M. and Putnam, F.W. (1986) 'Development, reliability, and validity of a dissociation scale.' *Journal of Nervous and Mental Disease 174*, 727–735.

Bonanno, G.A., Keltner, D., Holen, A. and Horowitz, M.J. (1995) 'When avoiding unpleasant emotions might not be such a bad thing: Verbal-autonomic response dissociation and midlife conjugal bereavement.' *Journal of Personality and Social Psychology 69*, 975–989.

Bowlby, J. (1969) *Attachment and Loss – Vol. 1: Attachment*. New York: Basic Books.

Bowlby, J. (1973) *Attachment and Loss – Vol. 2: Separation*. New York: Basic Books.

Bowlby, J. (1979) *The Making and Breaking of Affectional Bonds*. London: Tavistock.

Bowlby, J. (1980) *Attachment and Loss – Vol. 3: Loss*. New York: Basic Books.

Bowlby, J. (1988) *A Secure Base: Clinical Applications of Attachment Theory*. London: Routledge.

Bramble, D.M. and Lieberman, D.E. (2004) 'Endurance running and the evolution of Homo.' *Nature 432*, 345–352.

Brandon, M., Belderson, P., Warren, C., Gardner, R. *et al.* (2008) 'The preoccupation with thresholds in cases of child death or serious injury through abuse and neglect.' *Child Abuse Review 17*, 5, 313–330.

Bretherton, I. and Mulholland, K.A. (1999) 'Internal Working Models in Attachment Relationships: A Construct Revisited.' In J. Cassidy and P.R. Shaver (eds) *Handbook of Attachment: Theory, Research and Clinical Applications*. New York: Guilford Press.

Bretherton, I., Ridgeway, D. and Cassidy, J. (1990) 'Assessing Internal Working Models of the Attachment Relationship: An Attachment Story Completion Task for 3-Year-Olds.' In M. Greenberg, D. Cicchetti and M. Cummings (eds) *Attachment in the Preschool Years: Theory, Research and Intervention*. Chicago: University of Chicago Press.

Bronfman, E., Parsons, E. and Lyons-Ruth, K. (2004) *Atypical Maternal Behavior Instrument for Assessment and Classification (AMBIANCE): Manual for Coding Disrupted Affective Communication*, unpublished manual, Department of Psychiatry, Cambridge Hospital, Massachusetts.

Browne, K. and Saqi, S. (1988) 'Approaches to Screening for Child Abuse and Neglect.' In K. Browne, C. Davies and P. Stratton (eds) *Early Prediction and Prevention of Child Abuse*. Chichester: Wiley.

Busch, A.L. and Lieberman, A.F. (2007) 'Attachment and Trauma: An Integrated Approach to Treating Young Children Exposed to Family Violence.' In D. Oppenheim and D.F. Goldsmith (eds) *Attachment Theory in Clinical Work with Children*. New York: Guilford Press.

Carlson, E.A. (1998) 'A prospective longitudinal study of attachment disorganization/disorientation.' *Child Development 69*, 1107–1128.

Carlson, V., Cicchetti, D., Barnett, D. and Braunwald, K. (1989) 'Disorganised/disoriented attachment relationships in maltreated infants.' *Developmental Psychology 25*, 525–531.

Caspi, A., Sugden, K., Moffitt, T.E., Taylor, A., Craig, I.W. and Harrington, H. (2003) 'Influence of life stress on depression: Moderation by a polymorphism in the 5-HTT gene.' *Science 301*, 5631, 386–389.

Cassidy, J. and Shaver, P.R. (2008) *Handbook of Attachment: Theory, Research and Clinical Applications*, 2nd edition. New York: Guilford Press.

Cicchetti, D. and Curtis, W.J. (2006) 'The Developing Brain and Neural Plasticity: Implications for Normality, Psychopathology, and Resilience.' In D. Cicchetti and D. Cohen (eds) *Developmental Psychopathology: Developmental Neuroscience* (Vol. 2, 2nd edn). New York: Wiley.

Craik, K. (1943) *The Nature of Explanation*. Cambridge: Cambridge University Press.

Crittenden, P.M. (1996) *The Modified Adult Attachment Interview*, unpublished manuscript.

Crittenden, P.M. (2008) *Raising Parents: Attachment, Parenting and Child Safety*. Portland, OR: Willan.

Damasio, A.R. (1994) *Descartes' Error: Emotion, Reason and the Human Brain*. New York: Grosset-Putnam.

Deklyen, M. and Greenberg, M.T. (2008) 'Attachment and Psychopathology in Childhood.' In J. Cassidy and P.R. Shaver (eds) *Handbook of Attachment: Theory, Research and Clinical Applications*, 2nd edition. New York: Guilford Press.

Dennett, D. (1989) *The Intentional Stance*. New York: MIT Press.

Diamond, N. and Marrone, M. (2003) *Attachment and Subjectivity*. London: Whurr.

Diorio, J. and Meaney, M.J. (2007) 'Maternal programming of defensive responses through sustained effects on gene expression.' *Journal of Psychiatry and Neuroscience 32*, 4, 275–284.

Domes, G., Heinrichs, M., Glascher, J., Buchel, C., Braus, D.F. and Herpertz, S.C. (2007) 'Oxytocin attenuates amygdala responses to emotional faces regardless of valence.' *Biological Psychiatry 62*, 10, 1187–1190.

Dozier, M., Chase Stovall-McClough, K. and Albus, K.E. (2008) 'Attachment and Psychopathy in Adulthood.' In J. Cassidy and P.R. Shaver (eds) *Handbook of Attachment*. New York: The Guilford Press.

Dunst, C. and Kassow, Z. (2008) 'Caregiver sensitivity, contingent social responsiveness, and secure infant attachment.' *Journal of Early and Intensive Behavior Intervention 5*, 40–56.

Ekman, P. (2007) *Emotions Revealed: Recognizing Faces and Feelings to Improve Communication and Emotional Life*. New York: Owl Books.

Faraone, S., Biederman, J., Webber, W. and Russell, R. (1998) 'Psychiatric, neuropsychological, and psychosocial features of DSM-IV subtypes of attention-deficit/hyperactivity disorder: Results from a clinically referred sample.' *Journal of the American Academy of Child and Adolescent Psychiatry 37*, 185–193.

Farmelo, G. (2009) *The Strangest Man: The Hidden Life of Paul Dirac, Quantum Genius*. London: Faber and Faber.

Farnfield, S. (2009) 'A modified Strange Situation Procedure for use in assessing sibling relationships and their attachment to carers.' *Adoption and Fostering 33*, 1, 4–17.

Fauth, R., Jelicic, H., Hart, D., Burton, S. *et al.* (2010) *Effective Practice to Protect Children Living in 'Highly Resistant' Families*. London: C4EO (Centre for Excellence and Outcomes in Children and Young People's Services).

Fearon, P. and Mansell, W. (2001) 'Cognitive perspectives on unresolved loss: Insights from the study of PTSD.' *Bulletin of the Menninger Clinic 65*, 380–396.

Fearon, R.M.P., Bakermans-Kranenburg, M.J., van IJzendoorn, M.H., Lapsley, A. and Roisman, G.I. (2010) 'The significance of insecure attachment and disorganization in the development of children's externalizing behavior: A meta-analytic study.' *Child Development 81*, 435–456.

Feder, A., Alonso, A., Tang, M., Warner, V. *et al.* (2009) 'Children of low-income depressed mothers: Psychiatric disorders and social adjustment.' *Depression and Anxiety 26*, 6, 513–520.

Feeney, J.A. (1995) 'Adult attachment and emotional control.' *Personal Relationships 2*, 143–159.

Feeney, J.A. and Noller, P. (1996) *Adult Attachment*. London: Sage.

Feeney, J.A., Noller, P. and Hanrahan, M. (1994) 'Assessing Adult Attachment.' In M.B. Sperling and W.H. Berman (eds) *Attachment in Adults: Clinical and Developmental Perspectives*. New York: Guilford Press.

Feldman, R., Greenbaum, C.W. and Yirmiya, N. (1999) 'Mother–infant affect synchrony as an antecedent of the emergence of self-control.' *Developmental Psychology 35*, 223–231.

Fisher, H.E., Aron, A., Mashek, D., Li, H. and Brown, L.L. (2002) 'Defining the brain systems of lust, romantic attraction and attachment.' *Archives of Sexual Behaviour 31*, 413–419.

Fonagy, P. (2008) 'The Mentalization-Focused Approach to Social Development.' In F.N. Busch (ed.) *Mentalization: Theoretical Considerations, Research Findings and Clinical Findings*. New York: Taylor and Francis.

Fonagy, P. and Target, M. (1997) 'Attachment and reflective function: Their role in selforganization.' *Development and Psychopathology 9*, 679–700.

Fonagy, P. and Target, M. (2005) 'Bridging the transmission gap: An end to an important mystery of attachment research?' *Attachment and Human Development 7*, 333–343.

Forrester, D., Kershaw, S., Moss, H. and Hughes, L. (2007) 'Communication skills in child protection: How do social workers talk to parents?' *Child and Family Social Work 13*, 1, 41–51.

Fraley, R.C. and Phillips, R.L. (2009) 'Self-Report Measures of Adult Attachment in Clinical Practice.' In J.H. Obegi and E. Berant (eds) *Clinical Applications of Attachment Theory*. New York: Guilford Press.

Fraley, R.C. and Shaver, P.R. (1997) 'Adult attachment and the suppression of unwanted thoughts.' *Journal of Personality and Social Psychology 79*, 816–826.

Fraley, R.C. and Shaver, P.R. (1999) 'Loss and Bereavement: Attachment Theory and Recent Controversies Concerning "Grief Work" and the Nature of Detachment.' In J. Cassidy and P.R. Shaver (eds) *Handbook of Attachment: Theory, Research and Clinical Applications*. New York: Guilford Press.

Franzblau, S.H. (2002) 'Deconstructing Attachment Theory: Naturalising the Politics of Motherhood.' In M.R. Dunlap and J.C. Chrisler (eds) *Charting a New Course for Feminist Psychology*. Santa Barbara, CA: Praeger Press.

George, C. and Solomon, J. (1996) 'Representational models of relationships: Links between caregiving and attachment.' *Infant Mental Health Journal 17*, 198–216.

George, C. and Solomon, J. (1999) 'Attachment and Caregiving: The Caregiving Behavioural System.' In J. Cassidy and P.R. Shaver (eds) *Handbook of Attachment: Theory, Research and Clinical Applications*. New York: Guilford Press.

George, C. and Solomon, J. (2008) 'The Caregiving System: A Behavioral Systems Approach to Parenting.' In J. Cassidy and P.R. Shaver (eds) *Handbook of Attachment: Theory, Research and Clinical Applications*, 2nd edition. New York: Guilford Press.

George, C. and West, M. (2001) 'The development and preliminary validation of a new measure of adult attachment: The Adult Attachment Projective.' *Attachment and Human Development 3*, 30–61.

George, C., Kaplan, N. and Main, M. (1985) *The Adult Attachment Interview*, unpublished manuscript, Department of Psychology, University of California at Berkeley.

Gervai, J., Nemoda, Z., Lakatos, K., Ronai, Z. *et al.* (2005) 'Transmission disequilibrium tests confirm the link between DRD4 gene polymorphism and infant attachment.' *American Journal of Medical Genetics B, Neuropsychiatric Genetics 132B*, 126–130.

Goldberg, S. (2000) *Attachment and Development*. London: Arnold.

Gray, J. and Bentovim, A. (1996) 'Illness Induction Syndrome: Paper 1 – A series of 41 children from 37 families identified at the Great Ormond Street Hospital for Children NHS Trust.' *Child Abuse and Neglect 20*, 8, 655–673.

Green, J., Stanley, C., Smith, V. and Golwyn, R. (2000) 'A new method of evaluating attachment representations in young school-aged children: The Manchester Child Attachment Story Task (MCAST).' *Attachment and Human Development 2*, 48–70.

Grossmann, K., Grossmann, K.E., Spangler, G., Suess, G. and Unzner, L. (1985) 'Maternal Sensitivity and Newborn Orienting Responses as Related to Quality of Attachment in Northern Germany.' In I. Bretherton and E. Waters (eds) *Growing Points in Attachment Theory and Research*. Monographs of the Society for Research in Child Development 50(1–2), Serial No. 209, 233–256.

Gubman, N. (2004) 'Disorganized attachment: A compass for navigating the confusing behavior of the "difficult-to-treat" patient.' *Clinical Social Work Journal 32*, 159–169.

Haddon, M. (2003) *The Curious Incident of the Dog in the Night-time*. London: Jonathan Cape.

Hansen, E.W. (1966) 'The development of maternal and infant behaviour in the rhesus monkey.' *Behaviour 27*, 107–149.

Hart, S. (2008) *Brain, Attachment, Personality: An Introduction to Neuroaffective Development*. London: Karnac.

Hazan, C. and Shaver, P.R. (1987) 'Romantic love conceptualised as an attachment process.' *Journal of Personality and Social Psychology 52*, 511–524.

Hazan, C. and Zeifman, D. (1994) 'Sex and the Psychological Tether.' In K. Bartholomew and D. Perlman (eds) *Advances in Personal Relationships, Vol. 5*. London: Jessica Kingsley Publishers.

Heim, C., Young, L.J., Newport, D.J., Mletzko, T., Miller, A.H. and Nemeroff, C.B. (2009) 'Lower CSF oxytocin concentrations in women with a history of childhood abuse.' *Molecular Psychiatry 14*, 10, 954–958.

Hennighausen, K. and Lyons-Ruth, K. (2010) 'Disorganization of Attachment Strategies in Infancy and Childhood.' In R.E. Tremblay, R.G. Barr, R. de V. Peters and M. Boivin (eds) *Encyclopedia on Early Childhood Development* [online]. Montreal, Quebec: Centre of Excellence for Early Childhood Development. Available at www.child-encyclopedia.com/documents/Hennighausen-LyonsRuthANGxp_rev.pdf, accessed on 11 January 2011).

Hertsgaard, L., Gunnar, M., Erickson, M.F. and Nachmias, M. (1995) 'Adrenocortical response to the Strange Situation in infants with disorganized/disoriented attachment relationships.' *Child Development 66*, 1100–1106.

Hesse, E. (1999) 'The Adult Attachment Interview: Historical and Current Perspectives.' In J. Cassidy and P.R. Shaver (eds) *Handbook of Attachment: Theory, Research and Clinical Applications*. New York: Guilford Press.

Hesse, E. and Main, M. (2000) 'Disorganized infant, child and adult attachment: Collapse in behavioral and attentional strategies.' *Journal of the American Psychoanalytic Association 48*, 4, 1097–1127.

Hesse, E. and Main, M. (2006) 'Frightened, threatening, and dissociative parental behavior in low-risk samples: Description, discussion and interpretations.' *Development and Psychopathology 18*, 2, 309–343.

Hesse, H. and van IJzendoorn, M.H. (1998) 'Parental loss of close family members and propensities towards absorption in offspring.' *Developmental Science 1*, 299–305.

Hobson, R.P. (2002) *The Cradle of Thought: Exploring the Origins of Thinking*. New York: Oxford University Press.

Hodges, J., Steele, M., Hillman, S. and Henderson, K. (2003) 'Mental Representations and Defences in Severely Maltreated Children: A Story Stem Battery and Rating System for Clinical Assessment and Research Applications.' In R. Emde, D. Wolk, C. Zahn-Waxler and D. Oppenheim (eds) *Narrative Processes and the Transition from Infancy to Early Childhood*. New York: Oxford University Press.

Holland, S. (2000) 'The assessment relationship: Interaction between social workers and parents in child protection assessments.' *British Journal of Social Work 30*, 149–163.

Hopkins, J. (1996) 'The dangers and deprivations of too-good mothering.' *Journal of Child Psychotherapy 22*, 3, 407–422.

Howe, D. (2006) *Child Abuse and Neglect: Attachment, Development and Intervention.* London: Palgrave/Macmillan.

Howe, D., Brandon, M., Hinings, D. and Schofield, G. (1999) *Attachment Theory, Child Maltreatment and Family Support: A Practice and Assessment Model.* London: Macmillan.

Hrdy, S.B. (2009) *Mothers and Others: The Evolutionary Origins of Mutual Understanding.* Harvard: Belknap.

Jacobvitz, D., Hazen, N. and Riggs, S. (1997) 'Disorganized Mental Processes in Mothers, Frightening/Frightened Caregiving, and Disoriented/Disorganized Behavior in Infancy.' In D. Jacobvitz (Chair) *Caregiving Correlates and Longitudinal Outcomes of Disorganized Attachments in Infants.* Symposium conducted at the biennial meeting of the Society for Research in Child Development, Washington, DC.

Jones, D.P.H. (1997) 'Treatment of the Child and the Family Where Child Abuse or Neglect Has Occurred.' In M.E. Helfer, R.S. Kempe and R.D. Krugman (eds) *The Battered Child*, 5th edition. London: University of Chicago Press.

Juffer, F., Bakermans-Kranenburg, M.J. and van IJzendoorn, M.H. (eds) (2008a) *Promoting Positive Parenting: An Attachment-Based Intervention.* New York: Lawrence Erlbaum/Taylor and Francis.

Juffer, F., Bakermans-Kranenburg, M.J. and van IJzendoorn, M.H. (2008b) *Manual Video-feedback Intervention to promote Positive Parenting and Sensitive Discipline (VIPP-SD)* (version 2.0). Leiden University, Leiden, The Netherlands: Centre for Child and Family Studies.

Kaplan, N. (1987) *Individual Differences in Six-Year-Olds' Thoughts about Separation: Predicted from Attachment to Mother at Age One,* doctoral dissertation, University of California at Berkeley.

Kaplan, N. and Main, M. (1986) *Assessment of Attachment Organization Through Children's Family Drawings,* unpublished manuscript, Department of Psychology, University of California at Berkeley.

Kirschbaum, C., Pirke, K.M. and Hellhammer, D.H. (1993) 'The "Trier Social Stress Test" – A tool for investigating psychobiological stress responses in a laboratory setting.' *Neuropsychobiology 28*, 1–2, 76–81.

Klohnen, E.C. and John, O.P. (1998) 'Working Models of Attachment: A Theory-Based Prototype Approach.' In J.A. Simpson and W.S. Rholes (eds) *Attachment Theory and Close Relationships.* New York: Guilford Press.

Koenen, K.C., Moffitt, T.E., Caspi, A., Taylor, A. and Purcell, S. (2003) 'Domestic violence is associated with environmental suppression of IQ in young children.' *Development and Psychopathology 15*, 297–315.

Lakatos, K., Nemoda, Z., Toth, I., Ronai, Z. *et al.* (2002) 'Further evidence for the role of the dopamine D4 receptor (DRD4) gene in attachment disorganization: Interaction of the exon III 48-bp repeat and the 521 C/T promoter polymorphisms.' *Molecular Psychiatry 7*, 27–31.

Lakatos, K., Toth, I., Nemoda, Z., Ney, K., Sasvari-Szekely, M. and Gervai, J. (2000) 'Dopamine D4 receptor (DRD4) gene polymorphism is associated with attachment disorganization in infants.' *Molecular Psychiatry 5*, 633–637.

Leckman, J. (Rapporteur) (2005) 'Group Report: Biobehavioural Processes in Attachment and Bonding.' In C.S. Carter, L. Ahnert, K.E. Grossmann, S.B. Hrdy *et al.* (eds) *Attachment and Bonding.* Berlin: Dahlem Workshop Reports.

Leutenegger, W. (1987) 'Neonatal brain size and neurocranial dimensions in Pliocene hominids: Implications for obstetrics.' *Journal of Human Evolution 16*, 291–296.

Lewis, M. (1997) *Altering Fate: Why the Past Does Not Predict the Future.* New York: Guilford Press.

Lieberman, A.F. (2004) 'Traumatic stress and quality of attachment: Reality and internalisation disorders of infant mental health.' *Journal of Infant Mental Health 25*, 4, 336–351.

Liotti, G. (2004) 'Trauma, dissociation and disorganised attachment: Three strands of a single braid.' *Psychotherapy: Theory, Research, Practice, Training 41*, 472–486.

Lösel, F. and Bender, D. (2005) 'Resilience and Protective Factors.' In D.P. Farrington and J. Coid (eds) *Prevention of Adult Antisocial Behavior.* Cambridge: Cambridge University Press.

Luyten, P., Kempke, S. and Van Houdenhove, B. (2009) 'Stressonderzoek in de psychiatrie: Een complex verhaal [Stress research in psychiatry: A complex story].' *Tijdschrift voor Psychiatrie [Journal of Psychiatry] 51*, 611–618.

Lyons-Ruth, K. (2003) 'Dissociation and the parent–infant dialogue: A longitudinal perspective.' *Journal of the American Psychoanalytic Association 51*, 883–911.

Lyons-Ruth, K. and Jacobvitz, D. (2008) 'Attachment Disorganisation: Genetic Factors, Parenting Contexts, and Developmental Transformation from Infancy to Adulthood.' In J. Cassidy and P.R. Shaver (eds) *Handbook of Attachment: Theory, Research and Clinical Applications*, 2nd edition. New York: Guilford Press.

Lyons-Ruth, K. and Spielman, E. (2004) 'Disorganized infant attachment strategies and helpless-fearful profiles of parenting: Integrating attachment research with clinical intervention.' *Infant Mental Health Journal 25*, 318–335.

Lyons-Ruth, K., Bronfman, E. and Parsons, E. (1999) 'Maternal frightened, frightening, or atypical behavior and disorganized infant attachment patterns.' *Monographs of the Society for Research in Child Development 64*, 67–96.

Lyons-Ruth, K., Yellin, C., Melnick, S. and Atwood, G. (2005) 'Expanding the concept of unresolved mental states: Hostile/helpless states of mind on the Adult Attachment Interview are associated with disrupted mother–infant communication and infant disorganization.' *Development and Psychopathology 17*, 1–23.

Madigan, S., Bakermans-Kranenburg, M.J., van IJzendoorn, M.H., Moran, G., Pederson, D.R. and Benoit, D. (2006) 'Unresolved states of mind, anomalous parenting behaviour, and disorganized attachment: A review and meta-analysis of a transmission gap.' *Attachment and Human Development 8*, 89–111.

Magai, C. (1999) 'Affect, Imagery and Attachment: Working Models of Interpersonal Affect and the Socialisation of Emotion.' In J. Cassidy and P.R. Shaver (eds) *Handbook of Attachment: Theory, Research and Clinical Applications*. New York: Guilford Press.

Main, M. and Cassidy, J. (1988) 'Categories of response to reunion with the parent at age six: Predicted from infant attachment classification and stable over a one-month period.' *Developmental Psychology 24*, 415–426.

Main, M. and Hesse, E. (1992) 'Disorganized/Disoriented Infant Behavior in the Strange Situation, Lapses in the Monitoring of Reasoning and Discourse during the Parent's Adult Attachment Interview, and Dissociative States.' In M. Ammaniti and D. Stern (eds) *Attachment and Psychoanalysis*. Rome: Gius, Laterza and Figl.

Main, M. and Hesse, E. (1998) *Frightening, Frightened, Dissociated, Deferential, Sexualized and Disorganized Parental Behavior: A Coding System for Parent–Infant Interactions*, 6th edition, unpublished manual, University of California at Berkeley.

Main, M. and Solomon, J. (1990) 'Procedures for Identifying Infants as Disorganized/Disoriented during the Ainsworth Strange Situation.' In M.T. Greenberg, D. Cicchetti and E.M. Cummings (eds) *Attachment in the Preschool Years: Theory, Research, and Intervention*. The John D. and Catherine T. MacArthur Foundation series on mental health and development. Chicago: University of Chicago Press.

Main, M. and Weston, D.R. (1981) 'The quality of the toddler's relationship to mother and to father: Related to conflict behavior and the readiness to establish new relationships.' *Child Development 52*, 932–940.

Main, M., Goldwyn, R. and Hesse, E. (2003) *Adult Attachment Scoring and Classification System*, unpublished manuscript, University of California at Berkeley.

Main, M., Kaplan, N. and Cassidy, J. (1985) 'Security in infancy, childhood and adulthood: A move to the level of representation.' *Monographs of the Society for Research in Child Development 50*, 66–104.

Marvin, R.S. and Britner, P.A. (1999) 'Normative Development: The Ontogeny of Attachment.' In J. Cassidy and P.R. Shaver (eds) *Handbook of Attachment: Theory, Research and Clinical Applications*. New York: Guilford Press.

Marvin, R.S. and Pianta, R.C. (1996) 'Mothers' reaction to their child's diagnosis: Relations with security of attachment.' *Journal of Clinical Child Psychology 25*, 4, 436–445.

McCrory, E., De Brito, S.A. and Viding, E. (2010) 'Research review: The neurobiology and genetics of maltreatment and adversity.' *Journal of Child Psychology and Psychiatry 51*, 10, 1079–1095.

Melnick, S., Finger, B., Hans, S., Patrick, M. and Lyons-Ruth, K. (2008) 'Hostile-Helpless States of Mind in the AAI: A Proposed Additional AAI Category with Implications for Identifying Disorganised Infant Attachment in High-Risk Samples.' In H. Steele and M. Steele (eds) *Clinical Applications of the Adult Attachment Interview.* New York: Guilford Press.

Menzies-Lyth, I. (1959) 'The functioning of social systems as a defence against anxiety.' *Tavistock Institute of Human Relations Pamphlet No. 3*, IML, 1, 43–85.

Mickelson, K.D., Kessler, K. and Shaver, P.R. (1997) 'Adult attachment in a nationally representative sample.' *Journal of Personality and Social Psychology 73*, 1092–1106.

Mikulincer, M. and Shaver, P.R. (2007) *Attachment in Adulthood: Structure, Dynamics and Change.* New York: Guilford Press.

Miller, S.R. (1979) 'Children's fears: A review of the literature with implications for nursing research and practice.' *Nursing Research 28*, 217–223.

Mills-Koonce, W.R., Propper, C.B., Gariepy, J.L., Blair, C., Garrett-Peters, P. and Cox, M.J. (2007) 'Bidirectional genetic and environmental influences on mother and child behavior: The family system as the unit of analyses.' *Development and Psychopathology 19*, 4, 1073–1087.

Minnis, H., Millward, R., Sinclair, C., Kennedy, E. *et al.* (2006) 'The Computerized MacArthur Story Stem Battery – A pilot study of a novel medium for assessing children's representations of relationships.' *International Journal of Methods in Psychiatric Research 15*, 207–214.

Moss, E., Cyr, C. and Dubois-Comtois, K. (2004) 'Maternal Attachment Representations and Child Attachment at Preschool-Age: The Role of Mother–Child Discourse.' In A. Bernier (Chair) *A Further Look into the Attachment Transmission Gap: New Conceptual and Methodological Approaches.* Symposium conducted at the biennial meeting of the International Society for the Study of Behavioral Development, Ghent, Belgium.

Munro, E. (1999) 'Common errors of reasoning in child protection work.' *Ontario Association of Children's Aid Societies 44*, 3, 15–28.

Munro, E. (2002) *Effective Child Protection.* London: Sage.

Murray, L. and Andrews, L. (2000) *The Social Baby.* Richmond, Surrey: The Children's Project.

National Scientific Council on the Developing Child (2005) *Excessive Stress Disrupts the Architecture of the Developing Brain* (Working Paper #3). Cambridge, MA: Center on the Developing Child, Harvard University. Available at http://developingchild.harvard.edu/library/reports_and_working_papers/wp3, accessed on 4 December 2009.

National Scientific Council on the Developing Child (2007) *The Timing and Quality of Early Experiences Combine to Shape Brain Architecture* (Working Paper #5). Cambridge, MA: Center on the Developing Child, Harvard University. Available at http://developingchild.harvard.edu/library/reports_and_working_papers/wp5, accessed on 4 December 2009.

National Scientific Council on the Developing Child (2008) *Mental Health Problems in Early Childhood Can Impair Learning and Behavior for Life* (Working Paper #6). Cambridge, MA: Center on the Developing Child, Harvard University. Available at http://developingchild.harvard.edu/library/reports_and_working_papers/wp6, accessed on 4 December 2009.

Newton, R.P. (2008) *The Attachment Connection: Parenting a Secure and Confident Child Using the Science of Attachment Theory.* Oakland, CA: New Harbinger.

Oppenheim, D. and Goldsmith, D.F. (eds) (2007) *Attachment Theory in Clinical Work with Children: Bridging the Gap between Research and Practice.* New York: Guilford Press.

Orme, J. and Shemmings, D. (2010) *Developing Research-Based Social Work Practice.* London: Palgrave.

Out, D., Bakermans-Kranenburg, M.J. and van IJzendoorn, M.H. (2009) 'The role of disconnected and extremely insensitive parenting in the development of disorganized attachment: The validation of a new measure.' *Attachment and Human Development 11*, 419–443.

Pasquini, P., Liotti, G., Mazzotti, E., Fassone, G. and Picardi, A. (2002) 'Risk factors in the early family life of patients suffering from dissociative disorders.' *Acta Psychiatrica Scandinavica 105*, 110–116.

Patterson, G.R. (1982) *Coercive Family Process.* Eugene, OR: Castalia Publishing Company.

Perry, B.D. and Szalavitz, M. (2010) *Born to Love: Why Empathy is Essential – and Endangered*. New York: HarperCollins.

Pollak, S.D., Klorman, R., Thatcher, J.E. and Cicchetti, D. (2001) 'P3b reflects maltreated children's reactions to facial displays of emotion.' *Psychophysiology 38*, 2, 267–274.

Richter, L. (2004) *The Importance of Caregiver–Child Interactions for the Survival and Healthy Development of Young Children: A Review*. Geneva, Switzerland: Department of Child and Adolescent Health and Development, World Health Organization.

Sadler, L.S., Slade, A. and Mayes, L. (2006) 'Minding the Baby: A Mentalisation-Based Parenting Program.' In J.G. Allen and P. Fonagy (eds) *Handbook of Mentalisation-Based Treatment*. Chichester: Wiley.

Sagi-Schwartz, A., van IJzendoorn, M.H., Grossmann, K.E., Joels, T. *et al.* (2003) 'Attachment and traumatic stress in female Holocaust child survivors and their daughters.' *American Journal of Psychiatry 160*, 1086–1092.

Sayre, J.M., Pianta, R.C., Marvin, R.S. and Saft, E.W. (2001) 'Mothers' representations of relationships with their children: Relations with mother characteristics and feeding sensitivity.' *Journal of Pediatric Psychology 26*, 6, 375–384.

Schechter, D.S. (2003) 'Intergenerational Communication of Maternal Violent Trauma: Understanding the Interplay of Reflective Functioning and Posttraumatic Psychopathology.' In S.W. Coates, J.L. Rosenthal and D.S. Schechter (eds) *September 11: Trauma and Human Bonds*. New York: Taylor and Francis.

Schore, A.N. (1994) *Affect Regulation and the Origin of the Self: The Neurobiology of Emotional Development*. Hillsdale, NJ: Erlbaum.

Schore, A.N. (2000) 'Attachment and the regulation of the right brain.' *Attachment and Human Development 2*, 23–47.

Schore, A.N. (2001) 'Effects of a secure attachment relationship on right brain development, affect regulation and infant mental health.' *Journal of Infant Mental Health 22*, 7–66.

Shaver, P.R. and Fraley, R.C. (2008) 'Attachment, Loss and Grief: Implications for Theory, Research and Clinical Intervention.' In J. Cassidy and P.R. Shaver (eds) *Handbook of Attachment: Theory, Research and Clinical Applications*, 2nd edition. New York: Guilford Press.

Shaver, P.R. and Mikulincer, M. (2002) 'Attachment-related psychodynamics.' *Attachment and Human Development 4*, 133–161.

Shemmings, D. (2004) 'Researching relationships from an attachment perspective: The use of behavioural, interview, self-report and projective methods.' *Journal of Social Work Practice 18*, 3, 299–314.

Shemmings, D. (2006a) '"Quantifying" qualitative data: An illustrative example of the use of Q methodology in psychosocial research.' *Qualitative Research in Psychology 3*, 2, 147–165.

Shemmings, D. (2006b) 'Using adult attachment theory to differentiate adult children's internal working models of later life filial relationships.' *Journal of Aging Studies 20*, 2, 177–191.

Shemmings, D. and Shemmings, Y. (1996) 'Building Trust when Making Enquiries.' In D. Shemmings and D. Platt (eds) *Making Enquiries into Alleged Child Abuse and Neglect: Partnership with Families*. Chichester: Wiley.

Shemmings, Y. (1996) *Death, Dying and Residential Care*. Aldershot: Avebury.

Slade, A. (2008) 'Working with Parents in Child Psychotherapy: Engaging the Reflective Function.' In F.N. Busch (ed.) *Mentalization: Theoretical Considerations, Research Findings and Clinical Implications*. New York: Taylor and Francis.

Slade, A., Aber, J.L., Fiorello, J., DeSear, P., Meyer, J. and Cohen, L.J. (1994) *Parent Development Interview, Coding System*. New York: City University of New York.

Spangler, G. and Grossmann, K.E. (1993) 'Biobehavioral organization in securely and insecurely attached infants.' *Child Development 64*, 1439–1450.

Spangler, G. and Zimmermann, P. (2007) *Genetic Contribution to Attachment and Temperament*. Paper presented at the biennial meeting of the Society for Research in Child Development, 29 March to 1 April, Boston, MA.

Spinazzola, J., Ford, J.D., Zucker, M., van der Kolk, B.A., Silva, S. and Smith, S.F. (2005) 'Survey evaluates complex trauma exposure, outcome, and intervention among children and adolescents.' *Psychiatric Annals 35*, 5, 433–439.

Sroufe, L.A. (1997) 'Psychopathology as an outcome of development.' *Development and Psychopathology 9*, 251–268.

Sroufe, L.A., Egeland, B., Carlson, E. and Collins, W.A. (2005) 'Placing Early Attachment Experiences in Developmental Context.' In K.E. Grossmann, K. Grossmann and E. Waters (eds) *The Power of Longitudinal Attachment Research: From Infancy and Childhood to Adulthood*. New York: Guilford Press.

Steele, H. and Steele, M. (2008) 'On the Origins of Reflective Functioning.' In F.N. Busch (ed.) *Mentalization: Theoretical Considerations, Research Findings and Clinical Implications*. New York: Taylor and Francis.

Streeck-Fischer, A. and van der Kolk, B. (2000) 'Down will come baby, cradle and all: Diagnostic and therapeutic implications of chronic trauma on child development.' *Australian and New Zealand Journal of Psychiatry 34*, 6, 903–918.

Target, M., Fonagy, P. and Schmueli-Goetz, Y. (2003) 'Attachment representations in school-age children: The development of the Child Attachment Interview (CAI).' *Journal of Child Psychotherapy 29*, 2, 171–186.

Taylor, S.E., Klein, L.C., Lewis, B.P., Gruenewald, T.L., Gurung, R.A. and Updegraff, J.A. (2000) 'Biobehavioral responses to stress in females: Tend-and-befriend, not fight-or-flight.' *Psychological Review 107*, 411–429.

Tellegen, A. and Atkinson, G. (1974) 'Openness to absorbing and self-altering experiences ("absorption"), a trait related to hypnotic susceptibility.' *Journal of Abnormal Psychology 83*, 268–277.

Thomas, A. and Chess, S. (1977) *Temperament and Development*. New York: Brunner/Mazel.

Thompson, R.A. (1994) 'Emotion Regulation: A Theme in Search of Definition.' In N.A. Fox (ed.) *The Development of Emotion Regulation: Biological and Behavioural Considerations*. Monographs of the Society for Research in Child Development 59 (Serial No. 240), 25–52.

Toth, S.L. and Cicchetti, D. (1996) 'The impact of relatedness with mother on school functioning in maltreated children.' *Journal of School Psychology 34*, 3, 247–266.

True, M.M., Pisani, L. and Oumar, F. (2001) 'Infant–mother attachment among the Dogon of Mali.' *Child Development 72*, 1451–1466.

Tucker, D.M. (1992) 'Developing Emotions and Cortical Networks.' In M.R. Gunnar and C.A. Nelson (eds) *Minnesota Symposium on Child Psychology*, Vol. 24, Developmental Behavioural Neuroscience. Hillsdale, NJ: Erlbaum.

University of Wisconsin – Madison (1999) 'Mediator versus moderator variables.' Available at http:// psych.wisc.edu/henriques/mediator.html, accessed on 11 January 2011.

van IJzendoorn, M.H. (1995) 'Adult attachment representations, parental responsiveness, and infant attachment: A meta-analysis on the predictive validity of the Adult Attachment Interview.' *Psychological Bulletin 117*, 387–403.

van IJzendoorn, M.H. and Bakermans-Kranenburg, M.J. (2003) 'Attachment disorders and disorganised attachment: Same or different?' *Attachment and Human Development 5*, 3, 313–320.

van IJzendoorn, M.H. and Bakermans-Kranenburg, M.J. (2009) *Attachment Security and Disorganization in Maltreating Families and Orphanages*. Available at www.enfantencyclopedie.com/pages/PDF/van_IJzendoorn-Bakermans-KranenburgANGxp-Attachment.pdf, accessed on 13 October 2010.

van IJzendoorn, M.H. and Sagi, A. (1999) 'Cross-Cultural Patterns of Attachment: Universal and Contextual Dimensions.' In J. Cassidy and P.R. Shaver (eds) *Handbook of Attachment: Theory, Research and Clinical Applications*. New York: Guilford Press.

van IJzendoorn, M.H., Bakermans-Kranenburg, M.J. and Mesman, J. (2008) 'Dopamine system genes associated with parenting in the context of daily hassles.' *Genes, Brain and Behavior 7*, 403–410.

van IJzendoorn, M.H., Juffer, F. and Duyvesteyn, M.G.C. (1995) 'Breaking the intergenerational cycle of insecure attachment: A review of the effects of attachment-based interventions on maternal sensitivity and infant security.' *Journal of Child Psychology and Psychiatry 36*, 225–248.

van IJzendoorn, M.H., Schuengel, C. and Bakermans-Kranenburg, M.J. (1999) 'Disorganized attachment in early childhood: Meta-analysis of precursors, concomitants, and sequelae.' *Development and Psychopathology 11*, 225–249.

Vaughn, B.E. and Waters, E. (1990) 'Attachment behavior at home and in the laboratory: Q-sort observations and Strange Situation classifications of one-year-olds.' *Child Development 61*, 1965–1973.

Weaver, T.D. and Hublin, J.-J. (2009) 'Neanderthal birth canal shape and the evolution of human childbirth.' *Proceedings of the National Academy of Sciences of the USA 106*, 20, 8151–8156.

Walker, L.E. (1979) *The Battered Woman*. New York: Harper and Row.

Webster-Stratton, C., Mihalic, S., Fagan, A., Arnold, D., Taylor, T. and Tingley, C. (2001) *Blueprints for Violence Prevention*. Book 11: The Incredible Years: Parent, Teacher and Child Training Series. Boulder, CO: Center for the Study and Prevention of Violence.

Widom, C.S. (1989) 'The cycle of violence.' *Science 244*, 160–166.

Wimmer, H. and Perner, J. (1983) 'Beliefs about beliefs: Representation and constraining function of wrong beliefs in young children's understanding of deception.' *Cognition 13*, 41–68.

Winnicott, D.W. (1958) *Collected Papers: Through Paediatrics to Psychoanalysis*. London: The Hogarth Press.

Winnicott, D.W. (1974) 'Fear of breakdown.' *International Review of Psycho-Analysis 1*, 103–107.

Wortman, C.B. and Silver, R.C. (1989) 'The myths of coping with loss.' *Journal of Consulting and Clinical Psychology 57*, 349–357.

Zeanah, C.H. and Benoit, D. (1995) 'Clinical applications of a parent perception interview in infant mental health.' *Child and Adolescent Psychiatric Clinics of North America 4*, 539–554.

Zeanah, C.H., Benoit, D. and Barton, M. (1993) *Working Model of the Child Interview*. Available at www.oaimh.org/newsFiles/Working_Model_of_the_Child_Interview.pdf, accessed on 11 January 2011.

Subject Index

Author Index